D0282837

DATE DUE

BRODART, CO.

Cat. No. 23-221-003

More Advance Praise for *Continuity Management*

Continuity management is the missing link in knowledge management that will mean significant increases in productivity and knowledge creation—cutting-edge thinking regarding knowledge as a corporate asset.
> **—Newton F. Crenshaw**
> Vice President, Eli Lilly and Company, E.Lilly Division

This book will be immensely valuable to managers at all levels of the organization. Beazley, Boenisch, and Harden offer creative solutions for how to harness intellectual capital and transfer critical operational knowledge to new employees. *Continuity Management* is right on target.
> **—Kathleen T. Ross, PhD**
> Executive Vice President, Organization Effectiveness and Public Relations, Arbitron Inc.

Continuity Management addresses one of the greatest challenges all managers face: job turnover. In addition to defining the problem and its impact clearly and concisely, the authors provide practical strategies for documenting and passing along key operating knowledge to new staff. This is a landmark book that is also a pleasure to read.
> **—Marc Scorca**
> CEO and President, Opera America

This is the first book to provide a realistic path to leading with "continuity advantage"—as integral to the success of a large-scale enterprise as it is to a start-up entrepreneurial firm. It is not a matter of employee retention, customer satisfaction, or maintaining knowledge bases. You need dynamic systems that build human sustainability—keeping your feet on the ground while positioning competence with vision . . . and avoiding the inevitable knowledge loss related to downsizing.
> **—Debra M. Amidon**
> Founder of ENTOVATION International, Ltd., and author of *Innovation Strategy for the Knowledge Economy*

Continuity Management—a how-to manual for building and managing effective knowledge organizations—will be essential reading for companies large and small.
> **—Gary Strack**
> President and CEO, Boca Raton Community Hospital

Continuity Management

Preserving Corporate Knowledge and
Productivity When Employees Leave

Hamilton Beazley
Jeremiah Boenisch
David Harden

John Wiley & Sons, Inc.

Published by John Wiley & Sons, Inc., Hoboken, N.J.
Published simultaneously in Canada.

This publication is designed to provide accurate and authoritative information in regard to the subject matter covered. It is sold with the understanding that the publisher is not engaged in rendering professional services. If professional advice or other expert assistance is required, the services of a competent professional person should be sought.

Library of Congress Cataloging-in-Publication Data:
ISBN 0-471-21906-1

Printed in the United States of America.

10 9 8 7 6 5 4 3 2 1

To Herbert Malcolm Beazley (1932–2001), my big brother,
with gratitude for all our times together and with love. "Commodore."
—H.B.

To Deborah, my beautiful and loving wife, and to Kylie and Kate,
my precious daughters, who will always be Daddy's little girls.
—J.B.

To my beautiful bride who makes me the man I am, my best friend, Angie.
To my angel daughter Madison, you are always my little princess.
To my baby son Bradley, may I raise you to be a tender warrior.
—D.B.H.

Contents

Introduction

Scenario 1. Over the previous 12-month period, *70 percent of the employees in the sales department of your Fortune 100 company have left.* More alarmingly, you discover that they have taken their knowledge with them, leaving a knowledge vacuum of stunning proportions that their successors are struggling to fill—while productivity drops and revenue plummets.

Scenario 2. An internal survey reveals that *25 percent of your employees intend to look for a new job within the year.* But you have no way to harvest their knowledge—knowledge that is about to walk out the door when they do. And you don't even know who will be leaving.

Scenario 3. Your organization is about to implement a downsizing program that will result in the termination of hundreds of experienced individuals with critical operational knowledge. When their terminations are announced, they will leave quickly and unhappily, and their knowledge will leave with them. What will the organization do without that knowledge? What will you do?

These scenarios are not imaginary. *They have already happened.* Scenario 1 is based on a 70 percent annual turnover in the sales departments of some Fortune 100 corporations in the information technology industry for the year 2000 (Web-programmers rule, 2001, p. 154). Scenario 2 is based on the results of a survey by Development Dimensions, International, the Pittsburgh-based human resource consulting firm, reporting that 25 percent of the workers surveyed intended to look for a new job within the year even though fewer than 10 percent were unhappy with their present jobs (Geber, 2000, p. 50). Scenarios 1 and 2 reflect the high turnover rates of the dot-com boom years and the heated economy of 1996 to 2000, whereas Scenario 3 is typical of the downsizing, mergers, and reorganizations of the economic downturn that followed.

These scenarios reflect an irony of the knowledge economy: Even as knowledge has become more valuable, its loss has become more likely. But the irony deepens: The less knowledge that is captured regularly, the more urgently it must be captured with an employee's departure—at the very time when that employee may be unwilling to share it. These knowledge loss scenarios emphasize that the constant threat of knowledge loss may be a permanent feature of the Information Age. So, too, may be high job turnover. The high rates of the boom years may not be anomalous, but simply characteristic rates of the new knowledge economy. It may be the case that whether the economy is expanding and employees are job hopping or the economy is contracting and employees are being laid off, turnover will remain high. It is too soon to determine statistically whether high job turnover rates are a permanent or cyclical feature of the knowledge economy. Either way, however, job turnover poses a serious threat to knowledge continuity that must be countered. But it is not the only threat. Organizations in the public and private sectors of the U.S. economy face an unprecedented loss of critical knowledge for at least the next two decades from impending baby-boomer retirements. If not countered effectively, this threatened loss of critical organizational knowledge will disrupt corporate productivity, interfere with essential governmental services, and impede the growth of the American economy at least through the 18-year retirement cycle of the baby-boom generation. And perhaps beyond.

In the course of conducting the research for this book, we interviewed managers and executives from all sectors of the American economy—government, military, and the private sector—including organizations in both the for-profit and not-for-profit arenas. In virtually every case, we encountered the same question: "Is there something we can do to keep knowledge from walking out the door when employees leave?"

Our answer to that question became a confident, "Yes, there is." To the obvious follow-up question of "What?" we came to respond, "Continuity management."

This book expands on that two-word solution, *continuity management,* developing it into a comprehensive, highly effective means for preserving corporate knowledge and productivity *even when employees leave.* Operational knowledge no longer has to walk out the door with a departing employee. It can be harvested by the organization *prior* to an employee's departure and transferred to the employee's successor *after* that departure.

The growing concern with knowledge loss reflected in this often-asked question about departing employees and their operational knowledge grows out of an increased awareness that knowledge plays a critical role in the new economy and that threats to the preservation of that knowledge are threats to the organization itself. These threats take acute and chronic forms, both of which are more malignant than at any time in American history.

The Acute Threat: Catastrophic Knowledge Loss

The *acute threat* of knowledge loss arises from the impending baby-boomer retirements in the United States. The scale of this potential loss is so great that the U.S. Department of Defense and the U.S. Senate have declared it a crisis requiring immediate and decisive action to resolve. In a very real sense, the United States is facing a possible collapse of the operational knowledge on which it depends to maintain its productivity, its economic dominance, and its military might. The Bureau of Labor Statistics estimates, for example, that approximately *19 percent* of the entire American workforce holding executive, administrative, and managerial positions will retire by 2008.

Half of the 1.8 million federal employees will be eligible for retirement in 2005, including a majority of those in the highly experienced senior executive service and 50 percent of the civilian employees in the Department of Defense. Yet inchoate attempts to deal with the effects of this impending knowledge collapse have focused on setting higher retention goals, developing more persuasive recruitment and retention techniques, and instituting better corporate training rather than on *harvesting* the knowledge of departing employees before they depart. Such tactics, even if successful, will merely delay the inevitability of the baby-boomer retirements and the timing of the knowledge collapse.

The Chronic Threat: Knowledge Depletion

Equal in importance to the acute threat from impending baby-boomer retirements is the *chronic threat* to corporate productivity, profitability, and competitiveness posed by the loss of critical knowledge from the millions of annual transfers, resignations, and terminations that characterize the transient workforce of the Information Age. When these employees leave their organizations, for whatever reason, their operational knowledge is lost to the organization. In some low positions of the hierarchy, the lost knowledge is merely inconvenient for the organization. In higher, knowledge-based positions, however, it can be devastating.

Common sense suggests that organizations would provide for this inevitable contingency by developing systems to preserve the critical knowledge of departing employees and then to transfer that knowledge to successor employees. But *they do not*. Instead, organizations expect replacement employees to get up to speed using whatever knowledge scraps and data fragments remain in the files of the departed or the memories of their coworkers. In most cases, those scraps and fragments are incomplete and disorganized, and the information they contain is unhelpful or even counterproductive. This scenario of lost knowledge is repeated day in and day out in the departure of hundreds of thousands of employees in American organizations—and around the world—creating an organizational knowledge loss that is costly and enduring. Yet knowledge has never been more valuable.

The Value of Knowledge

Over the past quarter century, the American economy has moved from the Industrial Age to the Information Age and, in the process, from an industrial economy to what has been termed the *knowledge economy*. One of the indicators of this watershed transition is the amount of corporate investment in information technology. It was in 1992 that information technology expenditures exceeded, for the first time, expenditures on all other capital equipment combined (Manasco, 2000, p. 1). Knowledge has replaced capital as the scarce factor of production and so has become the dominant economic force in business. It is the new source of wealth—an asset category to be invested as carefully as capital itself.

As the importance of knowledge increases and knowledge loss accelerates, the negative impact of knowledge loss on organizations rises exponentially. The effects are predictable and costly. They include:

- Reduced efficiency
- Decreased productivity
- Increased employee frustration and stress
- Lower revenues

Together, these negative effects damage profitability, curtail innovation, impair responsiveness, and reduce the chance of surviving against quicker, more knowledge-savvy competitors.

The loss of knowledge that accompanies an employee's transfer, resignation, termination, or retirement is the single most pervasive and costly source of knowledge mismanagement in corporate America today. On the basis of job transfers and job hopping alone, it costs American companies billions of dollars a year in lost work hours and productivity. Yet despite intense interest in the knowledge economy, no comprehensive management approach has yet been developed to address either the acute problem of the impending knowledge collapse due to baby-boomer retirements or the chronic problem of knowledge depletion due to employee departures. Why not? Not because knowledge continuity is effectively handled in corporate America. It is not. Nor because knowledge discontinuity is not a problem. It is. Rather, it is because only in the new century has the problem of lost knowledge reached critical proportions.

A convergence of seven forces has turned what was once a troublesome problem of knowledge loss into a critical one of knowledge depletion and collapse. These forces include:

1. *The emergence of the Information Age and the knowledge economy, which have transformed knowledge into an asset and made it the basic economic resource.* In the new economy, the crucial hiring question is not "Where did you work (and for how long)?" but "What did you learn (and what do you know)?"

2. *The shift from relatively mechanistic organizational structures to more organic ones, which has ended job-function stability.* Job roles and responsibilities are continually redefined by technological change and other environmental forces. They have been expanded to include more and more activities and more and more decisions, many of which are increasingly complex and increasingly important to the organization. Networks, systems, and relationships have replaced rigid procedures and strict protocols in the performance of work. In such an environment, knowledge is controlling, and the loss of that knowledge can be permanently damaging to an organization.

3. *The emergence of data gathering and processing technologies, which have resulted in data and information proliferation and information overload.*

The pressing need is not for more information, but for better distillation, interpretation, and organization of that information, which is knowledge. It is knowledge, not information, that can be converted into savvy action. *Knowledge processing, preservation,* and *creation* have replaced *information processing* as the primary challenge for many workers.

4. *High employee turnover and brief job tenure due to job hopping and transfers, which create continuous knowledge discontinuities for the organization.* This characteristic of the mobile workforce has made knowledge loss a chronic problem.

5. *Layoffs and terminations due to downsizing, which create huge knowledge gaps in the downsized organization.* Downsizing often results in the best or most experienced people leaving an organization as they accept early retirement or voluntary separations motivated by lucrative severance packages. When these employees leave, institutional memory goes with them. If their operational and organizational knowledge have not been preserved, the resulting knowledge loss substantially reduces the value of the organizational knowledge pool and handicaps their less-experienced successors.

6. *Greater use of the contingent workforce (temporary and contract), which leads to frequent knowledge turnover and uncontrolled knowledge loss.*

7. *An emphasis on higher quality, continuous improvement, and organizational learning, which requires access to prior organizational knowledge, including the lessons learned from past successes and failures.* Unless existing knowledge is preserved, new knowledge cannot be constructed from it and must be rediscovered with every new employee.

These seven forces have converged to create a new management imperative, one that is consonant with the unique demands of the Information Age: the preservation of corporate knowledge and productivity when employees leave by preserving the operational knowledge of departing employees *before* they leave.

Countering the Threats: Continuity Management

Continuity management, which is a shortened form of *knowledge continuity management,* is defined as the efficient and effective transfer of critical operational knowledge—both explicit and tacit, both individual and institutional—from transferring, resigning, terminating, or retiring employees to their successors. Conceptually simple but extremely powerful, continuity management is an effective means of countering the acute and chronic threats of knowledge loss. It speeds the ramp-up of new employees, increases productivity, reduces the stress of job changes for new hires and incumbent employees, protects the organization's knowledge base, improves customer satisfaction, and creates other competitive advantages.

Four of the most important management concepts of the new century require effective knowledge continuity to fulfill their potential: continuous improvement, quality maximization, recurrent innovation, and organizational learning. Without knowledge continuity, no organization can be termed a "learning organization," because no organization hemorrhaging knowledge can maintain the essential knowledge base it needs to learn from its mistakes and build on its successes. Continuity management is critical to each of these concepts because it is about the *creation* of knowledge as well as its preservation. The analysis required by continuity management enables employees to identify their critical operational knowledge and to capitalize on their productivity leverage points. It clarifies job responsibilities, reduces nonproductive effort, and increases individual effectiveness. The analysis also identifies knowledge hoarders and employees for whom no redundancy exists and who, therefore, constitute a serious exposure for the organization.

Continuity management can be implemented at *any level* of an organization by *any manager* at that level or above. It can be scaled to fit teams and departments as well as entire organizations, and it can be implemented with varying degrees of technological and methodological sophistication. It can be productively integrated into existing planning, appraisal, and reward systems. Although organizationwide continuity management programs are more effective than localized ones, small-scale continuity management programs will nonetheless make a significant difference for individual managers and their teams, departments, units, and divisions. Some knowledge continuity is better than none and will produce significant rewards for managers and their organizations.

Overview

Continuity Management consists of three parts. Part I, "Knowledge Continuity in the Information Age," examines the chronic threat of knowledge loss from job turnover and the acute threat from impending baby-boomer retirements, why operational knowledge is both a capital asset and a commodity that can be harvested and transferred to successors, and how continuity management creates significant competitive advantages for individuals and organizations in the transient workplace of the Information Age.

Part II, "Confessions of a Continuity Manager," describes a step-by-step implementation of continuity management using the literary device of a manager's journal. It includes five get-started principles that underlie continuity management, five potential barriers to continuity management, and six steps to its implementation. It also describes a knowledge continuity assessment that managers can use to evaluate the extent of knowledge discontinuity in their organizations, and it explains the five process elements through which critical operational knowledge is harvested from incumbents, validated by their peers, and passed to successors.

Part III, "Knowledge Asset Management," continues with the practical application of the principles and concepts of continuity management. It complements the book's earlier focus on harvesting operational knowledge by focusing on the transfer of that knowledge to successor employees and on how that transfer can be achieved in the most effective way. It also describes the realignment of the organizational culture and reward system required to support continuity management, and it explores the integration of continuity management and knowledge management into a seamless process in the service of knowledge preservation and creation.

Business is a marathon. Success cannot be achieved by the sprinter who runs alone. The business marathon is made up of many races and many people. For each employee—for each runner—and for the organization as a whole, each race is a relay, and on the success of that relay depends the success of the organization. Competitive advantage in the Information Age belongs to the organization whose employees can hand off their knowledge to the next runner, who will hand off that knowledge to the next runner, and the next, in an endless succession of relays that preserve and pass on the key to victory in the marketplace: *operational knowledge.*

Our interviews with public- and private-sector executives, our analysis of organizations operating effectively in the turbulent business environment of the knowledge economy, and our study of the research on management, learning, productivity, and knowledge have provided ample evidence that continuity management is the missing piece in the complex mosaic of knowledge preservation, transfer, and enhancement that drives organizational success. Continuity management is an extraordinary opportunity for managers to outflank and outperform their competitors by seizing the knowledge advantage.

As more and more stories of individual and corporate successes built on continuity management emerge, we expect an ever-deepening understanding of its potential, greater levels of sophistication in its implementation, and a more powerful integration of its concepts and principles into daily management activities. The coming revolution in preserving knowledge continuity between incumbent and successor employees to achieve organizational knowledge superiority and dominant competitive advantage has begun. This book is about that revolution—and how to lead it.

Part I

Knowledge Continuity in the Information Age

To understand both the urgent need for—and the great potential of—continuity management is to understand the radically different environment in which contemporary organizations are required to operate. The new context created by this environment is transforming the nature of management itself. It is a context defined by the transformation of knowledge into a capital asset, the unique nature of that asset, impending baby-boomer retirements and chronic job turnover that threaten the asset, and the relationship of knowledge continuity to productivity and innovation in the Information Age. Part I provides this contextual understanding and sets the stage for the design and implementation of continuity management described in Part II.

1 | Knowledge Loss in the Information Age

Each generation of business leaders has had to deal with a characteristic threat to profitability and, sometimes, survival that came to define their era. War, inflation, depression, stock market collapse, foreign imports, and labor shortages were all serious threats to business enterprises in the past century that had to be countered if those organizations were to survive. The first decade of the new century offers no exception to the litany of threats; it merely adds a new one: knowledge loss. The loss of knowledge from departing employees poses a threat to the productivity and prosperity of contemporary organizations that is equal to the great business threats of the past century. Those organizations that can surmount this challenge by preserving their organizational knowledge base while job transfers, retirements, terminations, and resignations deplete the knowledge base of their competitors will be the business success stories of the century.

Knowledge Workers

Peter Drucker, perhaps the foremost management thinker of our time, coined the term "knowledge worker" in his 1959 book, *Landmarks of Tomorrow.* In 1994, he predicted that a third or more of the American workforce would be knowledge workers by the end of the century (Drucker, 1994, p. 53), a prediction that he confirmed in 2001 (Drucker, 2001, p. 2). Knowledge workers are the members of the labor force whose skills are primarily intellectual rather than manual. They *create and apply knowledge* rather than make things. As the defining characteristic of work shifts from repetitive actions governed by strict instructions or simple techniques to unique actions that require complex decision making grounded in understanding, knowledge becomes increasingly important. And more and more people become knowledge workers.

This shift to knowledge work has significantly enhanced the value of knowledge to an organization. As Chapter 2 explains, knowledge is now the primary economic factor in production, a capital asset to be carefully preserved and wisely invested. But knowledge resides largely in the heads of people—people who leave and take their knowledge with them. When knowledge walks out the door with departing employees who have left no "copy" for the organization, the results can be devastating. Mounting knowledge losses can create a knowledge crisis for the organization. In fact, contemporary organizations are facing just such a crisis: an acute threat of knowledge loss from impending baby-boomer retirements and a chronic threat from terminations, transfers, layoffs, resignations, and job hopping.

Acute Threat: The Impending Knowledge Collapse

The generation born in the post–World War II baby boom has had a profound effect on public policy, the workplace, and society at large throughout its life. Between 1946 and 1964, about 75 million children were born in the United States. Today, the baby-boom generation totals approximately 83 million, including those born in other countries but now residing in America. At each stage in its life cycle, this generation has shifted the demand for public services, changed the market for a wide range of products, and altered the nature of the workforce. For nearly 20 years, policymakers, analysts, and social scientists have been concerned about the effect the baby boomers would have on the economy and the nation as they retired.

Technically, the year 2005 marks the beginning of the baby-boom exodus from the workforce. Beginning that year, every seven seconds, another baby boomer will turn 60—and reach retirement age—a process that will continue for the next 18 years. What will these retirements mean? They presage a hemorrhaging of workplace knowledge and knowledge-based experience at a time when such knowledge and experience is increasingly important to the American economy and to the organizations that comprise it.

The Private Sector

The Bureau of Labor Statistics has attempted to estimate the number of baby-boomer retirements that will strike the private sector annually and to identify the most affected industries. The bureau's study indicates, for example, that 19 percent of the baby boomers holding executive, administrative, and managerial occupations are expected to leave by 2008. That's almost 1 in 5 management positions. But some industries will be even harder hit. By 2010, "as many as 60% of today's experienced management personnel will retire from the [oil and gas] industry even if various 'golden handcuff' incentives are initiated to retain perhaps 20% of them" (Clark and Poruban, 2001, p. 74). The Society of Petroleum Engineers estimates that the industry will lose 44 percent of its petroleum engineers between 2000 and 2010, a loss of 231,000 years of cumulative experience (Kornberg and Beattie, 2002, p. 19). Development Dimensions International, a Pittsburgh-based human resources consulting firm, projects that between 2000 and 2005, some companies (especially large, older companies) will see 40 to 50 percent of their executives retire, a decimation of management that will leave a knowledge void of unprecedented proportions (Geber, 2000, p. 50).

But many baby boomers—particularly in the management and executive ranks—are thinking about retiring *before* they reach 60, which foreshortens the retirement timeframe and amplifies the retirement threat from the baby-boom generation. According to the John J. Heidrich Center for Workforce Development at Rutgers University, 76 percent of the baby boomers would like to retire before they are 50 (working for fun, 2000, p. A1). Deloitte Consulting has discovered that by 2003, nearly one-third of its 800-partner firm will be over the age of 50—and some of the fiftyish partners are talking retirement (Geber, 2000, p. 48). The obvious prediction about the baby boomers is that they will not behave as a group; some will retire early and some will retire late. The sheer number of baby boomers, however, will generate millions of early retirees. Moreover, the general trend toward early retirement means that some of those in the generation following the baby boomers may themselves elect to retire early, exacerbating the effect of baby boomer retirements.

It is possible that estimates of early or "on-time" retirements are exaggerated because of future financial pressures that might force many baby boomers to change their minds about when they will retire. Their longer life spans, for example, might require more funding than retirement income alone can provide if baby boomers are to maintain the high standard of living to which many of them have become accustomed. Or baby boomers may incur extraordinary expenses associated with aging parents that will force them to continue working. Perhaps one of these circumstances will mitigate the threat. Certainly, a broad array of federal policies and programs have been developed or modified over the past several years to encourage baby boomers to remain in the labor force. Changes to the Social Security system, for example, have raised the official age of retirement, laws prohibiting age discrimination in the workplace have been enacted, and changes to pension and benefit regulations have removed many disincentives to continue working beyond age 65.

Even if baby boomers do work later than preceding generations, however, they are not likely to remain in the same job. They are more likely to choose a different full-time career or a part-time career that will utilize their experience while affording them the opportunity to do more of what they want to do. Either way, they will have retired from their primary organizations, taking their knowledge with them. And when they do, the results can be disastrous. Bill Gates, cofounder of Microsoft, recounts the potential loss to Microsoft that might have occurred from the retirement of just one employee whose operational knowledge had not been captured:

> A few years ago we discovered we were missing some blueprints for the existing buildings on our Redmond campus. We needed the blueprints as background for our next stage of construction. Our longtime head of real estate and facilities had just retired, so we had to call him up at home to see if he knew where the plans were. He directed us to an electrician who fortunately still worked with one of our outside vendors. Sure enough, the electrician had the blueprints. In fact, that electrician was the only person in the world who had all of the plans for all of our buildings.
>
> Traditional societies often rely on one or two people to remember the group's history and traditions, but modern organizations need a better way to record and pass on their folklore. Yet at Microsoft we were relying pretty much on oral tradition, too. Here we were, the largest developer of office space in the Seattle area, embarking on a period of construction in which we would put up between half a million and a million square feet of new office space a year, and our entire "knowledge base" of crucial information was being carried round in the heads of just a few people and in a few stacks of blueprints we didn't even have on file. (Gates, 1999, pp. 236–237)

In a similar vein, an account executive for a multi-billion-dollar company told us the following story. "We lost a high-performing client manager to retirement," this executive said. "When I took over the account, I discovered that we had also lost critical information relating to that account that we could not easily retrieve. With no continuity, I had to put off the customer for two weeks while I scrambled to recover the lost information. That didn't bode well for the client—or for me—because it stalled their important project. What were we missing? Just the thing we needed most—knowledge."

This loss of an experienced account manager to retirement exemplifies a mini–knowledge collapse. The phrase is not hyperbolic because the knowledge disappeared suddenly and with serious impact. It damaged the relationship with the client and delayed a major project. When these minicollapses are multiplied by the number of baby boomers eligible for retirement and the number of situations affected by the loss of their knowledge, they rapidly build into a knowledge collapse of major proportions. The depth and breadth of the baby-boomer knowledge base makes it a formidable corporate asset, one that cannot be easily replaced if lost and one that is currently at risk.

It can be argued that the knowledge base of the baby-boom generation is the single most valuable—and the most critical—organizational asset in America today, whether part of the public or private sector. Those organizations that fail to preserve baby-boomer knowledge are destined for rough sailing. They risk declining customer satisfaction, lost market share, lower revenue, and even potential bankruptcy. Such a scenario of companies faltering on lost knowledge was highly implausible in the Industrial Age. In the knowledge-driven Information Age, it is highly probable.

The Public Sector

The public sector is no more insulated from catastrophic knowledge loss than the private sector. By 2005, *more than half* the federal employees will be eligible for retirement, including an astounding 71 percent of the senior executive service, which is composed of the government's highest-ranking and most experienced career professionals (Walker, 2001c). According to the U.S. General Accounting Office, another 58 percent of federal employees at the GS-15 level (the highest-ranking managers beneath the senior executive service) and another 41 percent at the GS-14 level will also be eligible for retirement in the same year (Walker, 2001a). Debra Tomchek, director of human resources management at the Department of Commerce, warns that "we're going to have a crisis at the top" unless some strategy is devised to replace the knowledge lost from the retiring managers (Figura, 1999, p. 20). The Treasury Department's chief information officer reports that the department is "approaching a crisis in information technology skills" because of its "highly experienced workforce, which is moving in great numbers toward retirement eligibility" (Figura, 1999, p. 20). A U.S. Senate Governmental Affairs subcommittee issued a December, 2000, report entitled "Report to the President: The Crisis in Human Capital" that carried similar warnings about the high risk of baby-boomer retirements (Walker, 2001a). Since the federal government represents 20 percent of the U.S. economy, provides essential infrastructure functions, and ensures the national defense, major disruptions in its ability to carry out these responsibilities would have a highly adverse effect on the United States and its economy.

State and local governments throughout the United States face the same problem as the federal government. Described by a State of Wisconsin Workforce Planning Committee as "the most significant talent and brain drain ever experienced by government," 40 percent of all state and local government employees will become eligible to retire in the next 15 years (Wisconsin State Government Workforce Planning Team, 2001). The committee's report described the impending baby-boomer retirements as a "big locomotive," concluding that, "for the most part, states and municipalities are acting like they don't even see the train coming."

The Department of Defense faces a similar problem. The secretary of defense reported in May 2000 that "the Department of Defense is on the verge of a crisis that the rest of the public and private sectors will also encounter—a retirement-driven talent drain (Acquisition 2005 Task Force, 2000)." Furthermore, according to the report, it is "a crisis that can dramatically affect our Nation's ability to provide warfighters with modern weapon systems needed to defend our national interests" (Acquisition 2005 Task Force, 2000). In 2005, 50 percent of the civilians who work in defense acquisitions and 39 percent of the total civilian workforce of the Department of Defense will be eligible for retirement. "In some occupations," according to the Department of Defense, "half of the current employees will be gone by 2006" (Acquisition 2005 Task Force, 2000). Former Secretary of the Air Force F. Whitten Peters called the situation "a time bomb waiting to go off" (Grier, 2001).

Senator George Voinovich (R–Ohio), Chairman of the Senate Subcommittee on Oversight of Government Management, wrote in an op-ed piece for the *Washington Post* entitled "Dangers of an Aging Federal Work Force" (Voinovich, 2001), "The federal work force is in crisis. And nowhere is this erosion more evident, or potentially more dangerous, than in our national security establishment. . . . If we fail to respond to the formidable human capital challenges in our national security establishment in a thoughtful and deliberate manner, then our best strategies and billion-dollar weapon systems will afford us little protection in an already uncertain future."

Impending baby-boomer retirements in Europe, Australia, and Japan portend equally grave problems for these countries as they deal with similarly massive retirements in the public sector. In Western Australia, for example, a staggering 78 percent of the senior executive service will be eligible for retirement by 2009, with 45 percent of them eligible by 2004 (Ministry of the Premier and Cabinet, 1999, p. 6). According to the government study that reported these figures, the number of potential retirees over the next 5 to 10 years is so great that consideration should be given to developing a "senior management vacuum scenario."

As if the acute threat of baby-boomer retirements were not serious enough, it is exacerbated by a concurrent threat that is chronic in nature: knowledge depletion from high and continuing job turnover.

Chronic Threat: Ongoing Knowledge Depletion

The recurring loss of employees whose knowledge has not been harvested creates a chronic condition of knowledge loss that depletes an organization's knowledge base and so destroys its ability to effectively build on that knowledge base. Employees leave for many reasons, but generally, those reasons can be divided into four broad categories. They are:

1. *Employee terminations,* in which employees are laid off involuntarily because of downsizing, restructuring, mergers, reduced demand, budget cuts, unacceptable performance, or similar factors.
2. *Employee resignations,* in which employees voluntarily leave the organization because of dissatisfaction, better offers, changes in health status, changes in life style, or similar reasons.

3. *Employee transfers (reallocations)*, in which current workers are reassigned to new or existing positions within their organization and so must vacate their current positions.
4. *Contingency workforce resignations,* in which temporary or contract employees who have been hired for limited time periods leave the organization.

Collectively, these circumstances create a chronic problem of employee turnover and knowledge depletion in organizations. For example, approximately 34 percent of the staff at the Big Five accounting firms are either in their first year with the firm—in need of knowledge—or in their last year with the firm—soon to leave with knowledge (Hiltebeitel and Leauby, 2001, p. 17). The average annual turnover rate in the information technology industry in 1999 was 25 percent, according to a survey conducted by Sibson & Co., a Princeton, New Jersey, firm specializing in human capital, and confirmed by the American Management Association's mid-2000 job survey (Essex, 2000, p. 1). Even in the "Best 100 Companies to Work For," as reported in *Fortune,* annual turnover rates ran as high as 24 percent in business services, 17 percent in publishing, and 13 percent in finance, insurance, and real estate (Nobscot Corporation, 2001, p. 1). The annual *worker reallocation* rate in America exceeds 40 percent, which means that almost half of American workers change what they do for their employers every year. Of 5,000 executives surveyed by the Hay Group in 2001, 46 percent said they expected to remain in their position for only two to five years (Sahl, 2001, p. 6). Nearly 50 percent of those who constitute personal staff of the U.S. Senate have been in their current jobs for less than one year (Congressional Management Foundation, 1999, p. 95).

These statistics portray an appalling scenario of knowledge loss that is repeated over and over in daily employee departures. Consider, for example, these specific examples of lost knowledge from employee terminations in 2001 (That means I'm fired, 2001, p. 22):

- "Lucent," *Time* reports, "expects to reduce its net headcount . . . through a combination of force management actions and attrition." Translation: 10,000 employees gone. What happened to all that operational knowledge?
- Cisco reports that "the reduction in workforce will include . . . involuntary attrition and the consolidation of some positions." Translation:

3,000 to 5,000 employees gone. The employees obviously took their knowledge with them. But did they leave any behind?

■ Schwab confirms that "it plans to implement further restructuring to reduce operating expenses." Translation: 2,000 to 4,000 employees gone. Was the firm's knowledge base also "restructured"?

Many of those laid off in this round of downsizing were highly skilled, white-collar knowledge workers. "When they let these people go," Chicago outplacement expert John Challenger warns, "they scatter to the wind—all that training, all that corporate know-how gets lost" (McGinn, 2001, p. 37).

Or consider this example of knowledge discontinuity resulting from military job transfers. Air Force Colonel Michael Basla, former Joint Task Force Southwest Asia joint communications commander recounts:

Imagine stepping off a plane in Saudi Arabia knowing that you and only you are in charge of all the U.S. communication systems in Southwest Asia. This alone is a daunting task, yet what made it more daunting was knowing that every 90 days, 99 percent of my personnel were going to leave my organization and be replaced by new crews. Basically, my people would "high five" each other going in and out the door—that was the continuity I had. It wouldn't have been a big deal if we were digging ditches, but that wasn't the case. We were responsible for providing the commander with sensor information and his command-and-control capabilities. This complex enterprise was critical to the safety of friendly forces and to the accomplishment of the United Nation's "No Fly, No Drive" resolution against Iraq. (Basla, 2001)

Marc Scorca, president of Opera America, an association of opera executives from the country's major opera companies, observes that "chronic turnover among support personnel in marketing and fund-raising poses a serious threat to the health of the performing arts. It is as big a problem as the approaching retirements of those who have been founders and mainstays of performing arts companies for decades. We have reached a point where it is no longer tolerable to continue losing this kind and quantity of knowledge" (Scorca, 2001). Lieutenant General John Woodward, U.S. Air Force deputy chief of staff for communications information and deputy chief information officer, explains why knowledge loss is so costly to the military. "Knowledge is a key asset because virtually every person is a decision maker, and sound decision-making requires relevant knowledge. If we don't preserve that knowledge, we're wasting assets" (Woodward, 2001).

Another element in chronic job turnover is the growing corporate and governmental reliance on the contingency workforce, which creates special knowledge continuity problems for organizations. Contingency workers include self-employed individuals; those who work for temporary placement firms, contract engineering companies, and the like; and those who are relied on to perform outsourced functions through third-party firms retained for that purpose. More and more executive and professional positions (paying over $100,000 per year) and midlevel positions (paying in the $30,000 to $60,000 range) fall into the contingency workforce category, but at the high end; for example, "a growing number of CPI [chemical process industries] companies in the US are now hiring some senior-level managers, many with chemical engineering degrees, on an interim basis" (Shanley, 1999, p. 92).

As organizations change their employment strategies from full-term, permanent staffing to short-term, contractual staffing, the velocity of knowledge loss increases because of the shortened tenure of the contingency workers and the more rapid turnover they create. Because the government does not keep statistics on the number of individuals who provide work as so-called free agents, numbers are hard to come by. There are 14 million self-employed Americans, 8.3 million independent contractors, and 2.3 million who work daily through temporary agencies (Nakashima, 2001, p. A27). This combined figure of approximately 25 million, if accurate, would represent 1 out of every 6 working people in the United States. Not all of them are knowledge workers, but many of them are.

Loyalty in America at the beginning of the twenty-first century can't be taken for granted in quite the same way as in the twentieth century. Brand loyalty, for example, is fading; fans increasingly abandon losing sports teams; professional athletes change teams; independent voters have grown from 1 to 15 percent of total voters in the past 35 years; and even national politicians switch their party affiliation (sometimes with dramatic results, as happened in the case of Republican Senator James Jeffords, who tipped control of the U.S. Senate to the Democrats). A parallel societal trend away from loyalty to companies or birth cities and toward greater mobility and transience is reflected in the job hopping and career switching that increasingly characterize the American workplace. The new generation of employees does not consider long-term employment an issue of loyalty, but an example of naiveté. In fact, more and more employees under 30 see themselves as free agents, even when they are "regular" employees, because they know they can be laid off suddenly with a business slump, merger, or acquisition. Their solution? Actively managing their own careers, job hopping as necessary to further them. The new generation of knowledge workers don't see themselves as employees of the company as much as *employers* of the company, which they will dismiss whenever it works to their advantage to do so.

Disillusionment from the wave of downsizing in the late 1980s and 1990s, a strong economy at the end of the 1990s, portable 401(k) pension plans, instant access to many job listings on the Internet, and growth of the executive recruiter industry were all factors in creating a more transient workforce at the end of the century. Long job tenure "used to be an honor badge," says John Wilson, an executive recruiter with Korn/Ferry International in San Francisco. "It's changed to the point where recruiters now really scrutinize the background and wisdom of a person who's done that. These days, you have to wonder as a recruiter, 'Why was that person so happy there for so long? Were they challenged by a lot of different roles? Or were they just so comfortable that they stayed and stayed and stayed?' " (DeBare, 2000, p. 1). B. Lynn Ware, a recruitment retention expert with Integral Training Systems in Half Moon Bay concurs. She says that "two to three years [of job tenure] used to raise a red flag. Now, depending on the industry, it's one to 1.5 years. But what employers are really looking at is, did the person complete the project or commitment they made?" (DeBare, 2000, p. 3).

Clearly, the promise or even the hope of lifetime employment is a remnant of an earlier age. At one time, IBM boasted of its family atmosphere and its no-layoff policy. In 1992, it fired 120,000 workers (Whimper fi, 2001, p. C1). The unstated psychological contract between employees and employers that used to include the expectation of long-term, if not lifetime, employment with the organization has changed dramatically. The U.S. Post Office, for example, and the U.S. military once offered virtually lifetime employment if one weren't incompetent. Not anymore.

From 1989 to 1999, the civilian workforce of the Department of Defense was downsized by 38 percent, but the acquisition, technology, and logistics workforce was decreased by 49 percent. "Now what was the result of this downsizing?" Keith Charles, task force chief and director of acquisition, technology, and logistics, asked rhetorically. "We pushed people out the door, but when we looked inside their desks, we found that they were actually working on crucial projects for the Department of Defense that we could not just drop.

We had failed to maintain knowledge continuity for many of these positions, and we were left holding the bag. Knowledge loss is a serious problem that needs a robust solution" (Charles, 2001).

In the Information Age, job turnover is no longer just job turnover: It is *knowledge turnover.* "The churning of today's workforce is eating away at the profitability of even the healthiest corporations," writes B. L. Ware, president of Integral Training Systems. "Even when the bottom line isn't seriously impacted, the loss of several key employees who have special expertise or who maintain valuable customer relationships can shake an organization to its foundation" (Ware, 2001, p. 3). As with all knowledge loss, productivity suffers as the organization plays a continuous game of "knowledge catchup" in its managerial ranks. The continuity base on which corporate momentum is built and sustained is lost and then lost again and again.

Organizations that have been deeply concerned about organizational "learning" have been oddly negligent about its opposite: corporate "forgetting," which occurs with every departing knowledge worker. What kind of organizational learning can take place if the knowledge base on which it relies is subject to continual degradation or if the organization itself cannot remember enough to pass on its knowledge and its secrets to the newcomer expected to carry the torch? Yet this scenario is commonplace in contemporary organizations. In those organizations beset by significant job turnover, there may be more organizational forgetting going on than there is organizational learning. In the Information Age, as opposed to the Industrial Age, there is a lot more to forget.

Yet even as organizational forgetting increases, so does the value of the knowledge that is lost. So valued is knowledge in the Information Age that companies have instituted ongoing training and continuous learning programs to raise the level of employee expertise, a strategy that, ironically, increases the marketability of those employees. By building the knowledge of their workers—and so making those workers more valuable in the marketplace—contemporary organizations have made themselves more vulnerable to job hopping. Ironically, by failing to harvest the operational knowledge of those employees, organizations have also made themselves more vulnerable to knowledge loss. In fact, management has grown so accustomed to this knowledge loss that it seems largely accepted as an inevitable cost of doing business. In fact, job turnover *is* inevitable in organizations, but the devastating knowledge loss that accompanies it is not.

Significant numbers of departing employees send a shock wave of knowledge discontinuity through an organization. In the highly networked world of the Information Age, each employee is an integral part of the web of knowledge-based relationships that build core competencies and create competitive advantage for the organization. Whenever one piece of the knowledge web is eliminated, its loss inevitably affects other pieces of the web and shakes the web as a whole. The goal of continuity management is to maintain the integrity of the web by preserving the knowledge that sustains it and that would otherwise be lost with each departing employee.

Countering the Threats: Continuity Management

Chaos or continuity? The crippling consequences of knowledge loss from resignations, retirements, transfers, and terminations do not have to be an accepted part of doing business. Nor can they be for companies operating successfully in the Information Age. "The more an institution is organized to be a change leader," Peter Drucker writes, "the more it will need to establish continuity internally and externally, the more it will need to *balance* rapid change and continuity" (Drucker, 1999, p. 90). Preserving knowledge continuity between incumbent and successor employees creates that requisite balance. Continuity management reduces knowledge loss from employee departures and the negative impact of that loss on productivity and profits, yet it encourages creativity, innovation, and dramatic change grounded in lessons of the past.

Continuity management is more than a program, however, or an innovative management tool or even a process. It is a new management perspective, one that affects the structure, strategies, operations, and culture of an organization. By acknowledging the network of relationships that forms the heart of a successful enterprise in the Information Age, continuity management focuses attention on the critical asset of knowledge and how that asset can be preserved and enhanced. Ultimately, knowledge continuity and continuity management become part of the vision, goals, and mission of an organization. Continuity management is a powerful means for innovative managers to create opportunity out of crisis and to redefine the rules by which business is conducted and success is achieved. While competitors are first confounded and then stalled by knowledge loss, continuity-managed organizations move confidently and decisively, using knowledge superiority to seize opportunities, reshape environments, and outpace rivals.

It is rare for a completely new competitive advantage to emerge in the world of business. Quality improvement, process reengineering, organizational learning, and knowledge management are examples of competitive advantages developed in past decades. Each has wrought significant changes in the business landscape, catapulting some organizations to dominant positions and relegating others to the status of business-school case studies of what went wrong. The difference between these extremes was—and is— savvy management. Those leaders, executives, and managers who saw the potential of each of these enduring management advances profited handsomely in annual earnings, professional reputation, and personal satisfaction.

Continuity management offers a similar opportunity to the savvy managers of the Information Age.

2
Knowledge as a Capital Asset

Over the past 50 years, knowledge has replaced capital as the scarce factor of production, becoming the dominant economic factor in business. This dramatic shift in the value of organizational knowledge underlies the current knowledge crisis and the solution to it. In the Industrial Age, *physical labor* based on manual skills was the source of economic growth and the ability to perform such labor the key to employment. Knowledge was virtually synonymous with a set of skills—often limited—applied day in and day out on the assembly line or in a similar work environment. Knowledge, therefore, was *something that enabled work*.

In the Information Age, on the other hand, *intellectual* labor based on knowledge is the source of economic growth and the ability to perform such labor the key to employment. Knowledge, therefore, is no longer primarily the means to accomplish work; *it has become the work itself.* Executives, managers, service professionals and providers, technicians, sales and marketing experts, those who provide administrative support, and other knowledge workers all acquire and disseminate knowledge, which is the basic currency of their jobs. They analyze, summarize, create, hone, expand, or otherwise manage the intangible of knowledge. If the icon of the Industrial Age was a pair of hands, the icon of the Information Age is a pair of minds.

Peter Drucker has written that "the basic economic resource—'the means of production' to use the economist's term—is no longer capital, nor natural resources (the economist's 'land'), nor 'labor.' *It is and will be knowledge*" (Drucker, 1993, p. 8). "The most valuable asset of a 21st century institution, whether business or nonbusiness, will be its *knowledge workers* and their *productivity*" (Drucker, 1999, p. 135). This shift from an emphasis on trained physical capacities to an emphasis on trained mental capacities is mirrored in the shift in business goals of the past 100 years. The goal in the Industrial Age was to automate human labor. The goal in the Information Age is to develop and exploit human knowledge.

In 1996, the Securities and Exchange Commission (SEC) held its first symposium on "intellectual capital" and how it might be quantified to reflect its contribution to corporate performance and its role as a predictor of future performance. The SEC symposium reflected a growing awareness of knowledge-based assets as a key factor in corporate productivity. Knowledge, after all, is the basis of competency, which is the basis of high performance in a turbulent environment. Rote procedures or memorized responses quickly become obsolete and ineffective in a business context that is rapidly changing. The half-life of corporate procedures is increasingly brief, and what worked last week swiftly loses its validity. Improvisation, experimentation, and risk taking are essential to innovation and responsiveness; they grow out of knowledge—and also create knowledge.

In the knowledge economy, both the cost of goods and services and the value they create include an ever-increasing percentage of intangible assets, which include organizational knowledge as well as such intangible assets as patents and trademarks. The pharmaceutical industry is a good example. It invests huge sums of money in intellectual capital in order to develop the pills, powders, and injections that it then produces for a fraction of a penny in material cost. The two decades between 1980 and 2000 brought a transformation in the relationship between the value of tangible and intangible assets. The ratio of intangible to tangible assets jumped from 1 to 1 (meaning the market value of a company was roughly equivalent to the value of its physical assets) to a ratio of 5 to 1, meaning that the company's intangible assets were regarded as *five times* more valuable than its tangible assets. That ratio may have receded to 4 to 1 after the dot-com bust and market decline of 2000, but it still has not returned to anything like 1 to 1. This upward shift in the intangible-to-tangible-asset ratio recognizes the value of intellectual capital and an organization's earnings potential that is not directly related to its tangible assets.

Another example of the pure value of organizational knowledge is the spate of corporate acquisitions launched at the turn of the century by high-tech companies operating in the software, telecommunications, networking equipment, and biotechnology sectors. For the most part, these acquisitions were made to acquire knowledge, which took the form of the high-tech talent of people such as programmers, scientists, engineers, and marketing geniuses. In many cases, this talent—this knowledge—was the acquired firm's most valuable asset. In some cases, it was its *only* asset. Yet organizations treat this expensive asset in quite an unusual way.

If a company scraps 100 trucks before they are depreciated, they are written off as a loss on the corporate books. If the same company lays off 100 employees with extensive operational knowledge, they have no recorded value to write off. Yet, in reality, their value to the company was significantly higher than that of the trucks, which could be easily replaced. Ironically, a highly organized maintenance program was even instituted to preserve the trucks while they were in use, while virtually no effort went into preserving the operational knowledge of the employees while they were "in use." With every asset other than knowledge, organizations go to great lengths to prevent the loss of the asset or, at least, to salvage some of its value if the asset is discarded. Why should the asset of knowledge be treated differently?

It shouldn't be. Murray Martin, group president, global mail at Pitney Bowes, concludes:

> The business case for continuity management is really a back-of-the-envelope calculation. If you're growing at 20 percent a year and you lose around 15 percent of your people annually, that means that 35 percent of your staff in any year are new recruits. Getting them up to speed is a time-consuming and very costly exercise—in the millions per year. So if you could systematically capture knowledge from existing staff and make it easily available to new hires, and that would reduce their time to reaching full effectiveness by a few months, think of the savings you could achieve in this area alone. (Martin, 2002)

Unfortunately, many companies do not have this realistic perspective on the value of employee knowledge—or the cost to replace and grow it. Despite many CEO claims that "people are our greatest asset," people are more often treated as expenses. Recognition of knowledge as the primary engine of corporate productivity means recognizing "that people are not a cost, but rather an enabler for the creation of revenue and wealth," as James Copeland, CEO of Deloitte Touche Tohmatsu expressed it. Preserving the operational knowledge of employees is as critical as preserving the tangible factors of production. Because it is through operational knowledge—built day by day, employee by employee—that an organization utilizes its tangible factors of production to create competitive advantage.

The Knowledge Continuum

If knowledge is the "basic economic resource," then it is worth exploring what knowledge is and how it can be exploited by an organization. At its simplest, *knowledge* in a corporate setting is what employees need to know (and be able to do) in order to perform their jobs at maximum effectiveness. Knowledge includes basic data and essential information, but it is much more comprehensive than either. Knowledge is the foundation of competency and of wisdom, which are even more valuable to an organization than knowledge. The essential question for any organization that hopes to succeed in the knowledge economy is this: How can data and information be converted into knowledge and then into competency and wisdom? The knowledge continuum explains this process of conversion. Beginning with data and ending with wisdom, the continuum consists of the following components:

Data → Information → Knowledge → Competency → Wisdom

Movement along the continuum occurs through a series of processes that bring greater understanding, an enhanced ability to deal with complexity, and a more holistic perspective. The components of the continuum can be distinguished from each other as indicated in the following paragraphs.

Data

Data is the foundational element of knowledge. Data encompasses facts, representations, or forms of measurement about some aspect of the world provided without elaboration. For example, data includes the name of the organization (a fact) and the company's market share (also a fact, but expressed as a form of measurement).

Data → Information

Information is an *interpretation* of the data based on a change in conditions and the passage of time. By assigning patterns, relationships, and meaning to data, information is created. An example of information would be this statement: "Our analysis suggests that an increase in market share occurs with an increase in advertising expenditures. Therefore, increased advertising should lead to increased sales and increased market share."

Information → Knowledge

Knowledge is information *organized* into a framework, model, worldview, concept, principle, theory, hypothesis, or other basis for action that increases understanding of a situation, improves problem solving and decision making related to the situation, and increases the likelihood of task accomplishment. Knowledge, in other words, is the domain of understanding from which people act. For example, knowledge involves knowing *how* to increase market share by selecting the appropriate content and medium for the advertising expenditures. While information may be plentiful, knowledge is less so.

Knowledge → Competency

Competency is integrated, internalized knowledge based on experienced application or contextual familiarity that provides the capabilities necessary to handle problems, make decisions, and master tasks at the level required to succeed in a position. *Competency* is higher on the knowledge continuum than *knowledge* because it arises from an integration of multiple knowledge frameworks necessary for the achievement of complex tasks. Furthermore, it adds critical skill sets and abilities, many of them interpersonal, such as conflict management, emotional intelligence, negotiating, critical analysis, effective communication, and active listening, that make it possible to *apply* knowledge in a given situation with some confidence of achieving the desired outcome.

Competency develops out of social interaction, where it is created, tested, and validated. Competency is what makes it possible for a marketing executive to actually boost a product's market share. While a knowledge of marketing may create the plan, it takes competency to pull it off. Competency, therefore, is the ability to formulate and execute successful actions based on knowledge. At its simplest, competency is the difference between those with "book learning" and those who can make things happen.

Competency → Wisdom

Wisdom is the most amorphous of the five components of the knowledge continuum. It is difficult to define, yet easy to recognize, at least in retrospect. Wisdom is competency refined by experience, practice, and maturity into above-average judgment, keen insight, and a holistic perspective that leads to sound decision making in highly complicated, rapidly changing situations that demand a balance between long-term goals and short-term needs. Wisdom is examined experience from which valid conclusions about meaning and cause and effect have been drawn and insightful questions have been answered. Wisdom is comfortable with ambiguity and paradox, nuance and uncertainty, distant timeframes and profound complexity. It is grounded in an ethical framework and a historical point of view that override potential errors of judgment caused by human character failings such as greed, envy, hate, and revenge and by seductive errors of judgment driven by short-term needs and perspectives. Wisdom is the highest form of knowing and is virtually priceless to an organization.

It is wisdom that allows an executive to evaluate the plan to boost a product's market share based not just on the knowledge in the plan or on the competencies necessary to carry it out, but on the context in which the plan is to be implemented, balancing the short term against the long term and weighing all such factors to determine the best course of action. *Context* includes the plan's relationship to other product plans, to the mission and strategy of the organization, to the market itself, and to a host of other factors, some of them objective and some of them subjective and based on experience, but all leading to productive recommendations that will improve the plan or abort its implementation.

■ ■ ■

To summarize the knowledge continuum, raw data becomes information, then knowledge, individualized competency, and wisdom through a series of conversion processes. Those processes that convert one component into the next on the knowledge continuum are:

Data [interpreted]	→	Information
Information [patterned]	→	Knowledge
Knowledge [integrated]	→	Competency
Competency [with perspective]	→	Wisdom

The Asset of Knowledge

In the Information Age, knowledge has become a capital asset to be carefully acquired, conscientiously preserved, and wisely invested. An *asset* is anything owned by an organization that has monetary value. Assets on a balance sheet have traditionally been divided into four categories: *current assets* (e.g. cash and accounts receivable), *fixed assets* (long-term assets such as plant and equipment), *investments* (e.g. bonds and certificates of deposit), and *intangible assets* (assets without physical existence such as trademarks, copyrights, and patents). In the Industrial Age, this balance sheet, prepared on the basis of generally accepted accounting principles, did a reasonably good job of representing the assets of a company because the key assets (other than management and leadership) were tangible: cash, accounts receivable, equipment, plant, and inventory.

In the Information Age, however, the key corporate assets are not material; they are intangible. The knowledge asset is one component of larger asset groups such as *intellectual capital* and *human capital*. Whereas human capital emphasizes the idea that employees are assets whose organizational value can be enhanced through proper management and investment, *knowledge capital* emphasizes the idea that knowledge is an asset that can be enhanced through proper management and investment (i.e., created, purchased, traded, and sold). Knowledge capital generates *intellectual capital,* a term that refers to intellectual property (patents, trademarks, and copyrights) owned by the company.

The Canadian Imperial Bank of Commerce (with assets in excess of $100 billion) recognized the value of knowledge capital by creating a "knowledge-based lending group" for loans to knowledge-intensive companies. The 60-person group is tasked with examining the capacities and intangible assets of knowledge-intensive companies and determining new ways to define credit worthiness. The initiative is aimed at determining the value of such companies in a more precise manner. "It's a different way of measuring bankable value" says the vice president of learning, organizational, and leadership development (Manasco, 2000, p. 1).

Knowledge, however, is an unusual asset. To be properly valued and deployed, its defining characteristics must be understood:

- Knowledge is not a physical asset. It does not reside in a physical place within the company or even fully within the company's control but in the minds of its employees. Knowledge is a stream rather than a discrete entity that flows in, through, and out of an organization. It cannot, therefore, be tracked or measured except in terms of its effects, such as on performance and productivity.
- Because knowledge resides in the minds of employees rather than in a physical or virtual space accessible by the organization, it cannot be

owned by an organization, only *borrowed,* unless the organization has harvested and stored the knowledge for future use. In a sense, the entire operational knowledge base of an organization has been out-sourced to temporary employees (*temporary* because they can leave at any moment they choose). Because knowledge must be reborrowed every day, it is very easy to lose when an employee leaves—and calls the loan.

- Since knowledge is cumulative, present knowledge builds on past knowledge. Knowledge continuity is the link that connects these two knowledge tenses. A break in this link will impair development of future knowledge and so will reduce its utility and value. The financial metaphor is a loss of both principal, which is past knowledge that could have been invested to generate additional knowledge, and the interest it would have otherwise earned, which would have been the new knowledge.

- Although knowledge is hard to capture, preserve, or control, it is a critical resource for generating wealth and value. Knowledge activates the physical and intellectual assets of the firm so that they can generate revenue and profit. Without the application of knowledge, the tangible assets of an organization would have no productive value.

- Knowledge is the most volatile of all assets, because much knowledge is highly perishable and subject to rapid or even sudden obsolescence. Because turbulent change characterizes the Information Age, knowledge must be continually challenged, constantly renewed, and regularly validated if it is to remain current and retain its value. When the context in which specific knowledge is to be applied changes, the value of that knowledge changes.

- The value of organizational knowledge grows when it is shared and shrinks when it is hoarded. In other words, unlike other capital assets, knowledge does not depreciate from use; it appreciates. Shared knowledge increases in value, because it is subject to challenge, correction, and augmentation in the sharing. A simple example is a meeting in which a manager proposes a new program and then asks for feedback in the form of different perspectives, pro and con. Brainstorming sessions are another example of knowledge appreciation in which the juxtaposition of complementary or opposing thoughts creates new knowledge. Likewise, people learn from conversations and interactions with others (whether in person or on paper) because others' thoughts challenge, confirm, deny, or stimulate their own thoughts. Knowledge that is shared throughout an organization (as happens with best practices) is more valuable to the organization than hoarded knowledge (held by a single employee), because more employees can use it to benefit the organization.

- Knowledge can be grown (i.e., increased through training and education) and is self-generating through experience. The significance of this characteristic is that, unlike some assets, *all* knowledge assets can be increased in value if they are properly cared for and invested.
- Knowledge as a whole is not intrinsically scarce, but job-specific operational knowledge is.

Because knowledge is a unique asset and the basis of productivity, a strategic advantage accrues to any organization that can develop and maintain its knowledge base. The characteristics of knowledge, however, can make this objective difficult to accomplish. Perhaps the most troublesome aspect is the need to capture tacit knowledge, which is a key component of the operational knowledge that employees use in their jobs.

Tacit Knowledge

Tacit or *implicit knowledge* is knowledge stored in the heads of employees— knowledge that leaves the organization when employees leave. It can be contrasted to *explicit knowledge,* which is knowledge laid out in official procedures, steps, and standards (Dixon, 2000, p. 26) and contained in documents, databases, and formal processes. Tacit knowledge has several characteristics that distinguish it from explicit knowledge:

- Tacit knowledge is individualized, personal knowledge that develops out of on-the-job experience and reflects the means through which employees actually accomplish their work. It is based on improvisations, experiments, trial-and-error discoveries, inventive solutions, successes, and failures as well as on informal rules of thumb, stories, principles, and guidelines developed by colleagues and passed informally among them. It is a kind of organizational common sense or street smarts. As such, it often differs from official policies and procedures described in organizational manuals, taught in on-the-job-training sessions, or advocated by supervisors.

- Tacit knowledge includes content (such as job-specific knowledge generated from information), an understanding of context so that the content can be properly applied, and mastery of the processes through which knowledge is made productive.
- Tacit knowledge has a subjective component (insights, intuition, hunches, and so forth) as well as an objective component (technical skills and job-relevant data and information that is critical to the position).
- Tacit knowledge is often created in social settings such as informal meetings and casual gatherings at the water cooler, during breaks, over lunch, or at get-togethers after work. As the product of group conversations and employee collaborations, tacit knowledge grows out of the social fabric of the work experience. The process of social interaction adds to the pool of practical, collective knowledge that anyone in the group can draw on and incorporate into his or her knowledge base. But this tacit knowledge does not exist outside the group unless it is intentionally shared.
- Some tacit knowledge can seem such a natural part of what employees do that they may not be self-aware enough to articulate it. This characteristic of tacit knowledge suggests that that some formal, analytical means of extracting that knowledge (in other words, enabling its articulation) must be developed if it is to be captured for use by others. For example, employees may know, but not think to volunteer as part of their tacit knowledge, that they always provide a courtesy heads-up briefing to a particularly influential colleague of a key decision maker before presenting their idea to that decision maker.

The tacit knowledge that enables high performance in a given position exists only in the head of the employee holding that position. Explicit knowledge, by contrast, exists in formal documents available to many employees. Explicit knowledge, however, can be converted into tacit knowledge by any employee. This conversion occurs whenever employees recognize explicit knowledge as critical to high performance in their positions and therefore incorporate it into their personal knowledge bases. In the process, they convert the explicit knowledge to tacit knowledge. Because tacit knowledge is critical to employee performance—whether "tacit-born" or "tacitized" from explicit knowledge—some means of converting it into explicit knowledge must be devised so that it can be transferred to successor employees. The process itself requires that employees (1) first identify the tacit knowledge that is significant, then translate it into words that are meaningful to others, and (2) identify the explicit knowledge that has been tacitized. The process is difficult because the way people actually work in an organization is usually different from the way the organization thinks they work, at least as that work is described in handbooks, manual, training programs, organizational charts, and job descriptions.

John Brown and Estee Gray report on a study conducted by Xerox's Palo Alto Research Center (PARC) on how a group of field technicians performed their work (Brown and Gray, 1995, p. 78). This is what they found:

> When problems with copiers arose, the researcher asked to see the manuals the tech reps consulted. Early on, before they got comfortable with the PARC representative, the tech reps would pull out the "official" company manual—clean, pristine, neatly organized. Over time, though, they started showing the researcher their "real" manual. It was the standard book—but highlighted, dog-eared, filled with scribbles in the margins and annotated with notes and reminders.
>
> Each tech rep was keeping two sets of books: the formal and the informal, the official and the improvised. But isn't that true for work in general? Each of us, in our own way, keeps two sets of books. And too often, what is unofficial remains invisible—except perhaps to members of our own trusted community. In the Knowledge Era, what's invisible is often what's most valuable.

The tacit practices of these employees rather than the explicit procedures prescribed by their company were the basis of their success. If this tacit knowledge is not transferred to their successors, the successors will encounter difficulties at the outset of their employment and fail to achieve the productivity of their predecessors. Officially promulgated practices are often woefully inadequate to deal with the unpredictability and uniqueness of everyday work life. Employees make up the difference between the simple road map provided by official practices and the complex journey that reality demands by devising their own specialized approaches and storing them as tacit knowledge.

Operational Knowledge as a Commodity

Imagine people adrift on the ocean in a boat with all the necessities and amenities one could desire—except anything to drink. Although there is no drinking water on board, water is all around. But the water that laps teasingly against the side of the boat is undrinkable. As the passengers grow more and more parched, they become increasingly frustrated and increasingly angry. If only the saltwater in which they were floating could be converted into freshwater for drinking! Such is the allegorical plight of newly hired knowledge workers. They are awash in a sea of knowledge that they cannot use. How can the data, information, and knowledge that surrounds them in the organization be converted into job-specific knowledge that is meaningful in their new positions?

Continuity management provides the answer: By identifying critical job-specific, *operational* knowledge and then capturing it a meaningful form that can be transferred to the new hire. Operational knowledge can be thought of as the tacit knowledge required to perform well in a given position. It includes explicit knowledge that has been tacitized and tacit-born knowledge gathered from instruction, observation, application, failures, successes, and other forms of experience. Operational knowledge consists of the critical data, information, formal processes, informal processes, skill sets, applied experience, relationships, competencies, beliefs, values, and wisdom that create the domain of understanding that enables employees to excel at the tasks they undertake. It is as much a set of potentialities as anything else—knowledge potentialities that can be brought to bear to solve a problem or seize an opportunity. Operational knowledge is continually being revised to reflect the demands of a challenging, unpredictable environment.

Components of Operational Knowledge

Operational knowledge is multifaceted in its content and comprehensive in its scope. It draws broadly from across an organization, encompassing seven different types of knowledge and weaving them into a coherent whole:

- *Cognitive knowledge.* Content knowledge that includes job-specific data and information and their sources.
- *Skills knowledge.* The skills and training necessary to perform well in the position.
- *Systems knowledge.* An understanding of the interplay of cause-and-effect relationships that is essential for sound decision making.
- *Social network knowledge.* An understanding of the crucial social relationships that make it possible to get things done in the organization,

including those who can grease the wheels, provide inside information, clarify options, or offer reliable advice and counsel. When employees face an unfamiliar situation with which they feel unprepared to deal, they do not rely on databases or procedure manuals. They turn to their network of trusted colleagues for information, knowledge, and advice.

- *Process and procedural knowledge.*   Knowledge of formal and informal organizational processes and procedures, which are often more effective for getting things done in an organization.
- *Heuristic knowledge.*   A knowledge of shortcuts for accomplishing tasks, rules of thumb for decision making, and quick fixes that have come to constitute best practices for the position. Heuristic knowledge includes procedures that modify or circumvent obsolete, ineffective, or cumbersome official processes.
- *Cultural knowledge.*   Knowledge of organizational norms, values, roles, and standards of conduct that govern interaction with colleagues and other stakeholders.

Incumbents gather knowledge from a broad pool of organizational, personal, and external knowledge; analyze it for relevance; synthesize it for understanding; and structure it for applicability to the specific goals and changing situations that define their jobs. Out of the mass of knowledge spread across these seven categories, they extract a critical core that that is transformed by this process into an operational knowledge base that guides their decisions and determines their success. In so doing, they create a new commodity: *operational knowledge.*

Separating Knowledge from Employees

In the past century, it was thought that operational knowledge could not be separated from the employees who possessed it. The only way to preserve such knowledge was to retain the employee. From this perspective, knowledge is not a transferable commodity, but an amorphous, ever-changing resource that defies capture and transfer. Fortunately, that perspective is not valid for job-specific operational knowledge in the Information Age. While it is true that operational knowledge is dynamic and ever-changing, it is also true that it can be harvested using the proper tools and transferred using the proper vehicle (as is the case with any other commodity). Through careful analysis, it is possible to define critical operational knowledge, discern its primary knowledge categories, and identify the knowledge in each of those categories that is necessary for high performance in the position. It is also possible to harvest that knowledge from incumbent employees and convert it into a form that would be meaningful to their successors as well as transferable to them.

Through continuity management, operational knowledge can be *separated* from employees, *converted* into a commodity, and *transferred* to successors. It is impossible to capture an employee's total body of knowledge, of course. It is also impossible to capture all the operational knowledge in an employee's head. But it *is* possible to capture the critical operational knowledge that fuels productivity and performance in a given position, and transfer that knowledge to successor employees.

Five factors make it possible to identify, capture, and transfer operational knowledge for purposes of maintaining knowledge continuity. These factors are *content, context, format, competencies,* and *recipients.* They are explained in more detail in the following paragraphs.

Content   Critical operational knowledge does not lose its relevance when the person holding it leaves. Since it is the very knowledge that the incumbent used on the job, its content is position specific and inherently relevant for an immediate successor. Operational knowledge, in this case, was created by the incumbent for the purpose for which it will again be used by the successor. As a result, for the most part, the knowledge will be as meaningful to the successor as it was to the incumbent.

Context   The successor employee for whom the operational knowledge is destined will be operating within the same *general context* as the incumbent. Because the value of all knowledge is context dependent, the transfer of job-specific operational knowledge is easier than the transfer of knowledge created in one context but destined for use in another. The similarity of knowledge content and knowledge context that characterizes continuity management facilitates a successor's incorporation of the incumbent's operational knowledge into the successor's knowledge base. It increases the perceived relevance of that knowledge and makes it more meaningful in application. As a result, mistranslations and misunderstandings are greatly reduced, immensely increasing the value of the knowledge.

Format   A common problem with knowledge sharing is knowledge access. How are the people in need of knowledge to find that knowledge quickly and in a form that will be useful to them? This problem is solved with continuity management because the operational knowledge successors need will be presented to them in a structured, concise, and relevant format. People prefer to ask questions rather than access databases. One reason mentoring is so powerful as a knowledge transfer system is that it allows successors to ask incumbents specifically for the knowledge they need as they need it. Within limitations, continuity management delivers a similar capability, because the format in which this knowledge is transferred is designed specifically for the recipient. In sophisticated continuity management systems, successors have only to ask the continuity management system to obtain the critical operational knowledge they seek.

Competencies   The capabilities, professional skills, and general competencies of a successor employee will ordinarily be roughly comparable to those of the predecessor. As a result, a successor should find the transferred operational knowledge to be immediately understandable, relevant, and applicable. While knowledge management must often ignore—or somehow factor in—the diversity in talent and context involved in knowledge transfer, continuity management is able to capitalize on the similarities inherent in one-to-one intergenerational knowledge transfers between employees in the same position. This difference allows continuity management to build on the successor's competencies as well as the successor's knowledge base.

Recipients   A continuing problem area for knowledge management is identifying those employees who possess valuable knowledge and linking them with those who can benefit from that knowledge. By contrast, continuity management can easily identify and link employees who have valuable job-specific knowledge (by definition, incumbent employees and their peers in the same job classification) with those who will profit from accessing it (their successors). Continuity management avoids the problem of having to generalize local knowledge to an entire organization or to transfer knowledge across countries or cultures. Continuity management also largely avoids the problem of having to determine who should decide what knowledge is valid and worthy of transfer. As is explained in later chapters, operational knowledge transferred in continuity management is validated by peer incumbents to some degree and subject to specific review by authorized individuals in certain situations.

Commodity to Process

In continuity management, critical operational knowledge is transferred as a commodity to successor employees. At the moment of transfer, however, that commodity initiates a process—the process of knowledge acquisition and creation in the new hire. The knowledge transfer vehicle is designed to provide a knowledge core (the commodity) that forms a basis for the rapid acquisition and creation of knowledge (the process) through a structured presentation of knowledge and knowledge sources of immediate relevance. As is so often the case in the complex environment of the Information Age, an ability to understand paradox is the key to understanding strategy and operational advantages. In this case, the paradox is that operational knowledge can be a commodity when harvested and a process when transferred. An analog for this strange shift occurs in quantum physics, where light takes the form of either a particle or a wave, depending entirely on the conditions under which the light is measured.

The characteristics of operational knowledge exploited in continuity management and the paradoxical nature of operational knowledge harvested for transfer offer persuasive evidence that operational knowledge is a commodity—albeit a highly unusual one—that can be transferred between employee generations. Once transferred, that commodity initiates a process of knowledge acquisition and creation in the new hire to preserve knowledge continuity and build the knowledge asset.

The Value of Operational Knowledge

The transformation of knowledge into a capital asset and a key factor of production has dramatically increased the value of operational knowledge. It has also spurred an interest in learning (which is the acquisition of knowledge) and made the linkage of knowledge, learning, and productivity more obvious and more important to the business enterprise. This tripartite relationship of knowledge, learning, and productivity provides a conceptual means of understanding why knowledge drives productivity in the Information Age. In order to understand this relationship, however, it is first necessary to understand what productivity is and the factors that influence it.

Productivity is a measure of how effectively an individual (or a group or an organization or a thing) transforms its inputs (resources) into outputs (goods or services) through an intermediate conversion process. The conversion process may be manual, intellectual, chemical, or electronic, or it may employ some other means. The process can be diagrammed like this:

Inputs (resources) + conversion process = outputs (goods and services)

In the Information Age, operational knowledge is a *resource* (consisting of data, information, knowledge, competencies, and wisdom), and the *conversion process* (knowledge, competencies, and wisdom) through which that resource is converted into goods and services (outputs). In other words, knowledge workers use knowledge to process knowledge to create the good or service they offer. So a knowledge worker's equation looks like this:

Input (knowledge) + conversion process (knowledge)
= outputs (goods and services)

For some knowledge workers, however, knowledge is even more important, because it is the output, the input, and the conversion process. In other words, knowledge workers use knowledge to process knowledge to create knowledge. Innovation is one form of new knowledge that springs from this process. For example, when faced with a unique repair problem, employees who repair copiers may take knowledge acquired from their peers (as input), process that input through their own knowledge base (conversion process), and create a better way to repair the machine (new knowledge). Their equation is:

Input (knowledge) + conversion process (knowledge)
= outputs (knowledge)

Salespeople who develop better selling techniques follow this conversion process, as do engineers, attorneys, consultants, researchers, and others whose output is largely knowledge or knowledge-driven. The extraordinary role of operational knowledge as a resource factor, a conversion factor, and even an output factor helps explain why it has become the scarcest resource in the Information Age.

As an asset, operational knowledge is expensive to acquire and even more expensive to lose. The value of an employee's operational knowledge is the sum of the costs incurred to create that knowledge during the years of his or her employment with the organization, as well as the cost of creating the knowledge base that the employee brought to the organization in the first place. For example, the following costs are typically incurred by an organization in the creation of operational knowledge:

- The costs of training and continuing education incurred in bringing the employee's level of competency to its current level, including fringe benefits. Research conducted by the American Society of Training and Development (ASTD) reported in 2000 indicates that "the direct costs for formal training are typically on the order of 2 percent of payroll" (Bassi, 2000, p. 2).
- The value of an employee's productivity lost during the training and continuing education opportunities. ASTD reported in 2000 that "indirect and opportunity costs may raise the total [direct cost of training] to 10 percent or more [of payroll]" (Bassi, 2000, p. 3).
- ASTD also reports that "the cost of investments in informal learning are likely [to be] at least as large as investments in formal learning" (Bassi, 2000, p. 2).
- The cost of recruiting and selecting a successor employee and bringing that employee to the level of competency of the departing employee. This cost should also include the value of lost productivity of managers and colleagues who bring the new employee up to speed and reduce their own performance levels in the process.
- The cost of lost sales, processing delays, dissatisfied customers, and other missed opportunities that occur because the new employee lacks the requisite knowledge to perform well. These costs are in addition to the costs of reduced productivity.
- The intangible—but very real—value of the employee's contribution to the social capital of the organization that facilitate employee collaboration and cannot be immediately replicated by a successor.

The value of operational knowledge is more than the sum of the costs that the organization incurred to create it, however. The value of an employee's operational knowledge also includes the cost of an employee's own investments in its creation. For example:

- The value of all the investments that an employee has made on his or her own time to increase job competency, including the time and money invested in reading books, taking courses, participating in professional societies, and conferring with individuals in social settings unconnected to the company. This outside investment becomes an *inside* investment when its fruits are applied on the job and result in new procedures, insights, and innovations that enhance productivity.
- The value of an employee's integration of data, information, and knowledge over the period of his or her employment that have produced specialized competencies with high payoffs for the organization.

Another way to measure the value of operational knowledge is to calculate the net present value of the future revenue stream that operational knowledge generates. This number is the difference between the revenue stream generated by a new employee to whom operational knowledge has been transferred versus the same new employee who has received no operational knowledge transfer. Such calculations would be impossible to make, of course, but they provide a theoretical look at the tremendous value of operational knowledge lost to a firm through departing employees. When the cost of knowledge loss is multiplied by the number of people who annually leave an organization, the cumulative effect on the revenue stream is impressive. It ought to give pause to those who consider downsizing primarily an expense reduction rather than an asset giveaway. And it ought to give pause to those who would terminate employees or lose them through resignation or retirement without harvesting their operational knowledge.

A further way to value operational knowledge is to estimate the amount of lost revenue that can be tied directly or indirectly to lost operational knowledge from departing employees. Such calculations are impossible to make, of course, except in particularly disastrous cases. The Webb Partnership, a consulting firm, recounts one such case:

A consumer goods company was delayed by nine months with a new product as they struggled to resolve technical issues. They lost first-mover advantage and eventually launched after the "me-too" products.

The product never achieved the projected volumes or revenue. The company subsequently found that the technical solutions were already part of their own intellectual property. A review showed that research completed fifteen years earlier had covered the same ground, *but had been lost due to staff churn and retirements* [emphasis added]. The cost would be almost $1 billion. (Webb Partnership, 2002)

Operational knowledge has become more valuable in the Information Age because it has become more critical to effective problem solving and sound decision making. Turbulence, urgency, and unprecedented events preclude the use of narrow organizational rules as guides for formulating responses that are quick and effective. Rigid procedures, canned information, and distant hierarchies through which organizational knowledge can be passed to employees as fodder for operating decisions are no longer effective when, as is increasingly the case, the time to make complex decisions is short. As organizational hierarchies are flattened and decision making is spread lower and broader throughout the organization, the value of operational knowledge developed on the firing line increases exponentially in importance.

H. Cris Collie, executive vice president of the Employee Relocation Council, Washington, D.C., explains the relationship between the increased value of knowledge and the dispersion of decision making:

If you think the decisions that make or break a company are those made by strategists at the top, go back and read your Tolstoy. Whether in war or in commerce, it's the sum total of countless decisions made every day on the front lines that determine the course of future events. Success, in business or other large-scale endeavors, depends on good individual, daily decisions outweighing bad ones over time. And the most important thing top management can do to ensure success is to empower people throughout the organization to make good decisions. Partly, this is a question of simply granting the authority for decision-making—and establishing accountability for decisions made. But more importantly, it's a question of equipping people with the knowledge required to make decisions well. (Collie, 2001, p. 5)

The value of operational knowledge is so great in the Information Age that even *some* operational knowledge transfer from incumbent employees to their successors is preferable to *none*. Knowledge continuity is itself a form of knowledge. In a turbulent environment, it is the knowledge that underlies all other knowledge. Without knowledge continuity, chaos descends as organization members try frantically to determine what has happened in the past in order to know how to respond in the present. Employees cannot be prevented from leaving an organization. Nor can they be prevented from taking their knowledge with them. But they can be prevented from taking it without leaving a copy for their successor.

Some writers have suggested that knowledge cannot actually be transferred to successors—only information can be transferred. Our research indicates otherwise. Operational knowledge *can* be successfully transferred (because it is job specific) when transferred to someone with roughly the same competency (a successor). The key to successful operational knowledge transfer is the relative equality of the employee generations in terms of skills, experience, and knowledge requirements. It may not be possible to transfer operational knowledge to a less competent person and make it meaningful, but it is possible to transfer it to someone with similar competency encountering a roughly similar work environment calling for relatively similar skills. A predecessor's knowledge can be integrated into a successor's mental models and understanding with relative speed.

Job-specific competency is highly individualized, but it can be developed quickly when a new employee's base competency level is enriched by the addition of operational knowledge. In this sense, competency is also transferable from one employee generation to the next. The organizational goal of bringing an employee up to speed is really about increasing the employee's competency as quickly as possible. Operational knowledge is the commodity or process that converts a new employee's generalizable competency into the organization-specific competency that makes the employee a high-performer.

Job-applicable wisdom is even more valuable than competency. It is the highest evolutionary form of knowledge, the result of a transformation process that begins with data and ends with a comprehensive, experience-driven integration of all points on the knowledge continuum. The gift of wisdom is a set of principles that are valid in highly complex situations for very long timeframes. As the knowledge asset grows in importance, the great knowledge question becomes: Can the priceless asset of operational wisdom be captured? The answer is yes. Operational wisdom can be successfully harvested, but only when it is honored and when it is sought. Often, wisdom must be coaxed out of the wise with judicious questions. Organizations lose wisdom with departing employees because they do not honor it and do not seek it. Yet, inherent in wisdom—perhaps even cocreated with it—is a desire to share it when circumstances are right.

Knowledge, competency, and wisdom are all creations of the human mind, crafted by intellect, enriched by emotion, and forged in the experience of life. Often they are earned only as the result of great effort, even great pain and sacrifice. As such, they are meaningful creations that bring pleasure in sharing. That knowledge and wisdom are not preserved by organizations is not a testament to the difficulty of their harvesting and transfer, but rather to the organizational failure to encourage their preservation. In the Industrial Age, this failure was understandable. In the Information Age, it is unforgivable—not unforgivable in a moral sense, but in an economic sense. The marketplace will no longer forgive the failure to preserve and transfer operational knowledge. Why not? Because it cannot. The market *is* knowledge.

3 | Knowledge Continuity: The New Management Function

Management isn't what it used to be.

But what is it?

For the first time in 100 years—since Henri Fayol described the five functions of a manager and the fourteen principles of management—a new function has emerged to alter the basic configuration of a manager's responsibilities. This time, the change is not the work of one person, but of broad social and economic forces that have made knowledge a capital asset and dramatically shifted the way in which businesses operate. With knowledge as the new fulcrum on which organizational fortunes turn, preserving knowledge continuity has emerged as a basic management priority and, hence, a fundamental responsibility of management.

The effort to preserve knowledge and maintain knowledge continuity between employee generations may well stretch back to the beginning of recorded history, when official records were first kept of actions taken by rulers, governments, religious institutions, and armies. On December 31,

1600, Queen Elizabeth I granted a royal charter to the East India Company, the earliest example of a joint stock company, and so created the first need for knowledge continuity in a *public* company (a company, by the way, which is still in business after 500 years).

In the Industrial Age, attempts to preserve knowledge continuity included official records, formal policies and procedures, management directives, letters to employees, newsletters, wall posters, slogans, and so forth. All were efforts to spread knowledge throughout the organization as well as to maintain the continuity of that knowledge despite departing employees in the interest of aligning corporate and individual goals, setting the parameters of work performance, and ensuring continuity of vision and mission.

The concept of *knowledge management,* as we think of it today, developed out of seminal management themes in the 1980s and 1990s: best practices, Total Quality Management, continuous innovation, and organizational learning. From these efforts came an awareness of the critical nature of knowledge and a management conviction that it should be shared as widely as possible within an organization:

> The first conference in the United States which focused upon knowledge—beyond the theories of artificial intelligence—was entitled "Managing the Knowledge Asset into the 21st Century." It was convened by Digital Equipment Corporation and the Technology Transfer Society at Purdue University in 1987. The second on "Knowledge Productivity" was coordinated by Steelcase North America and EDS in April of 1992. The third was hosted by the Industrial Research Institute (IRI) in Vancouver, British Columbia in October, 1992. McKinsey & Company initiated their Knowledge Management Practice during the same timeframe. (Amidon, 1995, p. 1)

The first conference on knowledge management was held in 1993, organized by Lawrence Prusak among others. By the mid-1990s, knowledge management had emerged as an acknowledged theme in the management field. The goal of knowledge management (or *knowledge transfer* or *knowledge sharing*) is to get the right knowledge to the right person at the right time. That knowledge may be new (best practices) or highly specialized (problem-solving approaches that are not often needed, but critical when they are), foundational (knowledge that needs to be widely shared to improve decision making or align objectives), or some other category of knowledge. The appearance of the chief information officer (CIO), chief knowledge officer

(CKO), director of intellectual capital, and manager of knowledge as major players in the corporate hierarchy testify to the new and significant role of knowledge in the business enterprise.

The Twin Processes of Managing Knowledge

Effective management of the knowledge asset in any organization requires the integration of two related but different processes that combine synergistically and seamlessly to create a megaprocess. This megaprocess of knowledge asset management is analogous in some ways to breathing, which is a process created out of two integrated processes: inhalation and exhalation. One process without the other renders the organism dysfunctional, just as one knowledge process without the other renders the organization dysfunctional.

The two knowledge processes that form the megaprocess of knowledge asset management are:

- Knowledge transfer within the same employee generation (i.e., among *current* employees).
- Knowledge transfer between employee generations (i.e., *from* current employees to *successor* employees).

Knowledge management has traditionally emphasized the first process and largely ignored the second. There are exceptions, such as isolated cases where the impending loss of knowledge from departing employees was perceived in advance of their departure and recognized as a critical loss to the organization that had to be prevented. A second example is a knowledge-transfer effort that makes operational knowledge available to successors as a by-product of having made it available to incumbent employees. This relatively exclusive concern of knowledge management with knowledge transfer among current employees creates a problem. To the extent that critical operational knowledge has not been preserved between employee generations, each generation must start over by creating its own knowledge base. Employees cannot leverage current and past understanding to make more effective and imaginative decisions. The organization itself cannot reuse its own knowledge, and knowledge creation is hampered.

Continuity management specifically addresses the second process: the vertical transfer of job-specific operational knowledge from incumbent to successor employees. Together, the two processes of vertical knowledge transfer between employee generations and horizontal knowledge transfer among current employees ensures the preservation of the organizational knowledge base and its enhancement over time. Years of experience and best practices in the form of institutional knowledge and intellectual capital can be brought to bear on each new problem, enriching the decision-making process and stimulating new and more productive responses.

Knowledge transfer among current employees throughout an organization has produced some real successes, but also some impressive failures resulting from the complexity of the task and the frustration it can generate. The *why* of knowledge management has become clear; the *how* has proved to be more elusive. The problems that have plagued knowledge management programs and processes do not, in practice, have the same degree of impact on continuity management programs and processes. The primary reason is that continuity management is more manageable than traditional knowledge management because its scope is more limited. Rather than attempting to transfer knowledge across an organization, continuity management transfers knowledge between two people who are performing essentially the same work.

On the other hand, the achievements of knowledge management bode well for successful implementation of continuity management. The technologies used in successful knowledge sharing—and the nature of the knowledge shared—provide convincing evidence that the operational knowledge required to maintain knowledge continuity can be identified, harvested, and transferred to successor employees through a comprehensive program designed for that purpose. Furthermore, many aspects of existing knowledge management systems can be adapted to accommodate continuity management or can be completely integrated with it.

A simple example of integration between continuity management and knowledge management is an organization's "yellow pages," which are find-the-expert directories that summarize the job experience, histories, knowledge, and expertise of an organization's employees. When someone needs to know more about something—a customer, technology, operational process, business custom of a foreign company—or wants to bounce an idea or a conclusion off another person knowledgeable (or more knowledgeable) in the same area, yellow pages can provide the means for finding the answer. Yellow pages are generally low-cost in terms of time, technology, and people, and more and more organizations are employing them. Texaco, for example, uses PeopleNet, which is a search engine on the corporate intranet that is used for finding experts. Continuity management systems fit well with yellow pages because an important aspect of continuity management is the identification of experts to whom the incumbent turns to answer operational questions or for general advice. Expert contacts maintained by the incumbent—and regularly updated—for future transfer to a successor can be used to augment an organization's yellow pages or even as the basis for launching a yellow pages initiative.

One of the components of continuity management is a meeting of peer incumbent employees (that is, current employees with the same job classification). Peer incumbents meet to share, validate, and expand the critical operational knowledge they have identified that will be transferred to their successors. Included, of course, will be a discussion of the best practices they have developed or observed. This meeting reflects an essential principle of knowledge management, which is to validate and transfer existing knowledge, including best practices, among current employees (with continuity management, it is also a preparation for future transfer to successors). In this example of the integration of continuity management and knowledge management, the two processes have become virtually indistinguishable.

Many companies have made piecemeal efforts at implementing continuity management (these are discussed in more detail in Chapter 14, "Continuity Management in Practice.") For example, the Masters' Voices program in Ford Motor Company's Brake Division is designed to preserve the craft knowledge of retiring employees before they depart. In Ford's case, this knowledge is harvested to transfer to existing employees as well as to archive for future employees. It is a case of critical operational knowledge captured for the organization rather than for transfer to a specific successor employee. Efforts such as those at Ford are laudable, and they are multiplying in organizations. But they also lack the breadth, depth, and organizational support that characterize continuity management when fully implemented even as they foreshadow its potential.

The New Function of Management

While knowledge continuity is an old concept in skeletal form, it is a new concept in its fullest expression as a function of management. The emergence of continuity management as the *yang* process to knowledge management's *yin* can be found in a confluence of forces that have altered the management environment over the past half decade, driving organizations to seek new business models and scrap old perspectives on the nature and value of knowledge. Ten powerful forces converging at the end of the twentieth century created the "perfect storm" that rendered the Industrial Age concept of management incomplete and ineffective, pushing a reexamination of its meaning and adding knowledge continuity to its basic functions.

In the twenty-first century, preserving knowledge continuity will be as much a function of management as planning, organizing, controlling, and leading. Furthermore, it will be just as integrated as the four traditional management functions—fully incorporated into the daily activities of every manager. Whether one wants to talk about knowledge continuity as a new *responsibility* of management or, even more boldly, about a *new management* that encompasses knowledge continuity, the result is the same: a dramatic reassessment of what it means to lead and manage in the Information Age.

The reassessment of knowledge as the key economic factor in production and knowledge continuity as an essential component of knowledge preservation and generation was born of 10 forces acting on organizations at the end of the twentieth century:

1. The emergence of the Information Age and the knowledge economy
2. The shift from mechanistic organizations to organic ones
3. Data and information proliferation and overload, replacing the need for *information processing* with the challenge of *knowledge processing* and *creation*
4. High employee turnover and brief job tenure due to downsizing and job hopping, which result in huge organizational knowledge gaps
5. Impending baby-boomer retirements, which threaten to bring about potentially devastating knowledge losses
6. Knowledge turnover from greater use of the contingent workforce in all its forms, which depletes organizational knowledge
7. The drive for innovation and the emphasis on organizational learning, which requires knowledge of the past and quick access to existing resources
8. A commitment to higher quality and to continuous improvement, which requires knowledge continuity if it is to be achieved
9. The development of sophisticated computer technology that enables the capture and transfer of operational knowledge

10. The highly competitive global marketplace, which rewards quick responses, agile moves, and deft maneuvering, all built on operational knowledge continuity

These forces have reshaped the management landscape and created unique competitive opportunities for organizations canny enough to take advantage of them. The search for new business models, the race to enter new markets, and the drive to develop innovative products—all spawned by these factors—center around the critical asset of knowledge continuity and the need to preserve and enhance it. But the question remains: How to do it? The answer is through the development of a practical process that delivers results, preferably in the form of comprehensive knowledge harvesting and transfer with wide application.

Aart de Geus, chairman and CEO of Synopsys, an $800-million electronic design automation software company, posed an important question: "The key thing I'm interested in," he said, "is how do you tie the intellectual value and capital that you have in individuals into intellectual capital you have in the company? . . . On the one hand, you want to build up the individual as much as possible, to grow them and so on, and on the other hand, you don't want to be dependent on any of the individuals, so the intelligence [the company IQ] is really inside the company" (Haapaniemi, 2001, p. 64).

Continuity management provides an answer: by capturing the critical operational knowledge of each knowledge worker and ensuring the transfer of that knowledge to successor employees. Once that knowledge has been captured, it is then possible to share it with existing employees as well. In that act of knowledge sharing across the organization, the two complementary processes of continuity management and knowledge management have merged into the overarching process of knowledge asset management. The resulting synergy has a powerful effect on productivity and innovation.

Through continuity management, organizations can capitalize on the transformation in the business environment wrought by the 10 forces, building competitive advantage and outdistancing competitors. Because continuity management reflects a comprehensive understanding of the critical role that knowledge plays in organizational success in the Information Age, it positions organizations to fully exploit their knowledge asset. In the process, it requires something of a revolution in thought about what powers organizations, creates their core competencies, builds their productive capacity, and strengthens their competitive advantage. The knowledge analysis built into continuity management will lead to the rejection of some knowledge as irrelevant or tangential, the recognition of other knowledge as critical, and the maximization of knowledge leverage points wherever they exist. Ultimately, continuity management is a means of organizing other management functions—planning, organizing, controlling, and leading—around the primary asset of the Information Age: *operational knowledge.*

Knowledge Discontinuity Crises

Organizational knowledge resides in the heads of employees and in corporate documents and databases. According to the Delphi Group, a consulting firm that specializes in the emerging technologies of knowledge management and e-learning, about 70 percent of a company's knowledge resides solely in the minds of its employees, which leaves approximately 30 percent in externalized forms. Knowledge from both human and inanimate sources is critical to employee productivity, innovation, and performance. Continuity management enables access to both forms, ensuring that the critical operational knowledge required to perform at peak levels is harvested for transfer to successor employees regardless of whether it is tacit or explicit knowledge. If access to either knowledge bank is blocked and critical operational knowledge in either form is denied to new hires, the resulting knowledge deficit will seriously constrain their performance.

Many knowledge discontinuity problems could have been prevented had they been recognized and addressed before they arose. Undetected and unaddressed, however, they have the potential to disrupt operations and seriously degrade organizational performance. The following paragraphs explore seven knowledge discontinuity crises characteristic of many organizations. While they will seem very familiar, they are not preordained. Any organization can avert these potential crises through implementation of continuity management.

Knowledge Vacuum

The crisis of the knowledge vacuum develops when only one or two employees understand the procedures, processes, relationships, and systems that are essential to the work of a team, department, or division—and they leave. Unless this operational knowledge has been captured prior to the employees' departure, it disappears, creating a knowledge vacuum. That knowledge vacuum may have been brought about by management's inattention and carelessness. Or, more ominously, it may have resulted from *knowledge hoarding,* which is an employee's refusal to share essential knowledge in a deliberate attempt to become indispensable to the organization. Either way, the more critical the closely held knowledge or process is to the work of the group, the more severe the loss will be when the employee leaves.

A multi-billion-dollar company had failed to update and, ultimately, replace an aging financial accounting package on which it was completely dependent for its financial data. The financial package itself, affectionately known within the company as *BobWare,* had evolved over the years but had never been configuration managed. As a result, it was difficult, if not impossible, to know where all the functional capabilities were coded. "There is only one employee in the company," a manager admitted sheepishly, "who has any understanding of the financial package." His name was Bob, and it was the company's dependence on his knowledge of the software that had given rise to the nickname *BobWare.*

Such knowledge dependency is unacceptable, of course. While Bob was out of the country on a short trip, the server running the financial software went down, offering a preview of the coming knowledge vacuum when Bob leaves. Without Bob physically present, it took more than three days to get the software functioning again, during which time the company could produce no reports, purchase orders, or invoices. Just because the server went down. As unbelievable as it sounds, this true example of knowledge dependency—and the knowledge vacuum created by the three-day absence of a single employee—would not have happened with continuity management in place. The warning bells of such a dangerous vulnerability would have gone off years before.

A simple test for the existence of knowledge hoarding or knowledge scarcity created by organizational inattention is the *Bob test:* When "Bob" is out, can anything get done? If not, organizational knowledge flow has been severely constricted, and knowledge continuity will be a serious problem when Bob leaves for good. Neither the new hires nor their colleagues will know what to do in the ensuing knowledge vacuum. New employees will have to start from scratch to build the operational knowledge base they need to carry out their jobs. For them, it will be as if the organization had no history. Or, as one new hire in that position exclaimed, "It's like I've taken a job with a start-up company. Except that we've been in business fifty years."

Knowledge Panic

Knowledge panic develops when someone—or some document—in the organization holds the knowledge the new hire needs, but nobody but the departed employee knows who it is or where it is. The knowledge may even be in the predecessor's files, but the filing system is quirky, eccentric, or incomplete, and there is no index. This new-hire experience, repeated over and over, is the equivalent of repeatedly encountering the Internet message, "Error 404, File Not Found. The URL you requested could not be found on this server." The new employees' only alternative is to waste time searching for knowledge and information while deadlines slip and productivity falls. This crisis is similar to the knowledge vacuum, except that here the knowledge is actually in the organization—somewhere.

The knowledge panic crisis is captured by the story of a new employee who said, "Shortly after I took on my new job, I was given an assignment that assumed quite a bit of knowledge about a project we were involved in. The problem was, I couldn't find that knowledge and neither could anyone else. My coworkers repeated reassuring phrases like, 'We know it's around here somewhere' and 'I'm sure I've seen it.' 'Maybe so-and-so has it,' one of them would mutter, or 'Have you checked the files?' Meanwhile, people would call me, asking for information on the project, and I couldn't answer their questions. I had no knowledge, no background, no facts—nothing except a cubicle and a ringing phone. And escalating fear approaching panic."

Knowledge Bewilderment

Knowledge bewilderment develops when some operational knowledge is available to successor employees, but the knowledge is insufficient, inaccessible, or too poorly organized to be utilized effectively. This knowledge crisis mimics knowledge panic, except that the new hires do have *some* knowledge. It's just not enough to do their jobs. The new hires are bewildered, unsure about how to do whatever it is that they are supposed to be doing. Desperate for knowledge, all they can do is waste time hunting down information and the people or documents that presumably can supply it. The knowledge they need is somewhere in the organization, but little or no effort has been made to communicate that knowledge to them. Whatever knowledge exists is not accessible, and so it is worthless.

As a result, the new employees' fear rises and their morale plummets. As one new hire said, "I don't know what I'm doing. I don't even know how to know what I'm *supposed* to be doing. I have no knowledge, no context, no history. I feel like I've arrived in a spaceship on an alien planet. The natives are friendly, but they don't know very much. I keep wanting to say, 'Take me to your leader.' "

This frantic search for knowledge, which borders between the bitterly amusing and the truly desperate, is called *unicorn chasing* at one company. Because the search for knowledge is time-intensive, and there is no guarantee the knowledge will be found, the effects of knowledge bewilderment on productivity are dramatically negative. Overwhelmed by unicorn chasing and the sink-or-swim culture that creates it, new hires are rendered productively impotent. Their hoped-for productivity has been replaced by busyness as they try desperately to figure out what is required (without appearing confused) and to appear to be working (without the possibility of being productive).

Georgia-Pacific Corporation, an international forest products company based in Atlanta, forestalled a case of knowledge bewilderment by harvesting the knowledge of an incumbent who was going on indefinite medical leave. But what if they hadn't? In mid-1999,

> Senior management was notified that the company's veteran collections manager had been diagnosed with melanoma, a form of skin cancer, and had been ordered to start chemotherapy. In two weeks he would go on indefinite medical leave.
>
> This manager was the in-house expert in collections and dealing with delinquent accounts—an obviously important function directly related to the company's bottom line. Over the years, he had built a network of relationships with attorneys, collection agencies and credit managers and had developed instincts for such issues as when to send a past-due account to a collection agency.
>
> The manager's peers in the credit organization had expertise in their own specialties but only rudimentary knowledge of collections. Within two weeks, Georgia-Pacific had to find some way to make as much as possible of his know-how and work processes available to his colleagues in his absence. The key component of that solution was knowledge harvesting. (Eisenhart, 2001, p. 48)

Information Overload, Knowledge Deficiency

This knowledge crisis develops when the new employee encounters an overload of information, but no real knowledge. Furthermore, the information itself is worthless because it was organized and transferred in a format that rendered it unusable or indigestible. Poorly organized, misclassified, or nonprioritized information may as well not exist. In that state, it cannot be transformed into knowledge or used as information.

Knowledge Stuffing

This knowledge crisis develops when huge amounts of information and knowledge are dumped on the successor employee, but the knowledge is obsolete, incorrect, or immaterial. Highly relevant operational knowledge has been omitted. Much of it may be in the form of dusty continuity books. Some of it may be valuable, but who knows? Such knowledge is time-consuming to analyze, integrate, or reject. It is not worth tackling. Rather than being productive for the successor, the knowledge is counterproductive. This crisis is similar to information overload, knowledge deficiency except that it is an overload of disorganized knowledge rather than information.

Knowledge Fantasy

This knowledge crisis, which develops out of insufficient knowledge, is likely to emerge in varying degrees as a companion to the other knowledge discontinuities. Successors develop false assumptions, fallacious theories, and mistaken principles to guide their decisions and actions as they wander the labyrinth that operational ignorance creates. In place of data, information, and knowledge on which to base their decisions, new hires rely on knowledge fantasies and knowledge guesses about what might be true. Winging it with no basis for operating with confidence, errors are made, progress is stalled, and productivity is stunted.

Knowledge Rigidity

This knowledge crisis is somewhat different from the others. It results from an organizational culture that is closed to change and resists any modification of the way things are done. Innovative approaches, new solutions, and imaginative responses developed by incumbents to deal with the exigencies of a rapidly changing environment go unharvested, unreported, and unshared. Critical operational knowledge decays in relevance and applicability as new knowledge is ignored or twisted to conform to preconceived forms. Knowledge rigidity leads to corporate decay and extinction as the organization denies or ignores the changing demands of its environment that pressure its established products, markets, or distribution channels. Continuity management mitigates this slavish devotion to past knowledge, processes, and approaches because its comprehensive analysis of job requirements, activities, networks, and skills inevitably challenges the knowledge status quo and encourages innovation.

■ ■ ■

Year after year, these knowledge discontinuity crises breed knowledge dissipation. The level of organizational knowledge enabling high performance declines throughout the organization in the face of continued knowledge discontinuity accompanied by high turnover. Successor employee performance is marred by errors in judgment, firefighting, urgent requests for colleagues' assistance, and confusion about what to do next and how to do it. As knowledge declines, productivity drops, and competitive advantage is lost. Yet each of these knowledge discontinuity time bombs can be discovered and defused through continuity management, strengthening the flow of operational knowledge among current employees and ensuring the transfer of critical operational knowledge between departing and arriving employees.

The Competitive Advantages of Continuity Management

A *competitive advantage* is a sustainable difference between organizations recognized by customers as conferring a greater value on one organization than another, which leads to the choice of that organization as a provider of goods or services. The particular advantage may be a wider product selection, lower prices, higher quality, more responsive service, or any combination of these or other factors that allows one firm to triumph over its competitors. The heart of any competitive advantage in the Information Age, however—regardless of the nature of that advantage—is *knowledge,* and how deftly it is wielded to gain the upper hand in the turbulent shifts of the marketplace.

The emergence of knowledge continuity as a new management function arises quite naturally out of this transformation of knowledge into a key corporate asset. The same forces that made knowledge a scarce resource have made knowledge continuity a new management imperative.

Without some form of continuity management, the crises posed by knowledge discontinuities are irresolvable. But the strategic advantage of continuity management is not just in what it *prevents,* but in what it *creates.* By preserving knowledge, continuity management delivers a string of remarkable knowledge-related improvements that infuse the organization, providing a competitive edge uniquely tailored to the Information Age. The preservation and savvy application of corporate knowledge, competencies, and wisdom that continuity management promises is the most compelling reason for its implementation.

The remainder of this chapter describes the competitive advantages that continuity management delivers. These advantages reflect the web of relationships that knowledge both creates and demands, acting synergistically with each other to multiply their combined effect. For example, a corollary effect of bringing new employees up to speed faster is that it protects the productivity levels of established employees by reducing the time they have to spend answering questions from new hires. All of these effects are deeply interrelated, but together they culminate in bottom-line improvements in performance and productivity grounded in knowledge and its powerful role in the Information Age.

When implemented, continuity management:

- Speeds the ramp-up of new employees
- Results in better decision making and fewer mistakes
- Improves training effectiveness for new employees
- Lowers the stress, raises the morale, and increases the commitment of both new and current employees
- Preserves knowledge networks
- Focuses employee attention on identifying job-critical knowledge and productivity leverage points
- Prevents knowledge hoarding
- Preserves institutional memory
- Facilitates knowledge creation, innovation, continuous improvement, and organizational learning

- Reduces job turnover and increases a sense of employee value
- Lowers job-turnover costs
- Reduces organizational vulnerability when utilizing the contingency workforce
- Increases customer confidence and reduces customer attrition
- Sustains core corporate values, competencies, and mission
- Increases long-term organizational effectiveness

General Peter Cuviello, chief information officer of the U.S. Army, talks about the advantages of continuity management:

> Effective exploitation of the knowledge asset creates a decisive strategic advantage for any organization, including the military, and is one of our highest priorities. Preserving knowledge continuity is a crucial aspect of knowledge exploitation and a primary objective of the knowledge initiative that the Army has launched as part of its transformation process. To be quicker and faster, we have to apply past lessons with lightning speed in very different circumstances. Knowledge preservation between arriving and departing soldiers and civilians is essential to achieve that goal. In the Army, we don't have personnel *overlap;* we have personnel *underlap.* Most of the time, an arriving solider gets a handshake and a computer, and that's it. In fact, I should be able to pick up the knowledge where my predecessor left off. That's the capacity continuity management delivers and that's the capacity we're building.
>
> Our end-state objective is to enable new arrivals to sit down at their computers and call up critical operational knowledge they need, whatever it is and wherever it is. We can't afford a break in knowledge continuity, because we can't tolerate it in our environment. With a process like continuity management, we're leveraging knowledge instead of losing it. Reduced time lost to unproductive actions, faster ramp-up, higher productivity, sounder decisions—all come out from successor access to structured operational knowledge, which is what continuity management creates. Reinventing knowledge with every new person in the position is neither inevitable or sustainable. (Cuviello, 2002)

The following paragraphs explore the productivity advantages of continuity management in more detail.

Speeds the Ramp-Up of New Employees

According to a November 2000 report from Challenger, Gray & Christmas, a Chicago-based outplacement firm, 16 percent of managers and executives who were fired in the first three quarters of 2000 were terminated before their two-year anniversary (Rasmusson, 2000, p. 1). That 16 percent rate was double the percentage of 1990, a mere decade before. Meanwhile, the length of job tenure shrank by 36 percent over the eight-year period from 1992 to 2000, indicating a strong trend toward shorter-term employment. Some of the departures creating the shrinkage were voluntary, but employees who are about to be fired often quit first.

"Honeymoons are shorter and shorter," warns Margaretta Cullen, senior vice president of global human resources at TMP Worldwide, the New York executive recruitment firm that owns Monster.com. "When I started my career, I was told it takes a year to learn any new job. I still think that's true, but we don't give people that time anymore. You might still be learning, but you'd better be producing at the same time" (Rasmusson, 2000, p. 1). In the "prove it or lose it" job environment of the Information Age, new employees no longer have the luxury of months of ramp-up time. Yet they have more and more to learn.

As legislative liaison for mobility systems, Lieutenant Colonel Steve Arquiette had the critical task of interfacing with Congress on Air Force systems acquisition issues. During his two-year stint at the Pentagon, Arquiette learned a lot about the value of acquiring knowledge quickly. In a 2000 interview, he said:

> When you arrive at the Pentagon for a position like this, you don't know when you will be called upon to be an expert. It may be one month; it may be six months. The learning curve is steep. If you don't learn the ropes, get to know the people, and reach a productive stage in time, you have a problem. When the time comes to defend your systems before Congress, you can't. Your organization is then cut out of multi-million-dollar programs that are critical to its mission. You've failed. The mission-critical systems have been denied. No one cares whether you've been there three months or three years. (Arquiette, 2000)

Of the many ways in which continuity management contributes to increased productivity, one of the most significant is its reduction in the ramp-up time of new employees. Through continuity management, new hires begin immediately to tap the operational knowledge they need to reach the productive phase of employment. This quickened pace of knowledge acquisition, as compared to traditional start-from-scratch practices, is critical in the Information Age. The CEO of a privately held software company in Virginia terminated an executive vice president after only five months on the job because he didn't ramp up fast enough. "We expect our executives to move at market speed," the CEO explained matter-of-factly (Rasmusson, 2000).

Results in Better Decision Making and Fewer Mistakes

The Industrial Age glamorized difficult decisions made at the top as the determinants of organizational destiny. In the Information Age, however, it is no longer the decisions made at the top but the cumulative effect of the countless decisions made in the middle and on the front lines that determine an organization's future. This downward and outward dispersion of decision-making authority has altered the dynamics of organizational decision making, forcing a large number of employees to assume decision-making responsibilities once reserved for top executives, senior managers, and other shapers of corporate destiny. These critical day-to-day decisions made near or at the broad bottom of the hierarchy pyramid, often in circumstances of great uncertainty, are the new determiners of organizational destiny.

Mistakes are inevitable in organizations committed to innovation and driven by the lightning speed of the new marketplace. But unnecessary mistakes and judgmental errors caused by inadequate operational knowledge are costly, and they needlessly squander organizational resources. With continuity management, new hires are introduced to the operational knowledge they need from the start, presented in a structured format and at a measured pace that builds competence and confidence. No employee can function adequately without access to the operational knowledge that defines the employee's position. Job-specific operational knowledge is essential for dealing efficiently with recurring situations and effectively with unique situations where standard operating procedures do not apply.

Continuity management can prevent a number of management errors that develop from knowledge discontinuities. For example:

- Abandoning proven processes that are still effective
- Introducing "new" policies or procedures that have failed in the past
- Entering relationships with incompatible or unreliable partners long ago discredited
- Pursuing ill-considered initiatives that would not have been undertaken had the operational knowledge of long-term employees still been available in the form of institutional memory

These errors do not include the routine but costly mistakes that new employees make on a regular basis because of obsolete data, incomplete information, or inadequate knowledge that result from knowledge discontinuity. Since operational knowledge is based on prior failures as well as prior successes, employees who are aware of past initiatives can exploit their lessons and so avoid repeating what hasn't worked while building on what has. Experience is still the best teacher, but experiences can only teach when they are known.

Improves Training Effectiveness for New Employees

One of the components of the operational knowledge that is transferred to successor employees through continuity management is an understanding of the skill sets and competencies required to succeed in their new positions. By comparing these knowledge, skill, and competency requirements to their existing sets, they, in combination with their managers and human resources experts, can determine the tailored additional training that will make them more productive. This focused, specialized approach not only saves corporate funds from being wasted on unnecessary training, but prevents new employees from having to squander valuable time or suffer through the frustrating experience of being forced to "learn" something they already know. Knowledge continuity also provides a framework through which to organize the training pieces and match them to employee and organizational goals. Continuity management also supplies a context in which new hires can place their training, making it more meaningful to them and therefore more effective. Because they understand the training's purpose and can use its lessons immediately, new employees are often more receptive to training, more motivated during the training process, and more enthusiastic about applying what they have learned.

Lowers the Stress, Raises the Morale, and Increases the Commitment of Both New and Current Employees

Remember your first day on the job? The anxieties and excitement you felt, the expectations you had, and even the second thoughts you entertained? You were not alone. These feelings flood the early experiences of every new employee. Whether a new hire's first hopeful impressions are validated or repudiated, initial fears are resolved or exacerbated, and high expectations are met or dashed will determine, in large part, how well the new employee learns, performs, and commits to the organization. Research confirms the influence of initial experiences in shaping a newcomer's attitudes and behavior. The more positive those experiences are, the more likely the new employee will be able to commit to the organization and embrace its norms, values, and objectives.

Continuity management increases the commitment of new employees, lowers their stress, and raises their morale because:

- *It defines and clarifies their jobs.*   Role ambiguity (not being sure how one is expected to behave in a new situation), fear of looking ignorant or stupid, and fear of failing are high stressors for new employees. These stress factors are exacerbated by inadequate operational knowledge and alleviated by critical operational knowledge.
- *It makes new hires feel valued.*   The customized feel and comprehensive nature of the job-specific operational knowledge transferred to new hires confirms that they are recognized as being highly skilled and important to the organization. Continuity management also suggests a high level of trust and an organizational commitment to make employees feel like part of the gang as quickly as possible.
- *It integrates newcomers more quickly into the existing social network of the organization.*   Continuity management makes it easier for newcomers to meet members of their knowledge network and to rely on them for assistance in the early months of their new job. Knowledge of a prearranged affiliation facilitates initial contact and gives newcomers greater confidence in early discussions with colleagues. It also makes it possible for established employees to contact new hires or to say, "I was expecting your call."
- *It may reduce the cost of premature terminations.*   Frustration, early failures on the job, and high stress levels from trying to function with

insufficient operational knowledge can create such a negative impression that new hires lose their initial enthusiasm, replacing it with negativity that leads to performance deterioration, a new job search, and premature termination.

Continuity management also reduces the stress of job turnover for the remaining coworkers of the departing employees. When an employee leaves a team, the cohesion of the team is broken, valuable knowledge and skills are lost, productivity drops, and enthusiasm falls. Employee departures can stall entire projects and lead to disgruntled coworkers as remaining employees scramble to assume the duties of the lost employee until a successor is up to speed. Without continuity management, successor employees are thieves of time who distract coworkers from their primary tasks, add to their workloads, and heighten their stress levels.

Continuity management raises the morale and increases the motivation of surviving employees because it establishes a time limit on their extra work burden. Knowing that a burden has a definite end makes it less stressful and more bearable. Continuity management also brings new hires up to speed more quickly and therefore shortens the disruptive period. Rather than quasi-chaos of an indeterminate length, surviving employees experience a planned, orderly response to the knowledge loss that is reassuring and effective.

Preserves Knowledge Networks

Knowledge finds its value in human interactions and in the networks that power them. Knowledge moves through these networks—through the hundreds of people who ultimately connect thousands of others inside and outside an organization. Human networks are both sources of new knowledge and users of existing knowledge, and they form the basic structure of the new economy. Humans are the nodes that create these knowledge networks. As with all networks, some nodes are more critical than others. Key nodes exercise greater influence because they possess or have access to critical knowledge resources—data, information, knowledge, competency, or wisdom—either through formal authority conferred by the organization or informal influence resulting from their actions, abilities, or personalities. Identification of these key people will be time-consuming for the new hire and plagued by trial and error. Yet knowledge of them will be crucial to high performance.

Continuity management maintains the continuity of the network of relationships that powers productivity. When an employee leaves an organization without transferring knowledge of those internal and external contacts that create the knowledge web, the whole web—and the whole organization—suffers. If some of the nodes are known only to the departing employee, they will be lost forever, especially if they are contacts external to the employee's immediate area of influence or even to the organization itself. Unless knowledge of the network is maintained, the network must be rediscovered or reconstructed—sometimes year after year—by successor employees, at a terrible cost in productivity, effectiveness, and time.

Focuses Employee Attention on Identifying Job-Critical Knowledge and Productivity Leverage Points

Continuity management is an organizing framework for identifying, prioritizing, transferring, acquiring, and applying critical operational knowledge. One of its net effects is to identify the business-critical knowledge of the organization. As part of the continuity management process, employees analyze the objectives, functions, procedures, processes, performance measurements, contacts, and daily activities of their jobs. Through this analysis, continuity management can lead to refinements, even revolutions, in job definitions by helping employees discover their real work and the knowledge leverage points of that work, which are drivers of high performance. Continuity management thus alters the frame of reference through which knowledge is understood, transforming it from a useful tool into a critical asset and a focused means of achieving maximum productivity.

The *Pareto principle*—20 percent of the work is responsible for 80 percent of the output—applies to operational knowledge. Employees who identify the 20 percent of their knowledge base responsible for 80 percent of their productivity can refocus their attention on that critical 20 percent. Knowledge that is less important can be relegated to a low priority, ignored, or eliminated. The identification of job-critical knowledge is a major contributor to increased productivity. Since this process requires thinking strategically about job-specific knowledge, it subtly—and sometimes not so subtly—redefines the way an employee operates. Continuity management poses as its single most important question, "What do I need to know in order to succeed in my job?" This query leads to the development of meaningful questions about the job and about the data, information, knowledge, and competencies needed to perform well. It brings to the forefront what an employee does know (and doesn't know) and how his or her knowledge base can be enriched. Yet it achieves this objective in a personally rewarding way rather than in a punitive way, and so is itself motivational.

Continuity management also illuminates knowledge differences among employees in similar jobs that may correlate to differences in performance. It can lead to the correction of deficiencies and may produce new best practices or other insights that can be shared with peers through traditional knowledge-sharing techniques or through formal revisions of policy and procedure manuals.

Prevents Knowledge Hoarding

The analysis of knowledge needs and knowledge access that is an essential element of continuity management will reveal the existence of knowledge hoarding in an organization. With knowledge hoarding, critical knowledge is centered in—or controlled by—one person and cannot be obtained except through that person. Whether the knowledge hoard is by design (to increase that person's status or power) or as a result of obsolete procedures or past practices, its existence is a threat to the continuity of the organization's knowledge base and productivity. The potential consequences of this threat take several forms:

- If the knowledge hoarder leaves the organization, there is no backup source, and the knowledge is lost. In some cases, the hoarded knowledge is not the knowledge itself but how that knowledge can be accessed, filtered, or organized. Either way, the consequence of lost knowledge is the same.
- If the knowledge hoarder does not leave, many who could profit from the knowledge have no easy way to access it or may not know it exists and so must either do without the knowledge, squander valuable time trying to find it, or generate it from scratch as if it didn't exist.
- Because the free flow of knowledge increases its value, knowledge hoarding reduces the worth of the knowledge asset, lessens the likelihood of its enhancement, and prevents its widest utilization by the greatest number of employees.

Continuity management ameliorates or eliminates these threats by ferreting out knowledge hoarders so that the imprisoned knowledge can be freed and returned to an accessible state.

Preserves Institutional Memory

Without knowledge continuity, an organization lacks a solid institutional memory from which to grow its knowledge asset. When operational knowledge is preserved from one employee generation to the next, each generation makes the legacy knowledge more valuable to the organization by refining it, updating it, or using it to generate new knowledge. Operational knowledge thus becomes a corporate asset that is reinvested in and by each new employee. New knowledge is created as a return on the investment of that knowledge legacy and is added back to the principal.

Facilitates Knowledge Creation, Innovation, Continuous Improvement, and Organizational Learning

Continuity management preserves the tacit knowledge developed by individual employees and by groups of employees in formal teams or communities of practice (groups of people who meet together, often informally, to share knowledge). Such knowledge is constantly evolving in response to changes in the group's composition and to problems and opportunities in the environment to which group members respond. Improved services, new approaches to problem solving, or time-saving shortcuts are examples of tacit knowledge that emerge from teams and communities of practice. Without knowledge continuity, invaluable permutations of established procedures that constitute bottom-line best practices for the organization will be lost when the last member of the group leaves.

Long-term competitive advantage, however, does not reside in current knowledge but in new knowledge that improves existing goods and services and creates new ones. The purpose of continuous learning and the raison d'etre of the learning organization is the generation of new knowledge. Since learning is based on prior knowledge and developed through current experience, it is facilitated in an organization that maintains knowledge continuity. When incumbent employees organize their operational knowledge into an asset that can be passed to their successors, innovative solutions, tested responses, personnel insights, and other aspects of operational knowledge are preserved. Without the knowledge base of the status quo from which innovation springs, learning is retarded and change is haphazard and accidental rather than planned and intentional. Only with knowledge continuity can an organization function as a true knowledge network capable of learning. Knowledge continuity makes it possible for a new hire to tap the rich pool of operational knowledge developed by generations of employees.

Continuity management contributes to continuous improvement and organizational learning in another way. By harnessing the potential for innovation and positive change that comes with job turnover, continuity management can make lemonade out of the lemon of turnover. When knowledge continuity is maintained, job turnover can have a positive effect because it brings new people, ideas, and skills to the organization, which expands the organization's knowledge base and enhances knowledge creation. But such positive results can occur only when the critical operational knowledge of departing employees has been preserved, and the knowledge of arriving employees is honored and utilized. Otherwise, both new and existing knowledge will have been lost.

But continuity management does something more than preserve knowledge continuity. By virtue of the ongoing knowledge analysis inherent in its processes and the continuing peer reviews of the operational knowledge transferred to successors, continuity management counters the potential risk of preserving mediocrity. Without such analysis, mediocre performance might be maintained or created as conditions change, which is what happens when excellence is allowed to degrade. The objective of continuity management is not continuity of mediocrity but creation of excellence. It is from knowledge creation stimulated by the preservation of critical operational knowledge that innovation grows and excellence is achieved. Continuity management does not preserve the status quo, but challenges and changes it.

Reduces Job Turnover and Increases a Sense of Employee Value

A positive new-hire orientation experience can reduce job turnover. In fact, some research indicates that a well-developed and well-executed orientation program can improve employee retention rates by 25 percent (O'Toole, 2001, p. 1). One reason is that job orientation and training experiences are a visible investment in newcomers that demonstrates how much the organization values them. Continuity management personalizes these early training programs and enriches the orientation experience by customizing them to fit the operational knowledge needs of each new employee. It confirms organizational support for new hires by its commitment to expand their knowledge, develop their on-the-job competencies, and lead them to colleagues who are prepared to help them fit in sooner and learn faster. By providing clear paths to necessary knowledge sources, continuity management acknowledges each new employee as a critical link in the knowledge network of the organization.

Because continuity management makes it easier for new hires to reach higher productivity levels faster and because it reduces the stress associated with job transitions, it can be an effective recruiting tool. When properly promoted to potential employees, continuity management is an enticement that makes it easier to attract highly qualified workers. Top talent wants to move quickly and confidently into a new job, meeting performance measures well ahead of schedule, and surpassing expectations. The jump start that continuity management affords such employees is an inducement not only because of what it does for them but for what it represents: an organization that is genuinely concerned about their welfare and their success.

Continuity management provides another advantage for talented hires. By providing comprehensive operational knowledge quickly, it allows them to dive into the job challenges they crave. It supports them in the rapid acquisition of the operational knowledge they want so that they can expand, modify, and use it to its maximum effect as they build their new careers and establish their reputations.

Continuity management also increases the opportunities for employees to learn, to define and hone their knowledge, and to develop that knowledge in a strategic way based on their personal and professional goals. This ability to take a more direct role in shaping one's professional destiny is particularly important to younger talent with its free-agent mind-set. Dave Pollard, global director for knowledge innovation at Ernst & Young's Centre for Business Knowledge in Toronto, believes that offering employees more opportunities to learn is a key advantage to organizations that seek to attract and retain scarce talent.

Lowers Job-Turnover Costs

Continuity management lowers job-turnover costs by increasing the speed at which new hires become fully productive. It also lessens the cost of new employee mistakes, oversights, and judgmental errors and the cost of lost coworker productivity stemming from the time-consuming special attention and informal training that new employees often require. Knowledge continuity is particularly important in preventing lost sales. Recounting his experience with job turnover as a sales representative at Bayer Diagnostics, Anthony Cvitanich recalled, "The company faced the largest losses due to knowledge turnover from one sales rep to the next. When a company is losing market share in a $40 million-a-month business, every percentage point lost is a critical blow. Knowledge of the customer is so important in this business, and we lost it with the departing sales reps" (Cvitanich, 2002).

Reduces Organizational Vulnerability When Utilizing the Contingency Workforce

The contingency workforce is growing. A 2000 Towers Perrin survey confirmed an increasing organizational commitment to outsourcing, which poses a corresponding threat to knowledge continuity. Of the responding companies, 11 percent had outsourced noncore activities in the past two years, with 44 percent expecting to outsource such activities by 2003 (Samuells, 2001, p. 35). This mounting reliance on outside knowledge suppliers dramatically increases the risk of knowledge loss and productivity disruptions because of high turnover. Even more alarmingly, these losses have generally been regarded as beyond the control of the organization itself. Continuity management reduces an organization's vulnerability in utilizing the contingency workforce, allowing it to use outside knowledge suppliers without compromising the security of the organizational knowledge base. Continuity management achieves this objective because:

- It captures the critical operational knowledge of outside suppliers and internalizes that knowledge.
- It makes it easier to bring the outsourced function back in house when it is advantageous to do so, because the operational knowledge remains available internally. Hence, it is safer to outsource a function, because the organization never surrenders its capability of reclaiming that function.
- It makes it safer to switch external suppliers when their performance deteriorates, because a copy of their operational knowledge has been retained by the organization.

Increases Customer Confidence and Reduces Customer Attrition

Continuity management preserves service capabilities and customer confidence by transferring critical customer insights to the new employee for use at the outset of employment. By quickly restoring knowledge continuity between departing and successor employees, continuity management can reduce customer attrition by ensuring continuity of established service quality. A customer's special requirements and preferences are an important component of operational knowledge and costly to lose. Such knowledge makes it possible to cater to a customer's unique needs, render superior service, and maximize customer satisfaction.

Operational knowledge also makes possible the honing of product and service offerings by building on previous knowledge. The more an organization knows about its customers, the more it can shift its value proposition from providing goods and services (the model of the Industrial Age) to providing knowledge, experience, and expertise about those products and services (the model of the Information Age).

Sustains Core Corporate Values, Competencies, and Mission

Continuity of operational knowledge ensures that corporate values, core competencies, and mission objectives are sustained year after year. These values and competencies must be passed on to succeeding generations if the organization is to maintain its identity and competitive advantages while still responding to changing environmental stresses, demands, and opportunities. Continuity management preserves the organizational competence and wisdom that provide the decisive edge in navigating turbulent environments, allowing the organization to maintain its steady, forward course through recurring and unexpected storms.

An organization's culture—how things are done—is what defines the sense, feel, or spirit of an organization. It can be a significant factor in the differences in commitment and involvement between organizations in the same field. Organizational culture is one of the fundamental dimensions of organizational life that determines organizational performance and that creates the sense of belonging (or lack of it) that motivates employees. Organizational culture is transferred primarily through interpersonal contact and group experiences, not through formal rules and regulations. Formal policies and procedures provide a reference point for new hires, but they are not per-suasive. The real guidelines that determine behavior, set standards, and govern performance are prescribed by the group through unwritten group norms and role assignments and expressed in interpersonal relationships. Employee acclimation—assimilation into a new organization and a personal acceptance of its norms, missions, standards, and objectives—is facilitated by continuity management. This *buy-in* shapes a new employee's behavior and leads to conformity with the organization's culture, to identification with its members and goals, and to easier newcomer transition and increased organizational loyalty. Assimilation occurs more quickly through continuity management, which ensures a transfer of operational knowledge that translates official rules into real or operative ones that ease the newcomer's transition and build loyalty to the organization.

Increases Long-Term Organizational Effectiveness

The knowledge lost from a departing employee is not a short-term problem; it is a long-term problem that breeds other problems and reduces an organization's effectiveness. When an organization loses an employee's knowledge, it suffers a setback. The more significant the knowledge is to the organization, the more serious the setback. The greater the number of knowledge losses, the greater the total setback. The cumulative effect of lost knowledge from hundreds, even thousands of employee departures over months and years is substantial. It raises costs, decreases productivity, undermines competitive advantage, and erodes organizational competence.

■ ■ ■

Continuity management and *competitive advantage:* The two phrases will be synonymous in the new century, because continuity management delivers a decisive organizational capacity. It is the capacity to preserve, invest, exploit, and create knowledge—a capacity that will lead to unparalleled dominance in the uncertain times of the Information Age. The power to realign quickly, strike boldly, and forge resolutely ahead when opportunity beckons and others waver is the product of superior knowledge adroitly deployed. The rapier move, the creative punch, the audacious acquisition all spring from knowledge honed and perfected through organizational capacities generated and sustained by continuity management.

4

The Knowledge Learning Curve

With every new hire, an organization acquires that new employee's knowledge, which may include knowledge that is completely new to the organization and very valuable. But while the organization acquires this knowledge asset, it also takes on the employee's knowledge vacuum of job-specific operational knowledge. To fill this vacuum, organizations attempt to teach, train, and mentor their new hires and, thus, to inject new employees' existing knowledge bases with the job-specific operational knowledge they need to attain high productivity levels quickly. It is in this process of knowledge transfer (from the organization's standpoint) and knowledge acquisition (from the new employee's standpoint) that continuity management makes a major contribution.

"In every new job I start," confessed a midlevel manager, "I encounter the 'freshman effect.' The freshman effect occurs when the knowledge I have depended upon for success is no longer relevant, and I enter a condition of job ignorance. Job ignorance, however, is not an acceptable state. Not to me because I don't like to appear foolish or inept, and not to the organization because I don't appear productive. So what happens? I counter the freshman effect by attempting to pass as a 'senior,' which is what many organizations ask their new hires to do. They expect you to perform like a senior, but with a freshman's knowledge. It doesn't work. Only once have I ever been hired by a company that honored its freshmen by respecting their ignorance and offering them knowledge. It was the most exhilarating experience of my working career. It may also have been the most productive."

The Learning Curve

The lower productivity level of new hires is commonly recognized, of course, as is its cost to the organization. It is also commonly recognized that lower productivity results from inadequate operational knowledge. The increase in knowledge and experience that allows employees to increase their productivity over time has been depicted in a graph known as the *learning curve*. The learning curve was developed by the Boeing Company in the 1930s as a method for predicting the cost of building new aircraft (Anthes, 2001, p. 42). It illustrates the effect of improved productivity, over time, on the unit cost of production. Hence, the graph relates unit cost to time and productivity.

Boeing discovered that the unit cost dropped for each aircraft built after the first aircraft. Furthermore, it dropped at a predictable rate. With each subsequent aircraft, employees learned to work faster, make fewer mistakes, and waste less material until they reached a point of maximum productivity. The increased speed and improved accuracy of these employees resulted directly from their acquisition of operational knowledge. The learning curve of Boeing's aircraft workers was plotted as a graph, with the x (vertical) axis showing the cost of production and the y (horizontal) axis showing the units of production, as illustrated in Figure 4.1.

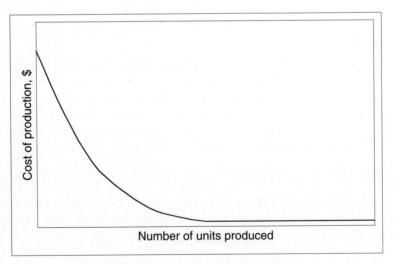

Figure 4.1   The learning curve.

The steeper the negative slope of the curve (the faster the curve falls), the faster the unit cost of production falls. Boeing created the learning curve to predict the cost of future aircraft production based on early production data. This learning curve is a critical forecasting tool in manufacturing industries because it allows a company to predict its break-even point, how much cash it will consume to reach breakeven, and how much profit it will make thereafter at a given price for each unit produced. Although the learning curve is essential in estimating production costs and in setting product prices, it can be used analogously in nonmanufacturing industries to describe the learning process that occurs on any job. Employee efficiency and effectiveness improve over time as a result of on-the-job experience that increases employee and organizational knowledge and hence produces employee and organizational learning. The importance of the learning curve is its recognition that *on-the-job knowledge acquisition* improves efficiency, effectiveness, and productivity.

The Boeing learning curve was very much a product of the Industrial Age, but it still has its use in manufacturing. The curve's original purpose in the 1930s was to predict the unit cost of producing something, a purpose it retains. The direction of the curve emphasized that it was a *reduction* in the cost of the manual labor required to produce a product that was important. Therefore, lower (and falling) learning curves were preferable to higher (and rising) learning curves because they meant lower costs from on-the-job learning. But people intuitively think of knowledge and learning as something that should be increasing, not decreasing. Ironically, Boeing's learning curve went down when learning went up. The counterintuitive nature of the Boeing curve resulted in the popularization among managers of a different kind of learning curve: one that *rose* with learning—that is, with the acquisition of job-critical operational knowledge.

The Knowledge Learning Curve

This new learning curve for the knowledge economy might be called the *knowledge learning curve*. It is a curve that managers and executives frequently talk about and use as a common frame of reference, even though, as far as we know, it has not technically been described before its appearance in this book. The knowledge learning curve can be graphed as illustrated in Figure 4.2.

While the knowledge learning curve takes the same concept of learning over time as the Boeing curve, it applies that concept to increased

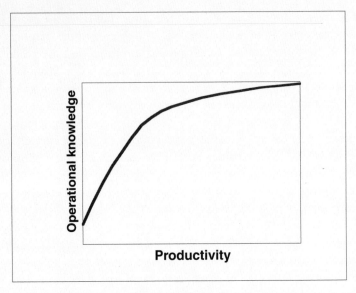

Figure 4.2   The knowledge learning curve.

productivity rather than to a drop in the unit cost of production. The knowledge learning curve depicts the *increased productivity* that develops as a function of the acquisition of *critical operational knowledge.* It illustrates the relationship between operational knowledge and productivity and between learning and productivity gain. As opposed to the learning curve, the knowledge learning curve starts on the *x* axis at a point near the *y* axis and *rises* with the acquisition of knowledge. The desired slope is positive rather than negative. The steeper the slope, the more desirable it is, because it indicates more rapid acquisition of operational knowledge and hence greater productivity.

With the knowledge learning curve, the objective is to move up the curve, because the higher the point on the curve, the greater the operational knowledge acquired and the higher the productivity. When executives say that they hope the learning curve isn't too steep, they mean that they hope the new employee doesn't have to acquire too much operational knowledge to get up to speed. When executives say with pride that new employees are quickly moving up the learning curve, they mean that the new hires are acquiring operational knowledge and proficiency at a rapid pace, which is bringing them quickly up to speed and high productivity.

The knowledge learning curve is not intended to be specifically predictive (as was the original learning curve in projecting actual per-unit costs), but descriptive of a process and predictive of a trend line. In theory, each new hire would have his or her own knowledge learning curve, a unique curve shaped by the characteristics of the job and by those of the new hire assuming it. Some employees might start higher on the curve and others might have a steeper curve, but the general shape of the curve should be something like the one shown in Figure 4.2.

Interestingly, the slope of the knowledge learning curve can be negative (the curve falls rather than rises). When the knowledge learning curve is dropping, it means that negative learning is taking place. Performance, of course, is deteriorating, and productivity is falling. The slope of an organizational learning curve is negative when organizational "forgetting" occurs, meaning that the organization is actually "unlearning." An unlearning organization will know less tomorrow than it did today. Organizational unlearning occurs on the micro level whenever an employee leaves and that employee's operational knowledge has not been harvested for transfer to the successor. It takes place on the macro level when knowledge discontinuities from downsizing or high employee turnover creates a net loss in the organization's knowledge base. Knowledge depletion from organizational forgetting can afflict a department, a business unit, or an entire organization, leaving the knowledge base in shambles and the organization vulnerable.

Knowledge Continuity as Productivity Continuity

The knowledge learning curve illustrates a central point: new-employee (and, ultimately, organizational) productivity is a function of the amount of operational knowledge available to new employees and the rate at which that operational knowledge can be acquired. This relationship between operational knowledge and productivity powers the potential of continuity management to create significant competitive advantage. If increased operational knowledge is equal to increased productivity in the early phases of a new job, then the more operational knowledge available to a starting employee, the higher that employee's productivity will be *from the beginning* and *the shorter will be the time necessary to reach maximum productive capacity* (everything else being equal).

Another way to express this principle is to say that *knowledge continuity makes it possible to move up the learning curve at a faster rate.* The knowledge learning curve explains the powerful effect of continuity management on productivity. Because continuity management increases the amount of operational knowledge transferred to a new employee and the rate at which that transfer occurs, an organization that employs continuity management will suffer less productivity loss from retirements and recurring job turnover than one that does not. The more critical operational knowledge is to an employee's performance, the greater will be the negative impact on productivity of that employee's departure. When organizations hemorrhage knowledge from departing employees whose operational knowledge has not been transferred to their successors, they hemorrhage productivity.

Just 1 additional hour of productivity per employee per day adds up to an average of 220 hours of additional productivity per employee per year. Assuming that it takes about a year to become fully productive in a new job, the annual effect of a daily 1-hour productivity gain on the organization's performance is impressive. When this gain is multiplied by the number of replacement employees hired each year, the cumulative effect on an organization can be substantial. In a firm with an annual turnover of 100 employees earning salaries and benefits averaging $45 per hour, a net increase in productivity that generates just 1 additional hour of productivity per day equals about $1 million per year of productivity gain. The value of that productivity increase, however, is even higher because the revenue derived from employee production is greater than the cost of production once the employee has passed the break-even point.

But the productivity gains are still greater than these figures suggest. Because new employees disrupt the productivity of their coworkers until they have acquired the operational knowledge they need to become productive, the sooner they reach full productivity, the sooner their coworkers' productivity will be restored. Hence, the value of operational knowledge that raises a new employee's productivity level is greater than the value of the employee's productivity itself. It also includes the value of the increase in coworker productivity that would otherwise have been lost because of the new employee's interference with the coworkers' productive capacities.

In addition to the added productivity of the new hire and the restoration of coworker productivity levels, there is a third source of increased productivity from rapid knowledge acquisition and application. That source is *group synergy*. Through synergy, the group's knowledge learning curve is greater than the sum of its individual curves. Therefore, the sooner new employees can achieve meaningful productivity, the sooner they can make a contribution to the group's synergy, which raises the whole group's productivity level. By the same token, the loss of a valued employee can have a greater negative impact on the team's total productivity than the loss of one employee might suggest. In this case, the positive effect of synergy turns negative. The faster that synergy can be reestablished, the sooner its productivity contribution to the group and its members can be restored. Lost productivity cannot be made up. Like an unsold seat on an airplane flight, the profit generated by the employee is lost, and, like the fare for the empty seat, it cannot be recouped. It is gone forever.

A new group member—no matter how capable—creates negative productivity for the group in the first few weeks. Negative productivity occurs because the new group member lacks the necessary knowledge to contribute to the team's productivity, while draining productivity from other group members, who are distracted from their primary work by their attempts to orient and instruct the new employee. If the new member's period of service is relatively short, his or her positive effect on productivity may never exceed the initial negative effect, and so the new employee may never have performed productive work for the organization. Indeed, the employee will have drained productive work from the group and the organization.

Phases of Productivity

A new employee's journey up the learning curve can be one of increasing exhilaration or of crushing frustration—or something in between. One of the single most important factors in determining a positive or a negative outcome is the employee's access to job-critical operational knowledge. When new hires start out, they confront a series of knowledge-based problems that stand between them and peak performance. It is the organization's responsibility to provide them with the operational knowledge they need to solve those problems and become productive.

Knowledge acquisition is not a random process. It occurs in recognizable phases. Research confirms the conventional wisdom that the productivity of new employees begins at a low level, increases over time, and finally plateaus as employees come to understand the job and bring their knowledge and competency to bear. This journey up the knowledge learning curve can be described conceptually in terms of four phases of increasing productivity—orientation, assimilation, productivity, and high performance—and a fifth phase of productivity decline that occurs as an employee prepares to leave the organization. Although the phases can be described as if they were discreet, they actually form a continuum. The length of time an employee spends in each phase depends on a variety of factors, such as intelligence, motivation, competency, and job complexity. But the key element on which all these factors act is the amount of operational knowledge transferred to the new employee.

The five productivity phases provide a framework for understanding productivity and the role of operational knowledge in achieving it. They can help new hires appreciate the limitations imposed on their performance by the knowledge learning curve, gauge the validity of performance expectations placed on them by others (as well as by themselves), and mark their progress along the productivity curve through recognizable achievements that characterize each phase. An understanding of the phases helps a new employee ask the right questions and seek the right answers. An appreciation of the phases breaks the journey up the curve into manageable segments, so that a new employee's motivation is not impaired by undue frustration or self-perceived failure. Indeed, success in each phase can provide motivation for moving to the next phase. By designing short-term wins into the early productivity phases, an organization can motivate its employees, reduce their stress, and speed their passage to high performance.

The phases of productivity are based on how operational knowledge in that phase is acquired by new employees and applied to increase their competency and improve their productivity. Several caveats are warranted regarding these phases.

First, there is no set timetable for the phases; their occurrence is dependent on a number of highly variable organizational, situational, and individual factors. The moment at which an employee can be said to enter a new phase does not depend on the passage of time per se, but on the level of productivity achieved. The phases, in other words, are productivity-dependent, not time-dependent.

Second, in an ideal scenario, employees progress through the first three phases into the fourth phase of high performance. But such is not always the case. Employees may get stuck in an earlier phase and never advance beyond it. Or they may leave the organization before reaching the high-performance phase.

Third, the lines of demarcation between the phases are subjective, fuzzy, and often difficult to determine other than in a general sense. In part, this is due to the fact that productivity is a complex phenomenon encompassing many complicated subtasks and affected by many interacting factors. At any given time, an employee might be in the orientation phase in one part of his or her work, in the high-performance phase in a second, and in the productivity phase in a third.

Finally, there is a window of opportunity in the early phases of productivity when a new employee's feedback becomes critical to the organization and should be solicited and honored. This feedback is important for two reasons:

- It allows the organization to better respond to the employees' learning needs.
- It encourages employees to suggest innovative procedures, policies, approaches, and solutions based on their fresh perspective *before that perspective is extinguished* by organizational pressures to conform. New employee feedback is an important source of creative ideas that lead to increased productivity and refinements in processes, products, and services.

"The objective," says Major General Michael McMahan, commander of the U.S. Air Force Personnel Center, "is to give everyone the opportunity to excel. You can't do that unless you also give them knowledge and unless you give it to them in an organized way" (McMahan, 2001).

Phase 1: Orientation

The orientation phase begins on the first day of employment as new hires start the process of assimilating a formidable amount of job-related data, information, and knowledge. New-employee productivity is low, and the productivity of established coworkers is adversely affected. Experienced employees are distracted from their primary tasks by the dependency of the new hires and the need to answer their questions or otherwise instruct them.

This phase generally includes formal and informal orientation sessions that introduce new employees to the organization and to the objectives, resources, skills, procedures, activities, performance measures, best practices, and so forth associated with their jobs. Special skills training, if required, begins in this phase. The more comprehensive and personalized the orientation, training, and knowledge-acquisition program, the more likely it will be to increase the new hires' productivity.

Continuity management provides the structured, job-critical operational knowledge that enables employees to progress quickly from the low productivity of the orientation and assimilation phases to the high productivity of the productivity phase. Without continuity management, new employees' progress in the orientation phase will be difficult and halting, as the novices struggle to figure out what knowledge they need and then how to acquire it. The vast reservoir of data, information, and knowledge in contemporary organizations is meaningless to newcomers without an organized means to sort through the overload. Continuity management is a Rosetta stone for interpreting and selectively accessing this ocean of information, helping new hires determine what they need to know, based on their needs and priorities. Metaphorically, continuity management is a Geiger counter that allows new employees to identify the "radioactive" knowledge they need and to find it in the knowledge landscape.

Continuity management makes it possible for new employees to exploit fully the existing knowledge management capabilities of their organization. Critical operational knowledge provided by the predecessor acts as an organizing framework, much like an index or catalog, that enables successor employees to identify and access the additional knowledge they need through existing knowledge management tools. Continuity management equips new employees with the operational knowledge their positions require by answering such questions as: What do I need to know? How can I find out what I need to know? And how can I find out what I don't know that I need to know?

EMC Corporation uses a knowledge management tool that it calls *My Sales Web,* which is an internal Web site for salespeople, directed toward their day-to-day needs. My Sales Web is a repository of product information, competitor analyses, training opportunities, how-to-sell techniques, best practices, productivity tools, solutions to specific sales problems, market news, late-breaking bulletins, and so forth. Its focus is on the practical and the successful. My Sales Web provides salespeople with a macrounderstanding of the corporation, its market, and its competitors as well as direct access to detailed information on the micro level. The site is refreshed continually and accessed frequently throughout the day by each salesperson.

My Sales Web could form the basis for a sophisticated continuity management system. By combining its existing data, information, and knowledge with job-critical operational knowledge transferred by predecessor employees, My Sales Web would deliver comprehensive knowledge continuity and knowledge creation capabilities to knowledge workers at EMC. It would link the operational knowledge captured by continuity management to the expanded knowledge captured by knowledge management, integrating the two into a seamless whole of guided knowledge acquisition and creation.

Phase 2: Assimilation

During the assimilation phase, employees become familiar with their jobs and begin to get a handle on them. They have progressed from the absorption of data and information to the acquisition of knowledge and competence. They are no longer a significant drain on organizational productivity, because their knowledge and productive capacity have reached the point that coworkers no longer have to do part of their job or spend significant time instructing them. Yet, the new employees are still not making major productivity contributions. Nonetheless, the insights, lessons learned, contacts, and knowledge analyses provided by continuity management form the basis for a quick ascension to the next phase: productivity.

A window of opportunity exists in the assimilation phase during which to harvest new employees' insights, perspectives, and ideas and, when appropriate, incorporate them into organizational operations. It is easy—perhaps inevitable—for established employees to accept the status quo, buy into how things are done, and fall into a rut that is resistant to challenge and change. Recent hires in the assimilation phase are not yet in that rut. They retain an outsider's perspective on their job that can now be integrated with an insider's understanding of that job's parameters, demands, and opportunities. This integration uniquely positions them to make objective judgments about the effectiveness of the status quo. From such judgments come innovation, increased productivity, and new ideas that keep the organization responsive and sharp—but only if the organization listens. Once new hires have been fully acclimated to their positions and have entered the productivity phase, they will be less likely to challenge basic assumptions or to propose new ways of doing things. As their routines become established and powerfully influenced by peer pressure and organizational culture, they will find it increasingly difficult to think outside the box that the organization is constructing around them. The pressures for conformity will be too strong.

Because a new hire's challenge to the status quo may be perceived as a threat and met with resistance, a formal mechanism needs to be established in this phase to encourage innovations, challenges to the status quo, and suggestions for change. Such a mechanism will ensure that the new employee's ideas are heard, evaluated, and acted on by adoption, modification, or rejection (with reasonable cause). This process of incorporating new insights and fresh perspectives into an organization's operational knowledge pool is the means by which knowledge continuity leads to excellence rather than to mediocrity. Through the infusion of new knowledge, employees create knowledge to add to the knowledge base to which they are heir, steward, and contributor. This challenge to the knowledge pool ensures its revitalization and therefore its currency and its value. There is nothing sacred about operational knowledge; it is always subject to change as the conditions in which it is relevant change. In the Information Age, the competitive edge belongs to those who take advantage of this potential to invigorate the knowledge pool.

Phase 3: Productivity

In the productivity phase, new employees convert the knowledge acquired in the orientation and assimilation phases into job-specific competencies that produce productivity gains for the organization. They are no longer net consumers of knowledge; they are producers. Knowledge of effective practices, critical cause-and-effect relationships, crucial knowledge networks, key resources, lessons from past failures, and an expansion of skills create the productivity levels that characterize this phase. Effective problem solving, sound decision making, and innovative solutions are the result. The phase is also marked by a strong motivation to add to existing knowledge, to build on previous successes, and to produce impressive operating results. Using a sports analogy, the phase begins with the new recruit on the bench, insisting, "Hey, Coach, put me in the game." It ends with the recruit saying, "I'm in!"

Phase 4: High Performance

In the high-performance phase, employees are at the top of their game, and exceptional productivity occurs. Elevated synergy levels, extensive operational knowledge, broad knowledge networks, comprehensive exchanges of knowledge in communities of practice, and cohesive groups all contribute to extraordinary performance. The commitment of these high performers to innovative approaches and creative solutions generates improved procedures, processes, products, and services. These employees create new knowledge at an accelerating rate, and they increase the productivity of others through the operational knowledge they share.

Since the level of productivity achieved in the high-performance phase depends on comprehensive operational knowledge and high levels of individual competence, continuity management's major contributions to this phase are the preservation of critical insights from generations of previous incumbents and the ongoing knowledge analysis that continuity management requires. That analysis facilitates continuous learning and skill building, more adept application of operational knowledge, and greater and greater knowledge integration.

Phase 5: Departure

Employees enter this phase when they decide to leave the organization or else discover that they will be forced to leave because of layoffs, terminations, or transfers. In the departure phase, motivation drops, productivity declines, quality of work suffers, and innovations cease as employees turn their attention to the next job, to finding the next job, or to retirement.

This productivity decline affects coworkers' productivity levels both because group synergy drops and because coworkers have to assume some of the work abandoned by the departing employees, perhaps even before they have left. If the departure is an angry one, or coworkers see the departing employees as having been mistreated, their productivity may also decline in response to that negative emotional reaction. Even if the departure is friendly, surviving employees will experience sadness and, to some degree, anger about the loss. All the parties affected by the departure must grieve the loss of the departing employees. Psychological and emotional withdrawal by either the departing employees or their coworkers or both may begin, defensiveness may increase, avoidance reactions may develop, and relationships will change as all parties attempt to adjust emotionally to the loss.

Continuity management's major contribution to this phase is its preservation of each departing employee's operational knowledge *even if* that employee's departure is on unpleasant terms. Since the operational knowledge captured by continuity management has been built up over time, it remains valuable to the organization, because its contents reflect the productivity or high-performance phases of the employee's tenure as well as the operational knowledge of previous employees in their productivity and high-performance phases.

■ ■ ■

The five phases of productivity provide a conceptual framework for understanding the process through which operational knowledge is acquired by new hires and how the acquisition of that knowledge relates to their productivity.

The phases emphasize that the knowledge acquisition rate of new hires has a profound effect on productivity and organizational performance. The phases explain why high job turnover without knowledge continuity reduces the knowledge asset, impairs productive capacity, and disables high performance. Continuity management maintains the operational knowledge base between incumbent and successor employees that sustains productivity and, at the same time, enables the generation of new knowledge that adds still more productive capacity. This relationship among knowledge, knowledge continuity, and productivity is one key to deciphering the mysteries of gaining competitive advantage in the Information Age.

Effective management in the knowledge economy requires a reorientation that focuses attention on the key role of knowledge and its preservation across employee generations. Chronic knowledge loss exacerbated by baby-boomer retirements threaten corporate productivity across the economic spectrum, and the situation is worsening. Yet the negative effects of knowledge discontinuity have persisted as a blind spot in the management field of vision. A new vision, however, is replacing the old as the crisis of knowledge loss comes into sharper focus, impairs productive capacity, and casts its red shadow toward the numbers on the bottom line.

Part II

Confessions of a Continuity Manager

In Part I, you came to understand the acute and chronic threats of knowledge loss to organizational productivity. You examined the unique importance of knowledge and its emergence as a capital asset in the new economy. You discovered that operational knowledge is a commodity that can be passed from one employee generation to another and also a process by which existing knowledge is acquired and new knowledge is created. Perhaps you've even become intrigued by the competitive advantages of continuity management. All of which leads you to . . . what?

To a knowledge hole. To the question of how to go forward, to implement, to make continuity management *happen*. After all the *whys* and *whats,* it's time for the *how-to's.*

Continuity management is made powerful by its application. Like any business model, framework, or paradigm, it is useful only if it can be implemented to achieve specific organizational objectives.

Whereas Part I is primarily about concepts, Parts II and III are about action. They describe how continuity management can be implemented in any organization by managers who recognize its potential and take advantage of it. Subsequent chapters thus focus on implementation—on the journey to continuity management—and on the road map for getting there. Part II depicts that road map through a literary device. Rather than the essays of preceding chapters, the next seven chapters employ entries from a journal—Brett's journal—as a narrative lens through which to understand continuity management and the means for putting it into practice.

As a singular account of how continuity management came to be implemented, Brett's journal chronicles the problems and opportunities, disappointments and successes, and conflicts and collaborations that are part of every change effort that results in organizational transformation. It explains the principles, guidelines, and procedures for implementing continuity management and the decisions and steps that convert its concepts into action. Although the journal is fictitious, its contents are the culmination of hundreds of interviews and conversations and thousands of hours of research involving real people facing real knowledge continuity problems in real organizations.

The stories in Brett's journal happened; only the names of the people and their organizations have been changed (the names of the people fictionalized and the names of the companies changed to the name of Brett's company). In cases where the names of these companies can be revealed, a footnote does so. Since some of the stories are knowledge continuity disasters, however, many of the executives who shared their experiences preferred not to have their companies identified. In these instances, a footnote is used to describe the company (e.g. one of America's largest banks), but not to identify it. In other examples, the names of the organizations have not been changed at all.

Brett's journal depicts a world of knowledge discontinuity that mirrors the everyday experiences of thousands of managers and executives who contend with the loss of valuable employees and the knowledge asset they take with them. You may recognize some of these situations—and even some of these people—because they are not uncommon in the turbulent world of job turnover and knowledge loss that characterizes the Information Age.

Before opening Brett's journal, there are a few things you might want to know about its author. Were you to meet Brett at a cocktail party, you would learn that he works for WedgeMark, a company you may know. It often appears in the pages of the *Wall Street Journal*. Were you to talk with him about your job or his, you would discover that he is slightly irreverent, often thoughtful, occasionally harried, and, in his own way, sincere and determined. Much later, you would find that Brett believes in what his company can be—even if he doesn't quite believe in what it is—and that he wants to make it more productive and a better place to work. He would wince if someone said he was searching for more *meaning* in his job, but the truth is that he is.

Brett is neither cynical nor naive, although he tends toward the former. He has put up with a lot that doesn't work over the past 15 years on the trail of jobs that has brought him to his midlevel manager's position at Wedge-Mark. During that time, he has seen many ideas come and go, and he doesn't want to have to put up with any more bad ideas that some idiot has dreamed up, pawned off, and left for dead on the steps of his cubicle. Yet Brett still searches for more productive answers, more innovative approaches, and more creative products that will allow him to serve his customers in a more personal and effective way and help him feel even better about himself and his work.

So the idea of continuity management resonated with him, and he remained intrigued but too busy to give it much thought after first reading about the concept. Then, at the end of a particularly difficult day, one of his best people announced that she was leaving unexpectedly. As he reflected on the coming loss, his thoughts turned to knowledge discontinuities, the price WedgeMark paid for them, and continuity management. In truth, Brett told himself, WedgeMark suffered crippling knowledge losses from high job turnover. Furthermore, the retirement of long-term employees from key positions posed an even greater threat. Finally, he admitted, WedgeMark wasn't even getting its new employees up to speed fast enough.

So Brett found the concept of continuity management appealing and resolved that he would look into it. If he became convinced of its potential, he told himself, he would try to bring it to WedgeMark. And, in the process, he would keep a journal to discipline his thinking. Like the journals of Lewis and Clark he had read as a youth, but on a much more modest scale, he intended it as a record of events and a personal account of an exploration into unknown territory. He would include key ideas, pertinent documents, memorable conversations, and anything else related to the implementation of continuity management at WedgeMark—should such implementation actually take place, of course. Only time would reveal whether his journal was to be abandoned on the road to continuity management—or tell the story of the biggest idea he had ever taken on.

5 | Getting Started

Brett's Journal Begins

Continuity management is a collaborative endeavor. So, once I had determined that I wanted to explore the idea, I rounded up a small group of colleagues to help. These were people whose opinions I trusted, who knew what they were doing, and who were cutting-edge enough to be intrigued by a big idea. I figured we'd get together, read those chapters on continuity management that I had seen earlier, and talk about how we could make it work at WedgeMark—if they believed in it the way I did. I knew some of them would catch the vision and others wouldn't. But I thought a majority would.

My first telephone call was to Andre, a buddy of mine who has the same job I do, but in a different unit. I told him that I wanted to talk to him about a new management concept I'd heard about that I thought might help us. He hung up on me. I called him back and told him I'd read about the management idea in four draft chapters of a future management book. He hung up on me again. So I called him a third time. I'm fairly persistent and I've known Andre—and his idiosyncrasies and distaste for management theories—for a long time.

Since we have caller ID at the office, he knew it was me. "Hey," Andre snapped into the phone, "if you're going to keep calling about a new management idea, then I'll have to put you on my appointments calendar for people with new management ideas. Let's see. How about Wednesday . . . of next year?"

"I'm serious, Andre," I told him. "It's a good idea, not a fad. Three minutes. You have three minutes?"

"Two minutes," he offered, as he put me on the speakerphone. Then I heard him typing. "The background noise you hear is me answering e-mail. It better be good. My attention is already wandering. . . ."

"Listen, Andre. Remember when Sue quit last year and nobody really knew what she did and everything was chaotic for a while?"★

"Yeah?"

"And remember how she had organized the client golf tournament and made it a big success? And then how her replacement didn't know what she was doing, and this year the clients complained, and the chairman chewed your butt out? And everybody said, 'Where the hell is Sue? It was a great tournament when she was here.' Remember that?"

"Of course," Andre replied, and the typing slowed. "How could I forget? It was a nightmare."

"No, it wasn't *a* nightmare. It was *your* nightmare. Because nobody but Sue knew how to put that tournament together, and nobody but Sue knew how to make that tournament work, and nobody but Sue knew all that *on your watch*."

"Yeah. . . ." He stopped typing and took me off the speaker phone. "Crandall was furious."

"Exactly. And then you finally tracked Sue down at her new job and asked her nicely to please come run the tournament next year as a consultant, and you would pay her the highest hourly consulting fee the company could—no, wait. Let's be honest—*you got down on your knees* and *begged her* to come back and run the tournament. I saw that. It was pathetic. Oh, yes, and now the good part. . . ."

"I remember," he groaned.

"When she wouldn't come back as a consultant for the amount of money the company could offer, *you agreed to pay her 40 percent more out of your own pocket if she would do it.* Remember that?"

"Yeah. I remember—"

"And how, this time, you assigned her replacement to write down how Sue did it so you'd never be chewed out again. Well, when you arranged that talk, what you did was to ensure knowledge continuity between Sue and her successor. That's what I want to talk to you about. Ensuring that the next time one of our employees leaves, we have harvested their operational knowledge to pass to their successor to keep our own success rolling. The goal is *knowledge continuity,* and the process is called *continuity management.* It's

---

★A true story from a national car rental company.

about maintaining knowledge continuity between employee generations. How simple is that?"

"Hummm," he said.

"Something else," I continued. "Remember when your administrative assistant left six months ago and nobody but her knew—"

"I can do lunch," Andre interrupted, panic slipping into his voice. "I can do lunch *today.*" He paused, then whispered into the telephone. "I just found out this morning that my top salesperson got a better offer. Can we meet at 11?"

My Lunch with Andre

The first thing that came out of the brainstorming meetings that developed out of that first lunch with Andre was the realization that virtually everyone we talked with understood that knowledge discontinuity was a problem. We had all experienced the chaos that ensued for a period of time after the departure of a good employee, and we realized how much valuable knowledge had been lost. Golf Tournament Sue was just one of many examples. So, we were in agreement right away that the problems were real. The only questions centered around whether a solution was possible, and, if so, how that solution would work.

The more we explored the solution, the more our conversations spread to others and then caught on. Soon, people were talking about our "stealth project"—which wasn't intended to be stealthy—and making inquiries about joining us. As turnover continued to ravage our knowledge base and disrupt productivity, people grew excited about the possibility of developing defensive measures. Our lunch twosome quickly expanded to a core group of seven, which we promptly dubbed the "KC Prime" as a play on *knowledge continuity* and *Kansas City* steaks, which Rob, our technowizard, favored above all food. My admiring colleagues promptly elected me Supreme Continuity Manager—United States. KC Prime met over lunch (without the steaks), at breaks, after work, and through e-mail.

As our thinking crystallized, we developed six "get-started" principles to guide us through the process of implementing continuity management in our unit at WedgeMark. To some extent, they were simply realizations that came to us as we talked through the implications of the process we were developing. The day we finalized the get-started principles was the day we knew we were onto something important and that we would ride it all the way to the end, wherever the end would take us. We expected it to be a happy ending, of course, but we didn't know for sure in the beginning amid all the uncertainty of trying to introduce a big new idea.

Here are the get-started principles, which we dubbed the "prime stakes" for anchoring a continuity management tent:

Prime Stake 1.   *Continuity management can be implemented at any organizational level, involving as many employees as necessary.*

We realized that continuity management could be implemented at any—or all—levels of WedgeMark and that it could therefore be initiated by any manager at his or her own level or below (e.g. at the level of the team, department, business unit, division, subsidiary, or the whole organization). It could be a companywide endeavor involving many levels and many people within those levels, or it could be the individual initiative of a single manager involving a few levels and a few employees within those levels. The difference between a small-scale and a large-scale continuity management implementation is negligible conceptually, but it can be quite different in practice because of the variation in available resources and the number of job classifications and people involved.

Prime Stake 2.   *Any degree of continuity management is better than no continuity management, but the more knowledge continuity, the better.*

Ideally, continuity management would include all of WedgeMark's knowledge workers. In the knowledge-based economy of the Information Age, *any* knowledge continuity between employee generations is better than *no* knowledge continuity. Consequently, any degree of continuity management implementation is better than none. As a general rule, the greater the number of employees participating in continuity management, the greater the likely return in increased productivity and profits. The truth of this principle was substantiated by our own experience, including the turnover among our peers and subordinates that had caused us problems. We could construct a highly sophisticated continuity management program or a very simple one, but either way, we would be better off than we were now, with virtually no knowledge continuity between employee generations.

In some cases and for some organizations, a program with less-than-full participation might be necessary because of various constraints, such as cost. Another approach would be to start simply, with small-scale programs that can be developed and tested prior to large-scale implementation. It is not necessary to think in grandiose terms to achieve reasonable and effective levels of knowledge continuity. But, of course, the usual economies of scale do apply, so the more comprehensive the implementation, the greater the effect it is likely to have.

Prime Stake 3.   *Continuity management should be customized to fit each job.*

We understood that continuity management in a given unit (whether a team, department, division, or the whole organization) would have to be customized to meet the specific needs of that unit, its job classifications, and its employees. While we intended to develop a general template for implementing continuity management throughout WedgeMark, we realized that the template had to be sufficiently adaptable to harvest and transfer job-critical operational knowledge for any job classification at WedgeMark.

Prime Stake 4.   *The continuity management process should be easy to understand and to utilize.*

While some people hoard knowledge because it is a source of power and status, many hoard it because they don't have the time or the means to share that knowledge with their successors. Their problem is not hoarding per se, but the lack of a knowledge-capture-and-transfer system that would enable them to share what they know with those who succeed them. Therefore, whatever continuity management structure we developed to harvest, preserve, and transfer operational knowledge from incumbents to successors would have to be easy to understand, easy to update, and easy to use. More than that, it would have to be inviting as well, offering significant advantages to incumbent employees (our next principle).

Prime Stake 5.   *Continuity management process should be rewarding to incumbent employees as well as to their successors.*

We concluded that the process of identifying and harvesting critical operational knowledge for each job would have to contain significant benefits for incumbent employees as well as for their successors. Our analysis suggested three approaches, all of which we intended to utilize. The first was to build operating advantages into the system that would make it worthwhile for incumbents to utilize and update the continuity management system regularly. These advantages would be constructed around an analysis of their critical operational knowledge and how to maximize the potential of that knowledge in their jobs.

The second approach was to develop a set of rewards that would support continuity management implementation and usage. Extrinsic rewards based on compensation, performance appraisal, and promotions would tie continuity management to the WedgeMark reward systems. Intrinsic rewards based on greater personal satisfaction from more efficient knowledge usage, higher productivity, learning opportunities, sharing with peers, contributing to the organization, and leaving a knowledge legacy were equally important and would be explained and supported.

The third approach was to build a culture that would support continuity management. While we did not underestimate the difficulty of this undertaking, we could not deny its importance. A related change effort to support knowledge management was already underway at WedgeMark, so we expected to be able to merge the two.

Prime Stake 6. *Continuity management can utilize varying degrees of technological complexity and sophistication.*

The question of what role technology should play in continuity management was a big one for KC Prime to tackle. *Continuity management, we realized, was not a technological solution involving managers, but a management solution involving technology.* In other words, continuity management will work with technology that is complex or simple, sophisticated or unsophisticated. On the other hand, the choice of technology will make a big difference in the nature and amount of critical operational knowledge that can be harvested and transferred and the ease with which that harvesting and transfer will take place. The more that technology can carry the manual burden of knowledge capture, organization, storage, and retrieval, the better it will be for incumbent employees and their successors.

WedgeMark had already undertaken a major knowledge management initiative, so we had various systems in place that could be adapted to pilot continuity management or even to launch a full-scale implementation of continuity management itself.

■ ■ ■

With the sixth prime stake, KC Prime had concluded its first formal task. Roger, one of our members, volunteered to keep the official minutes of our meetings and to provide executives summaries of the key points. We leapt at Roger's offer to serve as recording secretary and gave him a round of applause, because the rest of us dreaded that task. To say that Roger was fastidious, precise, and detail obsessed is an understatement on the order of calling the Grand Canyon a crevice.

"These summaries," Roger warned with an intense look as he warmed to his new role, "are critical to our work. They'll keep us on track and provide a permanent record of our efforts."

"*Summaries* is a boring term," Andre complained. "How about something more creative?"

"Call them *take-aways*, then," Roger said with satisfaction. "That's a business term. *Roger's* take-aways," he grinned.

We groaned.

"Roger's take-aways," Andre repeated. "Sounds like a take-out restaurant."

"It's a list of highlights—take-away ideas that summarize our main points."

"We know what it *is*, Roger," Sarah interrupted.

"No," Andre continued, "it doesn't sound like a take-out *restaurant*. More like a take-out *menu*, now that I think about it. Reminds me of a deli on Third Avenue I used to go to when . . ."

"Highlights! They're highlights. They're like having crib notes—you know, a cheat sheet for implementing continuity management."

"For God's sake, Roger," Sarah growled. "We know what they *are*. Just *give* them to us!"

And he did:

ROGER'S TAKE-AWAYS

Continuity Management Implementation Principles

- Continuity management can be implemented at any organizational level, involving as many employees as necessary.
- Any degree of continuity management is better than no continuity management, but the more knowledge continuity, the better.
- Continuity management should be customized to fit each job.
- The continuity management process should be easy to understand and to utilize.
- The continuity management process should be rewarding to incumbent employees as well as to their successors.
- Continuity management can utilize varying degrees of technological complexity and sophistication.

The Great Barrier Reefs

As our exploration of continuity management expanded beyond the early adopters who quickly favored it, we encountered pockets of resistance that both intrigued and concerned us. So KC Prime organized several informal focus groups of employees who didn't like the idea. After extended discussions with these people, we concluded that their objections to continuity management could be divided into five categories. Some of the barriers they raised to continuity management were perceptual and others were actual, but we discovered that they could usually be ameliorated and, in some cases, eliminated with the proper counterargument.

We called this research project our trip to the Great Barrier Reefs, because our goal was to determine the primary barriers to acceptance that employees were likely to raise to a continuity management initiative. Otherwise, we were afraid that our continuity management journey would end suddenly when our continuity ship struck a barrier reef we hadn't bothered to chart. And sank. This shameless use of a nautical metaphor developed courtesy of Cap'n Carlos. Carlos is a sailing nut, a wild marketeer, and a man who thinks of business in terms of wind, tides, tack, and trim. From our focus groups and discussions, we discovered five potential barriers to continuity management that constituted the Great Barrier Reefs. We identified each by assigning it a phrase that we thought represented the heart of the objection.

Reef 1.   *Where's the problem?*
    The first barrier is the most elementary. It results from a failure to recognize the cost of accumulated knowledge loss from departing employees. While those who raise this barrier admit that knowledge loss is a problem, they don't see how costly that loss is, so they dismiss it as a major problem.
    When we considered this barrier and how to respond to it, we realized that it developed from a lack of analysis. We decided that the barrier was best overcome by expressing the knowledge loss in terms that people could understand and that would have meaning for them. We began with corporate statistics relating to job turnover and anecdotal stories of knowledge continuity disasters, of which there were plenty at WedgeMark. Usually, the *bears* (our nickname for those who raise barriers to implementing continuity management, versus the *lions* who overcome them) can accept intellectually that WedgeMark has a knowledge continuity problem when we quote the number of people who departed last year (usually suddenly) and

the projections for those who say they're planning to retire over the next five years. The bears can certainly identify the cost and the lost productivity in their own cases when an administrative assistant, a coworker, or a subordinate leaves. When they see how knowledge loss affects them personally, they can often generalize those costs to the whole organization, and the full picture comes into focus. Now they recognize the problem, and they are ready to move to the next barrier.

Reef 2.   *So what can you do?*

Those who run aground on this reef accept the high price of knowledge loss, but they see it as an inevitable cost of doing business.

"There's no way to avoid it" is a typical lament.

"Everyone suffers from knowledge loss" is another.

"You have to live with it; it's part of high job turnover" is a third.

When we raised the issue of impending retirements (and we have many coming up at WedgeMark), the bears' response reflected the same pattern of futility and helplessness. Occasionally, this pattern was disguised in proactive terms. "Increase incentives and delay the inevitable as long as possible" is the standard fix they propose. Any other preventive remedy—like trying to harvest the knowledge of departing employees before their departure—is seen as too complicated, too difficult, or just too much work.

"Whoa," objected Cap'n Carlos. "What's the problem here? Are these people depressed, lazy, or just low scorers on the initiative scale?"

"None of the above," Sarah responded crisply. "They haven't thought through to a long-term solution."

After studying this reef, we found that the best response to these bears was the simplest: Some knowledge loss may be inevitable, but catastrophic knowledge loss is not. Some continuity management is better than *no* continuity management, a fact the bears can see for themselves in their own career-scarring knowledge-loss episodes. Even if continuity management is implemented at the most basic level, some critical operational knowledge will be preserved and transferred to successors. When these bears accept that continuity management *can* be implemented, at least theoretically, they are ready to sail toward the next set of rocks.

Reef 3.   *There's no more room on my plate.*

This response is a knee-jerk reaction to a deep fear that runs through most of the employees at WedgeMark—and not just the bears. It's a fear of being assigned more work when they are already overworked. And they *are* overworked. Too many of us at WedgeMark, for example, have had to take on the work of fired employees—*ghost work* we call it, because it belongs to the *departed* and won't leave us. Even people without ghost work are burdened by extra assignments that are dropped on them as we turn "lean and mean" or (my own favorite) "trim and triggered." Which *really* means "beleaguered and burned out." The fear among employees of "one more thing to do" that will result in extra work and no extra reward has reached clinical proportions. But the fear is legitimate and deserves to be addressed.

We proposed to answer the bears in this way: After analyzing continuity management, we concluded that it doesn't have to entail extra work because it will replace other, less important, non–knowledge enhancing work and so will create no net addition to the workload.

"Not a chance!" objected Cap'n Carlos. "Every management guru, consultant, and wacko who ever came, strolled, or sailed down the pike makes that claim, usually in an authoritative voice and a custom-made suit."

"Cynical?" Rob ventured.

"Nobody believes the 'no net addition to work' claim anymore," Carlos maintained. "That only happens at Disneyland when you visit Magic Management. And we've all been to Magic Management—with Mickey Mouse."

"I'm afraid the claim is true," Andre said matter-of-factly.

"It hasn't been true for the last 13 management fads, which would take us back about, oh, say five years."

"I can't be responsible for past idiocies embraced by the gullible," Andre offered smoothly. "I can be responsible for something highly innovative, very original, and hugely important—continuity management.

"Then you'll have to prove it," Carlos persisted. "Whenever a new management initiative, pet program, or infomercial idea is proposed, trotted out, or rammed down the throats of employees still hoarse from the last one, this claim is made."

"It's easy to prove to those with functioning minds," Rob said. "It's completely logical and totally demonstrable."

"Despite your comments, I admire your confidence," Carlos said. "So where's the proof?"

This conversation led to much discussion. Here is what we concluded:

Continuity management does eliminate certain tasks because it eliminates to-do items that are irrelevant or tangential to the productive heart of the work that's being done. This task elimination results from the knowledge analysis built into continuity management that identifies critical operational knowledge and its most effective utilization. At the same time, the same knowledge analysis increases productivity and so makes more time available for continuity management tasks. Finally, the analysis itself structures operational knowledge and organizes knowledge sources, making both more accessible and applicable for quick decision making.

The "no more room on my plate" barrier appears when continuity management is perceived as an add-on function rather than as an essential aspect of managing, a productivity generator, and a contributor to individual competence and advancement. At its fullest, continuity management is a means of calling into relief—and shaping—the essential elements of the operational knowledge that each of us works with every day, creating a new perspective on knowledge that increases leveraged productivity. Continuity management enriches the plate and leaves more room, rather than impoverishing it and leaving less.

Reef 4. *Not enough resources.*

We admired the combination of complexity and simplicity in this negative bear response. "Of course, why didn't I think of that!" the innocent are tempted to respond. Yet it sounds good only because it's a corporate truism. There are never enough resources for anything at WedgeMark, but that's irrelevant. This reef is born of a mental cramp trigged by something new the bear hasn't thought about. It appears in the *Bears Handbook* as Automatic Objection 4, and it can always be relied on to temporarily derail a great idea. Like all clichés, it contains an element of truth. In fact, genuine concern over the resource commitments required for continuity management is legitimate and can make a valuable contribution to any discussion about its implementation. The resources involved include the usual list of suspects: people, time, and technology.

The response that we developed to this bear claim reflects the KC Primers' earnest efforts to wrestle with the issue and resolve it. The answer is this: The amount of time and resources required for continuity management can be limited by the design of the continuity management implementation. Four factors determine the size of the committed organizational resources: continuity management's depth, breadth, technological sophistication, and organizational support (each of which is covered in more detail later). Because continuity management can be implemented at any level, it can be implemented within the cost constraints imposed on it. When launched as a pilot or incrementally, the results of continuity management can be measured as its implementation proceeds, and its value can be gauged in comparison to its drawdown of resources. For the grizzliest bears, the pilot program can often provide the proof they need to get beyond this barrier—and on to the next one.

Reef 5.   *It's not my problem, or what's in it for me?*

This reef came from a very candid bear who got right to the point and to the bottom line as he perceived it. In fact, the issue he raised is a good one and slightly difficult to handle, because the claim can be intuitively attractive. It also has an element of truth if the employee's career goals with the company are short-term. For short-term employees, continuity management *is* a sacrifice they're being asked to make for the sake of the company and the future—a sacrifice that will not benefit them personally, now or ever. Another version of that idea is "Why should I care about my successor?" Their thinking goes something like, "Continuity management is for future employees and has little or nothing to do with me." Still another version is: "What's in it for me? The answer to these bears will be explored in more detail as the implementation process unfolds, but, in a general way, the benefits of continuity management even to these bears are:

- Increased productivity from more effective use of their operational knowledge base and more efficient use of their time, which results from the knowledge analyses conducted as part of continuity management.
- Preservation of the operational knowledge of departing subordinates and more effective transfer of that knowledge to their successors, which preserves productivity in the incumbent's unit.
- Retention of operational knowledge when trusted colleagues leave, which reduces ghost work and improves the incumbent's own productivity.
- Rewards from a realigned organizational reward system that supports continuity management participation, including annual appraisals, compensation decisions, and promotions.

And now, here are Roger's take-aways on the Great Barrier Reefs:

> ## ROGER'S TAKE-AWAYS
>
> ### *Barriers to Continuity Management Implementation*
> - There's no problem.
> - There's nothing you can do about the problem.
> - I have too much to do to take on this problem.
> - There aren't enough resources to solve this problem.
> - It's not my problem.

KC Prime Caveat

The story that unfolds in the coming pages will describe how we planned and implemented continuity management at WedgeMark. I have provided significant detail about the thinking that went into developing continuity management so that you can clearly understand its rationale and its components. Your own implementation will be much less complicated than ours, because you will not have to engage in all these activities, and you can build on the models that we have developed. Each implementation of continuity management will be different, depending on such factors as organizational size, resources, culture, industry segment, and so forth. What we hope—speaking for KC Prime—is that you will learn from what we did right and what we did wrong and glean valuable insights should you want to implement continuity management in your organization.

While the principles and concepts described in this journal relate to WedgeMark, they are fully applicable to smaller-scale implementations, whether in a smaller company or in a business unit of a large company. Either implementation would follow the same principles that characterize the implementation that we describe.

Continuity management remains a work in progress. We do know this, however: The more we have explored continuity management, the more we have discovered its potential to increase productivity, enrich careers, and position companies to achieve industry dominance. Continuity management has surpassed all the expectations that Andre and I had the first time we met to talk about stemming the knowledge loss that was depleting our ability to meet the demands of the marketplace and the threats of our competitors. We believe that it holds the same promise for you.

6 | Six Steps to Continuity Management

Suggest an idea and you end up being the one instructed to do something about it. On your own time, of course, as if you weren't already completely loaded with things to do. I knew all about the "volunteer and you're it" phenomenon at WedgeMark when it was time to propose continuity management officially. I wasn't concerned that it would fall into my lap, however; I even welcomed it. There was something about continuity management that inspired me, if that's not too strong a word. It took me back to an earlier time when there weren't as many layoffs and people got excited about projects and wanted to do something meaningful and got a bunch of other enthusiasts together to help them do it.

Once our continuity management inquiry was officially recognized, more people joined us and KC Prime's size made it unwieldy as a think tank. So we divided it into prime teams, each with a set of responsibilities. Although officially sanctioned, KC Prime remained informal and somewhat irreverent. The first item on the agenda was planning, so we elected Cheryl Supreme Continuity Planner of the United States and put her in charge of it. Cheryl's planning team promptly met (out of spite, we think), and, after a period of time, developed a reasonable and generally coherent plan for implementing continuity management at WedgeMark.

I sat in as a member of Cheryl's planning team from the beginning. It was one of the most important of the teams we created out of KC Prime, because its charge was to design the continuity management initiative. The team's first step was to develop a set of get-started definitions for basic continuity management terms that would give us the beginnings of a common language on which to base our discussion of continuity management implementation. The choice of terms was easy. We selected *incumbents* to mean current employees who possess the critical operational knowledge that will be harvested and transferred to successors. *Successors,* obviously, are the employees who will replace the incumbents and receive the critical operational knowledge. And *peer incumbents* are current employees who share the same job classification, form a community of practice, and can serve as resources to each other in identifying (and later refining) the critical operational knowledge to be passed to their successors.

The next, more difficult step, was to develop a plan that would launch continuity management in our business unit and, hopefully, throughout WedgeMark. Since successful change initiatives follow a fairly standardized plan, Cheryl's team adhered to that template in developing the six steps to continuity management. Those steps are previewed here and discussed in more detail in subsequent paragraphs:

1. Conduct a knowledge continuity assessment to determine the state of knowledge continuity (and discontinuity) in the organization.
2. Determine the objectives and scope of the continuity management initiative.
3. Establish coordination responsibility for implementing continuity management.
4. Plan the continuity management implementation initiative.
5. Create the methodology to harvest and transfer the critical operational knowledge.
6. Transfer the operational knowledge.

While these steps are logical and, to some degree, self-explanatory, it remained to fit them to our organization. The ways in which we applied these steps at WedgeMark are described in later chapters. What follows here is an overview of the steps. The usual caveats apply to this neatly ordered set of steps intended to create change: They are not as discreet and sequential as they seem. For example, while it's true that the results of the knowledge continuity assessment (Step 1) will build a more powerful business case (from Step 2), it is also true that building the business case (from Step 2) makes a comprehensive knowledge continuity assessment (Step 1) more likely.

Step 1: Conduct a Knowledge Continuity Assessment

We had never formally addressed knowledge discontinuities at WedgeMark other than to acknowledge that we had an impending retirement problem and to make assorted efforts to grab the knowledge of some key people when we discovered they were leaving—if we discovered it in time. As a result, we had no real understanding of how serious the knowledge discontinuity problem was at WedgeMark. The first step, therefore, would be to determine the extent of that problem by conducting a *knowledge continuity assessment*. In essence, the knowledge continuity assessment was a form of risk assessment that sought to identify the critical operational knowledge that was most at risk of being lost. We began with the obvious positions: those with impending retirements, high turnover, unique operational knowledge, or knowledge with very high value. In each of these cases, knowledge loss would be unusually costly and disruptive.

As our assessment continued, we expanded the list of jobs. In the end, we came to the conclusion that the vast majority of WedgeMark employees were knowledge workers, so that virtually all of the operational knowledge that was critical to them would be critical to their successors. All of the knowledge did not have the same potential value to the company, however. Some knowledge was less complex or unique or difficult to harvest, so the loss of that knowledge was less important. All knowledge loss, in other words, was not equally disruptive. But the accumulated effect of the knowledge loss that WedgeMark suffered every year was beyond anything we had expected to find.

Chapter 7 describes the knowledge continuity assessment in detail.

Step 2: Determine the Objectives and Scope of the Continuity Management Initiative

Continuity management is highly flexible. It can be customized in many different ways to meet the diverse needs and resource limitations of an organization or its subdivisions. By design, the general template that Cheryl's team developed was suitable for all of WedgeMark, which meant that we had to customize it to fit our own business unit.

Objectives of Continuity Management

In the process of developing our own set of objectives for continuity management implementation, we proposed the following mission statement:

> To make knowledge continuity an integral function of managing at WedgeMark, seamlessly practiced and supported at every level of the company, in order to preserve operational knowledge continuity between employee generations and thereby protect and build the capital asset of knowledge for ourselves and for those who succeed us.

Scope

The scope of continuity management implementation can be described in terms of four factors: breadth, depth, technological sophistication, and support. *Breadth* refers to the *number of positions* for which critical operational knowledge is captured. *Depth* refers to *how much operational knowledge* is captured for each position. *Technological sophistication* refers to the degree of technological sophistication used in the capture and transfer of the critical operational knowledge. And *support* refers to the extent to which the organizational culture and reward systems are aligned to support continuity management implementation.

The following paragraphs explore each of these dimensions in more detail.

Breadth of Knowledge Capture and Transfer.   *Breadth* refers to the number of people who will be designated to participate in continuity management. It would be possible, for example, to ensure knowledge continuity for only a few top positions, such as the CEO or vice president of finance. Such a knowledge continuity program would have virtually no breadth, and continuity management would not have been implemented. At the other extreme, every employee in the organization could participate in continuity management, which would be the broadest possible implementation, but such breadth would be unnecessary. The knowledge continuity assessment will determine the appropriate breadth for a given implementation.

Three questions can be used to analyze the breadth of continuity management implementation:

- How many structural units of the organization will participate in continuity management? Will continuity management, for example, be implemented in single or multiple structural units (departments or divisions, for example)?
- How many levels of the hierarchy in each of the structural units will participate?
- How many people within each hierarchical level will participate?

We knew that continuity management could be implemented at any level of an organization and that it could be initiated by any manager at his or her level or below. Even rudimentary versions of continuity management will reap significant benefits in knowledge continuity and productivity. But implementation in one or two structural units or in a minority of the levels in those units does not have the salutary effect of implementing continuity management in the majority of the structural units or throughout the whole organization. The greater the breadth of implementation, the greater the synergy, and the greater the potential rewards are for the organization. This synergy results from five factors:

- Knowledge continuities in one unit reinforce and complement knowledge continuities in other units, so that the greater the number of participating units, the greater the effect of continuity management on an organization's productivity.
- The greater the number of people participating in continuity management, the greater the likelihood that valuable new knowledge will emerge that can be spread throughout the organization, using knowledge management tools that capture best practices or otherwise make knowledge available to others who need it.
- More sophisticated technology is likely to be employed with organizationwide adoption of continuity management. This greater sophistication makes it easier to capture, access, transfer, and utilize the operational knowledge.
- With organizationwide adoption, continuity management is more likely to be completely integrated into the operations of the organization, accepted as a function of management, and supported by the organizational culture.
- With organizationwide adoption, powerful extrinsic reward systems can be introduced to support continuity management.

The Information Age has transformed organizations into webs of knowledge, with nodes so interconnected that knowledge continuity improvements in one area of the web race throughout the knowledge web to other nodes, affecting them in unexpected but positive ways. By the same token, knowledge discontinuities in the web have a negative impact on other nodes. It is for this reason that knowledge continuity improvements at even the lowest level of a hierarchy can have a significant effect on the whole organization.

Depth of Knowledge Capture and Transfer.   The goal of continuity management is to harvest critical operational knowledge for a given position and transfer that knowledge to successor employees. But *how* critical should critical knowledge be? Obviously, there is a range of knowledge even within the *critical knowledge* designation. And once critical knowledge has been identified, how much of that knowledge should be harvested and transferred to successors? Any critical knowledge is better than none, but, within limits, the more comprehensive the knowledge, the better it will serve both incumbents and successors.

Additional critical knowledge, however, comes at a cost in time and technology. The fundamental question in determining the depth of continuity management implementation is: How much operational knowledge do we need to transfer to successor employees? Or, put another way, how deep do we want to drill down into the incumbent's critical operational knowledge base?

Technological Sophistication.   The third component is the degree of technological sophistication used in continuity management implementation. This issue is so important that it was tackled by a special team and is discussed in more detail in Chapter 11 ("Creating the Knowledge Profile"). Basically, the technology questions we posed were:

- How sophisticated should the technology be that is used to identify, capture, and transfer the operational knowledge?
- To what extent can continuity management technology be adopted from, or integrated with, existing knowledge management technology?

Support for Continuity Management Implementation.   The fourth factor in continuity management implementation is the extent to which it will be supported by the organization. This dimension involves three components:

- Realignment of the organizational recognition and reward system to support continuity management
- Changes in the organizational culture to support continuity management
- Time and training devoted to educating employees about continuity management and its related technologies

These factors indicate how seriously an organization takes its knowledge loss and how committed it is to preserving knowledge continuity between departing and arriving employees.

Building the Business Case

As we considered the objectives and scope of continuity management at WedgeMark, we were simultaneously developing the business case for implementing it. Building the business case is a key step in garnering the support necessary to initiate any new program, especially one as far-reaching as continuity management. Dave Pollard, global director for knowledge innovation at Ernst & Young's Centre for Business Knowledge in Toronto, describes the need for the business case in any attempt to persuade people to share knowledge. "Knowledge by itself," he advises, "is too abstract for many people to relate to. If you can tell them how their lives will be better or easier than today, then that really helps sell the concept. It makes the abstract concrete" (Buckler, 2001, p. 3). We heeded that advice.

We based our business case on the compelling need for continuity management described in the continuity management chapters I had distributed to members of KC Prime. In early discussions we held with respected colleagues, we used an approach that emphasized both the serious threats of knowledge loss and the rich opportunities they presented for maximizing the use of our knowledge capital. We began with the acute threat to productivity that impending baby-boomer retirements posed, resisting the attractive fantasy that the retirement problem would go away by itself or that it could be postponed. That forced us to confront what would happen to us when the institutional memories took their gold watches and said goodbye. We were the ones who would be left holding the empty knowledge bag, not them. This reality personalized the threat of knowledge discontinuity and provided an incentive for a knowledge continuity program that would benefit the company in the long term because it would benefit us in the short term.

The other threat we raised was the chronic loss of knowledge from rapid job turnover. The greener-grass syndrome was taking its toll at WedgeMark. So were the bouts of downsizing that struck like a recurring fever, leaving us more and more debilitated. Everyone recognized the severity of this chronic problem. They also recognized that the victims of downsizing weren't just the ones who left, but the ones who *were left*. Whether the turnover created new successors without sufficient knowledge to carry their load or transferred the work to remaining employees who also had insufficient knowledge, the results were equally nasty. We made the case that our own best protection from knowledge loss through job turnovers and downsizing was continuity management.

In addition to these threats, we talked about the opportunities. We emphasized the payoffs of the continuity management process: the positive effects of clarifying our knowledge needs, identifying knowledge leverage points, and eliminating work that was largely or completely irrelevant. We recounted stories of early successes related to continuity management. For example, I disclosed how my own continuity management initiative had revealed that a long-standing report I regularly received was no longer valuable. It might have been valuable to my predecessor or *her* predecessor, but not to me. I suggested to my boss that it be discontinued, thereby saving my subordinates the time it took to prepare it. In that vein, I also suggested that it was possible that I was providing him with reports that he didn't need or that he needed less often. At the same time, I requested additional information that would boost my productivity but that I had a hard time getting—if I could get it at all. Even as a proposal, continuity management gave us a forum in which to discuss our knowledge needs with one another. It was one of the most refreshing conversations I've had in my years at WedgeMark.

We all knew that good ideas and innovative approaches were being lost when our colleagues left. But they were also lost when *we* left. That was a problem for WedgeMark, but it was also a problem for us. Those creative solutions might have been a small legacy to leave, but it felt good to have our solutions and insights preserved for others. Whether it was a fleeting sense of immortality or a desire for recognition, the legacy idea resonated with people. A lot of our colleagues do take pride in their work and would like to see their insights passed to others. And some of them wanted to leave something when they left WedgeMark.

As we discussed the implementation of continuity management among ourselves, other potential advantages emerged. We knew that if we survived to experience another job at WedgeMark, we could access the operational knowledge of the people who had preceded us. That opportunity would increase our confidence in our new positions, an advantage that did not apply to everyone, of course, but that was important when it did. More and more people were being transferred internally, which was partly due to so many cross-functional teams and to a reinvigorated policy that encouraged internal promotions.

Step 3: Establish Coordination Responsibility

The members of KC Prime were not entirely sure where this step belonged in the sequence, but our experience indicated that, ultimately, someone had to assume coordination responsibility for implementing continuity management. That person might be a manager if continuity management were launched in a single department, or it might be a vice president if it were launched in a division, or it might be someone else. But someone had to assume the role. I took it on informally at first, but a formal arrangement finally became necessary. Implementing continuity management was not an onerous task, but it was time-consuming. The degree of required coordination depends on the level of implementation, but even the simplest requires someone to get it started.

It was our belief that whoever took the coordinating position would eventually work himself or herself out of the job, although it might take half a decade or more for that to happen. As we conceived the process, continuity management would start as a program but would finally evolve into a function of management, as much a part of what a manager does as planning, organizing, controlling, and leading. At that point, continuity management would be an integral part of how things worked, supported by the reward systems and the culture of the organization, and no one would be required to coordinate it. That conclusion was based to some degree on WedgeMark's experience with quality improvement, which we thought might be analogous. Richard Leinert, CEO of Deloitte & Touche LLP, pointed out this analogy between knowledge management and the quality initiative, although we applied his comments to continuity management rather than to knowledge management. "If we look back at corporate America 10 or 15 years ago," he observed, "many organizations created senior vice presidents of quality. . . . What they did over the ensuing 10 years is essentially work themselves out of a job. They served as change agents, cheerleaders, focal points to elevate the attention and emphasis on quality, and then over time that responsibility was embedded back into the operating units" (Haapaniemi, 2001, p. 65). That vision was one that some of us had for continuity management, but not everyone on the team agreed.

"Fantasy," Sarah called it. "Even if continuity management were fully operational, it would require someone to oversee and maintain it," she said. "The analogy between continuity management and quality improvement isn't valid. Quality improvement is important, but it's not a function of management; it's a goal. The true analogy is another organizational function. In other words, there will have to be a VP–continuity management just like there has to be a VP-finance or VP-marketing. That's how critical the function is. In fact, there may be a chief knowledge continuity officer or even a chief continuity management officer."

Andre disagreed. "Continuity management is an integral part of knowledge management," he said, "perhaps, in fact, the foundational part. There won't be a chief knowledge continuity officer, except possibly as an interim measure. The duties that would be assigned to such a position will be assumed by the chief knowledge officer or chief information officer. Continuity management and knowledge management will ultimately be regarded as a *single process*, which will be under the CKO."

Our differences in perspective regarding the ultimate disposition of the continuity management start-up coordinator were based on timing rather than function. We all agreed that someone was necessary to coordinate the initial implementation of continuity management. As the role of continuity management expanded, the responsibilities of that position would also expand, at least for awhile. We were confident that continuity management itself would continually evolve, because the operational knowledge it captured and transferred was continually evolving, just as the circumstances that made that knowledge valuable were evolving. Whether the coordinating position became a permanent position in the executive hierarchy, became another function of the chief information officer, or disappeared as continuity management became an accepted management function was something we would have to wait to find out. We could predict, however, that until continuity management was well established as a process, it would require someone to plan, implement, and coordinate it.

The person chosen to lead the continuity management initiative has the fundamental responsibility of coordinating the work of the teams responsible for the design and implementation of continuity management. Small-scale implementations (as would be the case with a pilot for the whole organization or an implementation in a single business unit or a small organization) would call for fewer teams than a large-scale implementation (in which continuity management is implemented throughout the organization, for example). In small-scale implementations, multiple functions can be assumed by the same person or the same team. But the functions that are necessary to carry out the six steps to continuity management described in this chapter remain the same. Once implemented, various elements of the knowledge-harvest-and-transfer system that preserve operational knowledge have to be updated, revised, and enhanced if the value of the knowledge asset is to be protected and multiplied.

Step 4: Plan the Continuity Management Implementation Initiative

As one of Cheryl's planning team members pointed out, continuity management is a major change initiative, which means that its implementation has to be well planned if it is to succeed. Even continuity management on a small scale requires this strategic approach. In our own case, we followed the eight-stage plan for bringing about change that John Kotter describes in his book *Leading Change* (Kotter, 1996). We had each of the team members read the book and relate it to continuity management at WedgeMark. Although there are other change models, we would suggest this book to anyone intending to implement continuity management.

Just as Kotter suggests, we established an urgent need (the business case for continuity management), built a guiding coalition (which we later expanded to include a large group of people), developed a continuity management vision, and employed all the means at our disposal to communicate that vision to the people in our unit. We were also careful to restructure, retrain, and retool wherever necessary (including aligning the organizational reward systems) to encourage implementation of continuity management.

We built in short-term wins for employees who implemented continuity management (and communicated those successes through as many different media as possible) so that they would be encouraged and would encourage others. We consolidated the early gains we achieved with continuity management (easy when we had retained the critical operational knowledge of someone who had left the company) to increase enthusiasm and support for it. And, finally, we tried in every way possible to anchor continuity management in our corporate culture. The eight-stage process for leading change that Kotter describes is straightforward, although, as we discovered, its stages are less sequential and have more simultaneity than he suggests. Once you have read Kotter's book, it will be clear how to apply these steps to continuity management.

Step 5: Create the Methodology to Harvest and Transfer the Critical Operational Knowledge

After the knowledge continuity assessment identified key knowledge discontinuities, it was time for a more complicated task: creating the methodology to harvest and transfer critical operational knowledge from incumbents to successors. Since the design of the methodology was crucial to the success of continuity management, Cheryl appointed a specialized team to handle it. While all the team members agreed on the general parameters of their assignment, they were not sure what they should call the process or processes they were creating.

Roger favored *operational knowledge audit* because, in his view, the process of harvesting operational knowledge was, in fact, an audit of an employee's operational knowledge.

But Andre objected. "Nobody likes to be audited," he said. "Besides, our process is more inclusive than an audit, which might analyze knowledge, but wouldn't gather or transfer it. What we need is something to harvest operational knowledge from incumbents and a knowledge profile to transfer it to their successors."

We liked the term *knowledge profile* and promptly adopted it. With that endpoint in mind, it was easy to determine the additional instruments that were needed to create the profile. The first was a set of questions that would identify and harvest an incumbent's critical operational knowledge. Since these questions would ultimately result in the knowledge profile, we called them the *knowledge profile analysis questions,* or *K-PAQ* for short. K-PAQ and its development are described in Chapter 9 ("Developing K-PAQ: The Knowledge Profile Analysis Questions").

The second instrument we needed was the questionnaire that would contain questions from K-PAQ that were relevant to the knowledge profile for a particular job classification. We dubbed this instrument, logically enough, the *knowledge questionnaire,* which we shortened to *K-Quest.* The process of creating the knowledge questionnaire from the questions in K-PAQ is described in

Chapter 10 ("Developing K-Quest: The Knowledge Questionnaire"). An integral part of developing K-Quest is choosing the proper technology for its administration, since the answers to K-Quest will be converted by technology into the knowledge profile.

Our objective in administering K-Quest was to harvest a comprehensive body of operational knowledge and to focus the attention of Wedge-Mark employees on knowledge as a critical asset—one to be preserved, enhanced, and adroitly exploited. With that in mind, the process of administering K-Quest assumed special importance. The complete administration process that we envisioned included an orientation day for explaining continuity management and for administering K-Quest to designated employees (described in Chapter 10, "Developing K-Quest: The Knowledge Questionnaire"). It also included follow-up meetings of peer incumbents so they could share their answers to K-Quest and validate the critical operational knowledge they had harvested (described in Chapter 11, "Creating the Knowledge Profile").

Step 6: Transfer the Operational Knowledge

The dual objectives of continuity management are (1) the identification and analysis of critical operational knowledge by incumbents and (2) the transfer of that operational knowledge to their successors. Implicit in the knowledge transfer process is the successful acquisition of knowledge by the successor. In continuity management, the design of the knowledge transfer (and acquisition) process focuses on the format of the knowledge profile through which the operational knowledge will be transferred, the context in which that transfer will occur, and the organizational reward systems that support or undermine the transfer. (These issues are addressed in Chapter 12, "Operational Knowledge Transfer and Acquisition").

With the completion of these six steps, we were ready to move the continuity rocket to its launching pad. Except that we had no rocket yet, just the design for one. We were enthusiastic about our progress and impatient to move forward, but the devil is in the details. There was a great deal more to do before we could launch continuity management at WedgeMark. Our next project would be to design the knowledge continuity assessment. First, however, we received Roger's take-always. Then we celebrated with a hearty lunch of KC Prime steaks, baked potatoes, Caesar salad, and the desserts of our choice. The company even picked up the tab.

ROGER'S TAKE-AWAYS

Six Steps to Continuity Management
1. Conduct a knowledge continuity assessment to determine the state of knowledge continuity (and discontinuity) in the organization.
2. Determine the objectives and scope of the continuity management initiative.
3. Establish coordination responsibility for implementing continuity management.
4. Plan the continuity management implementation initiative.
5. Create the methodology to harvest and transfer the critical operational knowledge.
6. Transfer the operational knowledge.

7 | The Knowledge Continuity Assessment

We gathered as the A-Team to take on the specialized task of designing the knowledge continuity assessment. Roger was take-away-ready, and Cap'n Carlos sailed in just before the meeting began with the announcement of another retirement.

"What's our objective with the knowledge continuity assessment?" Cheryl asked as she opened the meeting.

"To determine how serious the knowledge discontinuity problem is," Roger quickly answered.

"Which means?"

"What's our annual job turnover rate?" Cap'n Carlos suggested. "Who at WedgeMark has unique knowledge? How big a knowledge hit do we take every time somebody leaves? What procedures do we have in place to prevent knowledge from leaving when people jump ship or walk the plank? Things like that."

"This is beginning to sound complex," Roger said, possibly with delight.

"No, it isn't," Cheryl reassured him. "It's a straightforward assessment with known criteria. We'll break into groups and brainstorm a knowledge continuity assessment. What is it? What does it require? How do we accomplish it?

As we explored developing the knowledge continuity assessment, we found that it was less complicated than we had thought, but just as critical.

In fact, it is the assessment that sets up and guides the continuity management initiative, serving 10 important functions:

1. Develops the business case for continuity management by providing evidence of organizational knowledge discontinuities and their associated costs.

2. Identifies operational knowledge that is critical to the organization, including knowledge that relates to core competencies, and assesses the negative impact of the loss of that knowledge on operations when knowledge discontinuities occur.

3. Provides an assessment of the extent to which employees analyze their knowledge base in relation to their job functions and performance. Do they, for example, understand the knowledge leverage points in their jobs? Have they evaluated their knowledge needs, including skills enhancement, and have they analyzed how they spend their time in relation to job priorities? Have they analyzed their knowledge strengths and weaknesses? Such analyses are all part of continuity management.

4. Identifies specific job classifications where the most serious knowledge discontinuities exist and therefore defines the breadth of the continuity management implementation (that is, how many job classifications should participate in continuity management).

5. Determines the extent to which knowledge is critical in each job classification and therefore defines the depth of continuity management implementation (that is, how much knowledge should be harvested for each job classification).

6. Analyzes the process of operational knowledge transfer between incumbent employees and their successors, pinpointing strengths and weaknesses in each phase of that process. This analysis examines everything from the means by which operational knowledge is identified and preserved to how new hires are oriented and mentored to how much job-specific operational knowledge new hires actually receive.

7. Identifies those areas where continuity management can build on or supplement knowledge management efforts or where continuity management can be productively integrated with knowledge management initiatives.

8. Surveys existing information technology capabilities to determine which systems can be adapted to continuity management. If a pilot program were to be launched, for example, what kind of technology would be required, and what would it cost to develop that technology through purchase, creation, or modification?
9. Generates statistical and anecdotal data on knowledge discontinuities and their costs that can be compared with similar data after continuity management implementation as one measurement of continuity management's effectiveness.
10. Provides an assessment of the extent to which the organizational culture values knowledge and knowledge sharing and so previews changes in the organizational culture and reward systems that may have to be made to develop support for continuity management implementation.

The knowledge continuity assessment requires the collection of two types of data: *statistical data* and *anecdotal data*. Anecdotal data is necessary because statistical data is not always available and because statistical data alone will not capture the full extent of the knowledge discontinuity problem. The data-gathering methodologies we employed were questionnaires, structured interviews, and focus groups. Because we were starting on a small scale, we used the entire organization for some data (such as annual job turnover statistics), but concentrated on three job classifications for our in-depth analysis and pilot implementation. We surveyed every employee in those classifications, using structured interviews and focus groups to determine the extent of their knowledge discontinuities. In large organizations, random sampling may suffice, but regardless of the scale of implementation, the fundamentals of the assessment remain the same.

The knowledge continuity assessment process consists of seven steps:

Step 1.   *Calculate annual turnover statistics by job classification.*

Annual turnover statistics show the number of "knowledge hits" the organization takes each year through resignations, layoffs, downsizing, terminations, transfers, and retirements. A breakdown by job classification is especially revealing. Virtually every employee who leaves the organization represents lost knowledge, but we didn't know the size of the turnover among our knowledge workers—or where that turnover was concentrated—and therefore how pervasive the knowledge discontinuities were. We also examined our use of the contingent workforce and outsourced knowledge suppliers to determine how well the company was managing knowledge continuity with these employees.

Step 2. *Calculate retirement eligibility statistics by job classification.*

Retirement eligibility statistics indicate how many people will be eligible for retirement over the next 3- to 10-year period. Baby boomers are such a high percentage of our experienced workforce, and so many of them could leave within the next five years, that their departure will create a potential knowledge crisis unless we act soon. Job turnover usually involves relatively short-term employees who take significant operational knowledge with them, but relatively short-term knowledge built up over a few years. Retirements, on the other hand, can steal years of operational knowledge and corporate wisdom. The accumulated organizational experience of these employees is our institutional memory, on which we constantly depend to maintain our competitive edge. It is of inestimable value to us, and we have made no effort to capture it except in a very few cases. Because organizational knowledge loss through baby-boomer retirements is concentrated, it can threaten the fundamental knowledge base of the company. However, with these impending retirements, we have both warning and the potential for a physical overlap between incumbents and successors that we could mine to great effect. Both of these characteristics are advantages that can be seized with continuity management.

Step 3. *Determine which job classifications warrant participation in continuity management and to what degree.*

After we had completed our knowledge continuity assessment, we reached a surprising conclusion: the majority of WedgeMark employees possess operational knowledge that is critical to high performance in their jobs. This discovery was something of a revelation to us. We began to look at continuity management as a process with broader application than we had originally conceived, but with more complex criteria for determining individual participation than we had anticipated. The question of whom to include was not as clear-cut as we had imagined it would be. The issue was complicated by such factors as how much operational knowledge the job required, how often that knowledge changed, whether the knowledge was tacit or explicit, and how much variation existed in the job's activities. Some employees, for example, held relatively routine jobs that, once mastered, required little additional knowledge for high productivity, whereas other employees faced many unique situations requiring extensive new knowledge.

Where to draw the line? Should every employee at WedgeMark participate in continuity management to some degree? How extensive and how unique did the operational knowledge have to be to warrant its transfer to a successor employee? For example, should successor employees requiring primarily explicit knowledge receive simple knowledge transfers as opposed to the complex knowledge transfers for employees using primarily tacit knowledge? Questions such as these led us to develop a set of criteria for determining which job classifications should participate in continuity management. All the criteria are derived from two basic questions: How critical is operational knowledge to the job, and how critical is the job to the organization? The more critical the knowledge or the job, the more likely that the job classification will be included in continuity management.

- *How strategic and essential to ongoing operations is the job?* In other words, does the job, for example, support the organization's core competencies? How seriously would poor productivity affect co-workers or the organization?
- *To what extent is knowledge rather than skill or information essential to the job?* That is, to what extent would missing knowledge have a negative impact on a successor's performance? Is the job largely intellectual rather than physical?
- *How complex is the knowledge base needed for an employee to perform well in the job?* In other words, is the job relatively routine, or does it involve many unique events requiring complex decisions based on complicated factors? A correlated question is: How stable is the knowledge base required for the job? That is, how quickly does the operational knowledge have to be supplemented or replaced if the employee in that job classification is to perform well in the job?
- *How much of the operational knowledge is* tacit *(in the employee's head) and how much of it is* explicit *(in corporate documents or databases)?* Tacit knowledge is often unique and is more difficult to capture and transfer than explicit knowledge. The greater the tacit knowledge involved in a position, the more critical the operational knowledge for that position is likely to be.
- *How unique is the knowledge base required for the job?* In other words, how many other employees are performing approximately the same

job, how long have they been with the organization, how specialized is their training, and so forth? The more unique the knowledge base is, the more likely the job classification will be included in continuity management.

On the basis of this analysis, we could determine the number of people at WedgeMark whose operational knowledge should be preserved and transferred and so calculate the number of job classifications and employees who should participate in continuity management. But the analysis accomplished something else as well. It pointed out that the depth of continuity management (that is, how much operational knowledge should be harvested) could vary significantly among job classifications. Because not every position would require the same degree of knowledge harvesting and transfer, we needed to develop a template that could be widely applied. Some positions simply required less operational knowledge or less complex operational knowledge than others.

Another big lesson came out of the knowledge continuity assessment. We realized that continuity management would lead us through a process of analysis that, in the end, would transform the way we thought about and managed knowledge. When continuity management was fully implemented, WedgeMark employees would be more knowledge-savvy than they had ever been before. In the process, WedgeMark would be transformed into a knowledge-driven organization with powerful competitive advantages.

Step 4. *Determine the extent of knowledge continuity or discontinuity between incumbent and successor employees by job classification.*

This process, which we called *knowledge gap analysis,* examines the difference between the operational knowledge a successor needs for peak performance and the operational knowledge made available to that successor at the time of employment. We looked at two aspects of the operational knowledge transfer: the *content* (how much knowledge was transferred and what the nature of that knowledge was) and the *process* (the mechanisms by which the transfer was accomplished).

Regarding the transfer process, we were interested in how the circumstances of the incumbent employee's departure affected the knowledge transfer. For example, we wanted to determine the content and mechanism of the knowledge transfer when:

- The successor is not known at the time of the incumbent's departure.
- The successor is known prior to the incumbent's departure.
- The incumbent knows nothing of his or her impending departure.

To obtain this data, we used focus groups and conducted structured interviews with representative employees. We raised four core questions and required specific examples:

1. How much operational knowledge was available from your predecessor or from the company to help you ramp up when you were hired?
2. If, in your opinion, you were not provided with adequate operational knowledge, to what extent was your productivity adversely affected?
3. To what extent has your productivity been negatively affected by the departure of peers or subordinates who did not provide their successors with adequate operational knowledge?
4. To what extent have you provided for a systematic transfer of critical operational knowledge to your successor?

A long list of adverse effects surfaced, along with many examples of insufficient operational knowledge transfer that had proved costly to WedgeMark. We discovered, for example, that in many cases there was nothing left for the successor but the incumbent's files and the contents of the computer. Even in those instances, there was often no way to make sense of the records other than through trial and error or through whatever assistance colleagues of the departed might provide (usually not much). When there was no formal successor to the lost employee, the problem was even greater. Why? Because, except in unusual circumstances, there is *always* a successor. When no formal successor is hired, one is *conscripted*—yanked from the ranks of the still-employed, saddled with additional work about which the hapless conscript may know little or nothing, and provided with no organized way to access the knowledge that has been left behind somewhere in somebody else's files.

When we faced head-on what we all had known intuitively, we were appalled at how carelessly we had treated operational knowledge at Wedge-Mark. The stories we collected were tales of knowledge-loss horrors. Henry, for example, was a new hire and a highly competent manager. He started on the first day of February and had to make a rapid series of important decisions by the end of the second week—all without sufficient operational knowledge. His predecessor had left him with disorganized, incomplete information that hobbled decision making and caused him to make several serious errors. The truth is that nobody could have done better, given the facts that Henry had to work with, but his superiors weren't interested in the facts, only in Henry's results. And the results were not good. Henry told us the story with regret, but also with bitterness, because the company had failed to give him the basic operating knowledge he needed to do his job. "It wasn't a job I came to," he said. "It was a knowledge hole. And it was ridiculous."

The results of the survey and the structured interviews showed us how deeply immersed we were in the past-century perspective that had ignored the importance of knowledge continuity. The survey results also revealed how hard it might be for us to dig ourselves out of that mind-set and confront the new realities of the Information Age.

"We are living in an old paradigm," Andre pointed out, "when manual skills or formulaic mental processes were the keys to career success. We're acting as if we can still go from job to job like traveling journeymen. All that mattered in those days was carrying the tools of the trade with you. The problem is that the tools of the trade are no longer static abilities, but ever-changing knowledge."

In a recent downsizing at the company where a buddy of mine works, two vice presidents and a managing director vanished.* Or at least they seemed to vanish. The three execs were called out of their upper-floor offices and sent to the basement for a meeting with Human Resources. No one knows for sure what happened there on the Floor of Regret, but the assumption is that the three were terminated and ordered to leave the building immediately. Because *they never came back.* Only their screen savers remained. It's as if they were vaporized, beamed up to the starship *Enterprise,* or sucked into a hole in the space-time continuum. No one ever *saw* them again, at least not in the hallways of the firm. So what do you suppose happened to all the operational knowledge the two vice presidents and the managing director possessed about the clients and the projects they were working on? Well, I can tell you, because my buddy knows. It vanished right along with them.

---

*A true story from an investment banking firm headquartered in New York City.

Step 5. *Generate a knowledge-loss damage assessment.*

A knowledge-loss damage assessment uses turnover and retirement statistics to estimate the damage to productivity, quality, and innovation that knowledge discontinuity inflicts on an organization. Because quantification is difficult, a qualitative appraisal may have to suffice, although it is possible to quantify the knowledge loss in some cases. When it is, the results can be dramatic. For example, we could directly link the loss of two big customers to sales reps who had quit and taken their customer knowledge with them. The successors' insufficient operational knowledge impeded their ability to ramp up quickly enough to accommodate the clients' unique product and service demands within the timeframe the clients required. In one case, the client had gone through two reps in three years and was tired of starting over. The client declined the opportunity to try it a third time.

In another example, we had hired a hot-shot guy in his early thirties and handed him a $6.5 million start-up project we were running for one of our clients.* It sounds like a lot of money, but it isn't for us. He did a brilliant job of planning the project and overseeing its design. He was about to launch the development phase when—he left. A competitor, you see, had observed the same capabilities in this fast-track manager that we had. The project was quickly handed off to a successor, who was unprepared because he had virtually no operational knowledge about the project. Oh, some of the explicit details where there—in hundreds of pages of dispersed documents. But there was no organized way of accessing the knowledge, of understanding it, or of putting it to use. All the tacit operational knowledge in the head of our star performer was gone. Suddenly, after $3.0 million in expenditures, it was start-over time. The client, shall we say, was not amused. Neither was the accountant who recorded the lost contract.

Step 6. *Identify areas where continuity management can be linked to knowledge management systems.*

Continuity management is a set of processes that harvests an incumbent employee's critical operational knowledge and transfers it to a successor. Because the focus of continuity management is on knowledge capture and transfer, it shares many principles with knowledge management and can often be integrated with it. Such integration is highly desirable, because it

---

*A true story (including the dollar amount) from an organization in the communications field.

maintains a free knowledge flow throughout the organization. As an example, continuity management harvests critical operational knowledge from each employee and validates that knowledge through a knowledge-sharing process that includes the other employees in that job classification. As a result, the continuity management function of harvesting critical operational knowledge for future transfer to successor employees has merged with the knowledge management function of transferring best practices. The logical knowledge management extension of this continuity management knowledge process is to make those best practices available throughout the organization.

In pilot and small-scale implementations, the cost of developing technology to harvest, store, and transfer the operational knowledge between incumbent and successor employees may pose a problem. For this and other reasons, it is worthwhile to seek creative modifications to existing knowledge management technology that will convert that technology to continuity management use.

Step 7.   *Assess the extent to which the organizational culture values knowledge and knowledge sharing.*

During the structured interviews and focus groups we conducted for the knowledge continuity assessment, we also examined how well WedgeMark's organizational culture and reward systems supported knowledge sharing, knowledge management, and knowledge continuity. We looked at all three issues because they are interrelated. The more an organization is open to knowledge sharing, the more likely it is to engage successfully in knowledge management activities, and the more likely it is to embrace continuity management activities, as well.

Therefore, we explored why WedgeMark employees might or might not be willing to analyze their critical operational knowledge and to make it available to their successors. By the end of our work and the launch of continuity management in our business unit at WedgeMark, we had the answers. We didn't have them in the beginning, but the results of our investigation into organizational rewards and cultural support for knowledge continuity laid the groundwork. (Organizational culture and rewards are discussed in more detail in Chapter 12, "Operational Knowledge Transfer and Acquisition.")

These seven means of assessing knowledge continuity at WedgeMark are shown here in the earnest efforts of our favorite detailmeister.

ROGER'S TAKE-AWAYS

Knowledge Continuity Assessment Process

1. Calculate annual turnover statistics by job classification.
2. Calculate retirement eligibility statistics by job classification.
3. Determine which job classifications warrant participation in continuity management and to what degree.
4. Determine the extent of knowledge continuity or discontinuity between incumbent and successor employees by job classification.
5. Generate a knowledge-loss damage assessment.
6. Identify areas where continuity management can be linked to knowledge management systems.
7. Assess the extent to which the organizational culture values knowledge and knowledge sharing.

As we looked at our knowledge continuity assessment plan, it was clear that the assessment could be as comprehensive as we wanted to make it. In a small-scale or pilot implementation of continuity management, the research task is not onerous because the number of people sampled is small. Even in a large-scale implementation, random or convenience samples of various job classifications can be used to develop an overall picture of knowledge discontinuities. Our own experience was that the assessment appeared more complicated and time-intensive than it was. When we had finished, we prepared a report of our findings that included these elements:

- An assessment of the extent of knowledge discontinuity between employee generations that exists in the organization.
- The estimated damage that knowledge discontinuity inflicts or is projected to inflict on productivity, quality, and innovation. In part, this assessment is based on retirement eligibility data, annual turnover by job classification, and anecdotal evidence gathered from structured interviews and focus groups.
- A proposed scope for continuity management implementation (that is, how many job classifications should participate in continuity

management and how much knowledge should be harvested for each classification).

- A report on those areas where continuity management can be linked to, or integrated with, knowledge management initiatives.
- Proposed technology for harvesting and transferring critical operational knowledge, including potential modification of existing information technology.
- An assessment of the extent to which the organizational culture values knowledge and knowledge sharing and of any realignment in the organizational reward system that might have to be made to support continuity management.

The results of the knowledge continuity assessment confirmed statistically and anecdotally that we had serious knowledge discontinuity problems at WedgeMark. The piecemeal efforts we were making individually and sometimes collectively to repair the damage of lost knowledge were often creative, but they were largely ineffective—Band-Aids on a sliced artery. We were awash in knowledge loss, and that loss was driving more of what we did every day than any of us had imagined when we began. The truth was that our daily activities were directed to a disproportionate extent by the problems created by knowledge loss. We consumed immense amounts of time and energy trying to recover knowledge. And, tragically, it was largely unnecessary.

This stark report on the state of knowledge continuity at WedgeMark was eye-opening. Confirmatory statistics were supported by poignant stories of recurring knowledge discontinuities, the lost productivity they spawned, and the frustration they bred. *Enduring* was one of the words used in the report to describe the knowledge loss. With these findings, our team moved quickly to the next step: figuring out how to preserve, through harvest and transfer, the critical operational knowledge we were hemorrhaging.

8 | Designing the Knowledge Profile

What do we need to know in our jobs and when do we need to know it?

What is the essential knowledge that makes us productive in our positions at WedgeMark?

What knowledge is critical, what knowledge is merely helpful, and what knowledge is tangential?

And, as one of the more eccentric members of our team put it, if you discovered that your house of knowledge was on fire, what knowledge would you choose to save?

These were the questions we asked each other as we wrestled with categorizing operational knowledge and developing a means to harvest and transfer it. They led us to the conclusion that the process of knowledge harvesting and transfer has three components:

- A means for identifying critical operational knowledge and organizing it into knowledge categories
- A methodology for harvesting the critical operational knowledge from incumbent employees
- A "container" to store the critical operational knowledge and transfer it to the successor employee

We began with the container, which was the third component, because it described the knowledge categories that set the objectives for the knowledge harvest. Andre had already called it the *knowledge profile*.

The challenge of designing the profile was intriguing because none of us had ever systematically examined our operational knowledge needs. Some people intuitively understood those needs and some did not, but no one had ever tried to categorize them. In order to accomplish this task, we turned to our colleagues, casting a broad net in our effort to understand the meaning of job-critical operational knowledge. Over lunch, during breaks, at breakfast, through e-mail, and in informal focus groups, we asked people, "What is the critical knowledge you use on your job, and how would you categorize it?" Or, "If you had started your job, and your predecessor handed you a profile of the knowledge you needed for that job, what would that profile look like?"

From these conversations, we created the knowledge categories that defined critical operational knowledge at WedgeMark. We also developed a set of eight organizing principles to guide the design of the knowledge profile and determine its contents.

Principle 1: *Knowledge profiles should contain only critical operational knowledge.*

In the daily conduct of our jobs, we use a vast amount of operational knowledge. Most of it is easily acquired and of little real consequence, but some of it is critical to the work we do. It is the critical knowledge that the profile is designed to hold. If criticality is the criterion for including knowledge in the profile, then a definition is warranted. Unfortunately, a precise definition is not easy to frame. The effort to define *critical* for purposes of the profile is further complicated by two conflicting objectives of the profile design: *conciseness* and *comprehensiveness.* We wanted to keep the knowledge profile as short and easy to use as possible, but, at the same time, make it comprehensive enough to transfer the critical operational knowledge that successors needed.

We proposed three criteria for determining criticality: (1) knowledge that is essential to effective job performance, (2) high-impact knowledge that makes a significant difference in productivity or quality, and (3) knowledge that would have a big negative effect on performance if it were missing. In other words, we used phrases to define *critical,* understanding that they were hardly definitive, and left it up to the incumbents to determine criticality for the knowledge in their profile.

Sarah pointed out that the resulting knowledge profile would reflect the knowledge biases of the incumbents and the ways in which they had shaped their jobs to their own particular strengths.

"True enough," Andre agreed, "but that's inevitable."

There was another perspective, however, that proved reassuring. We concluded that some of the biases and individual differences would even out as knowledge profiles were built up over generations of employees. We also counted on meetings of peer incumbents to correct the most egregious errors or omissions in individual knowledge profiles, a process that is explained in more detail in Chapter 11 ("Creating the Knowledge Profile").

Principle 2: *Incumbent employees require a structured means of identifying their critical operational knowledge.*

Our interviews with colleagues at WedgeMark confirmed that incumbent employees cannot be relied on to identify critical operational knowledge for their positions without a structured means of analysis to assist them. There are four major reasons for this phenomenon:

- Productive incumbents are so fluent in the operational knowledge they use—in the data, information, skills, knowledge, and competencies required to perform well—that their decisions and actions often seem instinctive. The knowledge and knowledge sources they use are so familiar to them that they make the false assumption that everyone else has the same knowledge. Because they take the knowledge for granted, they may fail to recognize it as critical or to identify it as knowledge someone else would need. Therefore, it can be difficult for productive incumbents to transfer what they know to their successors without a disciplined, systematic approach that provides a structured methodology for identifying and harvesting critical knowledge.

- Incumbents may have difficulty drawing a distinction between *critical knowledge, useful knowledge,* and even *irrelevant knowledge.* As James Pollard, CEO of Deloitte Touche Tohmatsu, has pointed out, "What needs to be shared may not be as important as knowing what doesn't need to be shared" (Haapaniemi, 2001, p. 68).

- Even if incumbents are aware of their critical operational knowledge, they generally do not know how to organize that knowledge in such a way that it can be efficiently and effectively transferred to their successors.

- Many incumbents are not aware of the operational knowledge weaknesses that negatively affect their productivity and performance.

These weaknesses, which take the form of missing, insufficient, inaccurate, or obsolete knowledge, reduce the utility of their operational knowledge, whether for them or their successors. The knowledge analysis built into the profile development process will identify these weaknesses.

Principle 3: *The nature of employees' contractual arrangements affects their profiles.*
Once upon a time, the word *employee* had a clear meaning. An employee was someone who worked full-time for a company in the company's offices or on the road selling the company's products. A person who worked part-time for the company was not spoken of as an employee, but as a *part-time employee.* Like so much else in the knowledge economy, even the meanings of *employee* and *part-time employee* have changed. Five types of potential employment arrangements are discernible in contemporary organizations, and each presents special knowledge continuity challenges that should be reflected in the contents of the knowledge profiles for those positions. But even these employment categories are not the whole picture, because they can be subdivided into full-time and part-time employees. The employment categories are shown in Table 8.1.

Part-time employees pose somewhat different knowledge challenges from full-time employees and constitute a special area of knowledge-loss exposure. Continuity management is valid for each employment category and for both full-time and part-time workers within those categories, but the knowledge profiles will be different for each.

Table 8.1 Employee Contractual Arrangements

Type	Full-Time	Part-Time	Description of Employment
On-site	✔	✔	Physically goes to the office or the factory
Telecommuter	✔	✔	Works at home or an outlying office
Road warrior	✔		Is in the office 4 or 5 days a month and otherwise on the road
Loaned	✔		Located at the facilities of a supplier, strategic partner, or customer
Outsourced	✔	✔	Contractors, part-timers, consultants, and temporary and leased employees

Principle 4:   *Knowledge profiles should reflect an analysis and prioritization of operational knowledge.*

Because we wanted the knowledge profiles to benefit incumbents as well as successors, we built an analysis of operational knowledge into continuity management. The purpose of the analysis is threefold: (1) to prioritize operational knowledge, (2) to pinpoint knowledge holes, and (3) to identify knowledge leverage points, which consist of knowledge with exceptional potential to increase operational efficiency, effectiveness, and productivity. This inventorying process spotlights high-payoff knowledge areas that warrant attention. It also makes it possible for incumbents to find and discard obsolete knowledge or ignore tangential knowledge and focus on the acquisition, development, and application of knowledge that is critical to their productivity. This analytical process is described in Chapter 9 ("Developing K-PAQ: The Knowledge Profile Analysis Questions").

Principle 5:   *Knowledge Profiles should include an analysis of strengths, weaknesses, opportunities, and threats (SWOT).*

Knowledge profiles should include an analysis of corporate strengths and weakness as well as opportunities and threats facing the organization and incumbents. This analysis provides a context for determining present and future action and is a critical component of operational knowledge. The SWOT analysis is described in Chapter 9 ("Developing K-PAQ: The Knowledge Profile Analysis Questions").

Principle 6.   *The criteria for requiring a knowledge profile should be the significance of the knowledge to the employee's job and the significance of the job to the success of the organization.*

Which job classifications should have profiles? Two general criteria govern the choice: (1) how critical operational knowledge is to success in the job and (2) how critical the job is to the success of the organization. In practice, these criteria are hard to measure, because *critical* is difficult to define.

"It's a matter of context," Sarah said. "It's looking at the big picture and asking if it's worth creating a knowledge profile for that position. It's all subjective, it seems to me."

"Not entirely," Andre countered. "In fact, the knowledge continuity assessment gives us a very good picture of knowledge discontinuities and the positions where they occur most frequently and with the greatest consequences for WedgeMark."

"In the final analysis, we may have to leave it up to each manager to determine," Cheryl suggested.

"Maybe," Andre replied. "But the one thing we do know from the knowledge continuity assessment is to err on the side of caution. Knowledge loss through departing employees is more costly than we have realized or been willing to acknowledge."

Our reexamination of the knowledge continuity assessment led us to this conclusion: Virtually all the employees at WedgeMark had knowledge that was critical to their positions, but the impact of knowledge loss would be considerably greater on some positions than on others (obviously). We decided that the critical operational knowledge in all these positions was ultimately important to WedgeMark if we were to build a high-performing organization in the knowledge economy. In some cases, the operational knowledge was not complex, and the depth of knowledge would not be great, but the knowledge itself was worth preserving and transferring.

Did that mean that it was knowledge profiles for everyone? Not necessarily, but perhaps for the vast majority of employees. After all, the complexity of preparing the knowledge profile generally parallels the complexity of the job. Less complicated positions require less complicated profiles. And some knowledge continuity is better than no knowledge continuity. We ended our discussion by agreeing with Andre's conclusion: It was better to err on the side of caution. A knowledge profile, however reduced in scope compared to those for more complicated positions, was still important to new hires with a knowledge aspect to their jobs. It still reduced their ramp-up time, increased their productivity, and made them feel like valuable members of the WedgeMark team, which they are.

Principle 7. *Knowledge profiles should be easy to understand and access and should be meaningful to both incumbents and successors.*

Obvious, but important. The content of the knowledge profile should be organized in a format that is meaningful to incumbents who prepare the profile and to successors who receive it. Profile content should be current, easy to understand, and simple to use—an interactive resource rather than a file somewhere in storage.

Principle 8. *Access to portions of the knowledge profile should be restricted.*

We found early on that we would have to confront a touchy issue regarding the knowledge profiles: Who would have access to them? Only the incumbent? An incumbent's boss? An incumbent's boss's boss? Someone from HR? A fear of putting some operational knowledge into the written word surfaced early.

"I might—*might*—be willing to tell someone certain things about past failures at the company, about the incompetence of some of our suppliers, and dumb moves by witless managers, but I'm sure not going to put it in writing," was an early response from a member of the focus groups.

Another person said, "If I thought just anybody could look at my profile, I might put some neutral stuff in there, but wouldn't put down anything private."

"It depends on whether I have to. If I have to—you know, if my evaluation depends on it—I guess I would, but I wouldn't want to unless two things were true. First, everybody else was doing it, and second, people needed my permission to look at my profile."

"This is a serious issue," confirmed a long-time employee. "Who's going to monitor these profiles to be sure we're doing them? And what are they going to do when they read some of the things in there?"

Access to the knowledge profile raised other concerns in the focus groups, most of them centering around creating new conflicts or resurrecting old ones, exposing untouchable topics, inflaming highly emotional issues that simmered just below the surface, or exposing errors in judgment that could jeopardize an incumbent's career (or someone else's). Other concerns rose from misguided loyalty to customers, suppliers, or bosses that prevented an accurate assessment of their performance—an assessment that might seem foolish or be held against them.

These concerns led us to a sustained discussion on the issue of who should be permitted to access a knowledge profile. Unfortunately, we were not able to completely resolve the question. Many different perspectives and opinions emerged, and we were unable to reach consensus until much later, when we resolved the issue in larger forums and in a way that was right for WedgeMark. Our own solution might not work for your organization, but it worked for us because it fit our culture, mission, goals, and traditions. From the standpoint of reporting our discussions and the decisions we made, perhaps the most effective approach is to summarize the areas in which the members of KC Prime agreed and disagreed.

The central question we asked ourselves was: Who but the incumbent should have access to a knowledge profile? The answer to that question seemed to depend largely on the job classification of the person providing it. The HR people had one set of views, the attorneys for the company another, and the incumbents themselves a third—although, ironically, the HR people and the attorneys were *also* incumbents, so they took a some-times schizophrenic approach to the question. Furthermore, not all the incumbents agreed—and, as might be expected, some incumbents thought they should have more access to the profiles of their subordinates than they thought their supervisors should have to theirs.

We approached the issue by sorting though the access options. Who were the people who might have a claim on some portion of an incumbent's knowledge profile? Our answers were:

- The incumbent
- Peers of the incumbent
- Subordinates of the incumbent
- The direct supervisor of the incumbent
- Higher-level supervisors
- Managers (if not the higher-level supervisor)
- Vice presidents (if not the higher-level supervisor)
- HR representatives
- Corporate attorneys (on demand)
- Successors and those who would work with incumbents in assimilating the knowledge in the profile
- Other WedgeMark employees for whom some of the operational knowledge in the Profile might prove useful

The only category we could agree on as having a right to access the entire knowledge profile was the first—the incumbent. On the other hand, almost everyone agreed that peer incumbents should *not* automatically have complete access to any knowledge profile other than their own. The reasoning was uniform: The profile would likely contain confidential information that we might be willing to transfer to our successors but not to some of our peers, with whom, frankly, we might be competing for future promotions. (This conclusion was an early indicator that the organizational rewards and culture at WedgeMark were not amenable to knowledge sharing and would have to be addressed.)

As we thought through our positions, however, and learned to listen more closely to what those with opposing views were saying, we began to see larger possibilities. We had the first glimmer, for example, that the knowledge profile could be linked to, or even integrated with, knowledge management databases and that real synergy might result. Our network of contacts, for example, or our sources of expert advice could benefit many people. As we became more collaborative in our thinking, we began to see that there might be advantages to having supervisors access our profiles. By providing a concise summary of our work experience, skill sets, and past projects, the profiles could be an important tool in making assignments. The more we thought about it, the more we realized that the operational knowledge in our profiles was, to a large extent, common knowledge that could be shared with incumbents and others and that it could, in fact, be enhanced by that sharing.

We recognized, for example, that the contents of the profiles revealed significant information about job-related skills and activities that could be of use to HR in recruitment, selection, and training and, especially, in developing continuous learning opportunities that would enhance our existing skills or teach us new ones. HR access could be positive rather than just regulatory. The profiles could also be helpful to others who might be recruiting members of a team in which we had an interest. Over time, we came to see that sharing the profiles and parts of the operational knowledge they contained could work to our advantage.

However, we all had a proprietary feeling about our knowledge profiles. It wasn't so much that we wanted to keep them secret as that they felt very personal to us, and they had to be managed with those feelings in mind. Our profiles might be our legacy to a successor or they might just represent our best thinking, but they still were our stuff, and we didn't want just anyone messing with them or looking in on them without our permission. We had all regressed, perhaps, but we felt that the profiles should be fundamentally private, with certain parts accessible to others who had a need to know. The question was how broad that need to know should be. We did agree that corporate attorneys should have access to the profiles and that HR should under certain circumstances, because we knew it was hopeless to think that any organization would allow mystery comments to float around without any check on them, especially when such mystery comments were contained in official corporate documents.

In the final analysis, we decided that there should be no access to any knowledge profile without the permission of the person who had created it or else an established purpose for the look. It was possible for the creator of a profile to offer blanket access permission or, alternatively, to restrict access to some or all of the profile during his or her tenure at WedgeMark. Blocking total access, however, would be discouraged. Toward that end, we recommended three security levels for the knowledge categories and subcategories contained in the Profiles. These designations were simple:

- *Available.* Knowledge that was accessible to any WedgeMark employee authorized to access a knowledge profile.
- *Restricted.* Knowledge that was restricted to peers, designated peers, or others of the profile creator's choosing.
- *Confidential.* Knowledge that was unavailable except to individuals with a need to know, such as corporate attorneys on demand, HR people with good reasons to view the profiles, and our direct supervisors as part of our performance evaluations.

As we thought through access to the knowledge profiles, the risks did not seem as great as they had at first, and they were considerably outweighed by the potential benefits. Meetings of peer incumbents that facilitated cross-sharing of operational knowledge among peers had vetted much of the knowledge in the profiles (described in more detail in Chapter 11, "Creating the Knowledge Profile"). And most of the knowledge in the profile wasn't particularly personal. What we finally realized was that we had to design the profile and the context in which it was created, transferred, and applied so that it would be a respected creation perceived as adding value to the organization. We wanted people to have a sense of pride and accomplishment in their profiles.

Does that mean that we were completely honest about what we put in the knowledge profiles? The answer to that question is yes and no. Yes, we were honest in what we inserted. Based on conversations in peer incumbent meetings, our communities of practice, and informal gatherings, we determined that most of us had been truthful in what we had revealed, and each of us had revealed a lot. Did that mean that we had revealed everything? No, it did not. But once the profile creation process was over, we could see that few of us had intentionally withheld very much and that what we had created was immensely valuable to ourselves and to our successors. The profiles might not have been absolutely complete, but they were very *accurate,* and so much more complete than anything we had ever had before.

We also addressed the potential for intentional dishonesty that would skew operational knowledge in one direction or another for political purposes or to advance private agendas. How was the knowledge profile to be protected from dishonest incumbents with grudges or from disgruntled incumbents about to leave and bent on sabotage? The dishonest incumbents were difficult to defend against, but not impossible. Direct supervisors offered some oversight protection in performance evaluations. Also, the individual assigned to help the successor to assimilate the operational knowledge in the profile would afford additional protection. For the most part, we simply banked on there not being too many such incumbents.

Disgruntled incumbents who might sabotage their profile by destroying its contents or altering the data prior to their departure would be foiled by regular backup profiles stored outside of their reach and retained for a period of 18 months. These measures were some of those we developed to preserve the integrity of the knowledge profile, but we were confident that more would emerge as we began to implement continuity management at WedgeMark.

■ ■ ■

These principles for developing the knowledge profile were captured by Roger for the take-aways with which he was now identified:

ROGER'S TAKE-AWAYS

Principles for Developing the Knowledge Profile

- Knowledge profiles should contain only critical operational knowledge.
- Incumbent employees require a structured means of identifying critical operational knowledge.
- The nature of employees' contractual arrangements affects their profiles.
- Knowledge profiles should reflect an analysis and prioritization of operational knowledge.
- Knowledge profiles should include an analysis of strengths, weaknesses, opportunities, and threats (SWOT).
- The criteria for requiring a knowledge profile should be the significance of the knowledge to the employee's job and the significance of the job to the success of the organization.
- Knowledge profiles should be easy to understand and access and should be meaningful to both incumbents and successors.
- Access to portions of the knowledge profile should be restricted.

Content of the Knowledge Profile

With the principles to guide us, we turned to the task of creating the content of the knowledge profile. As a summary of the knowledge assets that an employee deploys in his or her job, the profile was intended to capture all types of knowledge, including cognitive knowledge (content knowledge), skills knowledge (know-how), systems knowledge, social network knowledge, process and procedural knowledge, heuristic knowledge, and cultural knowledge (discussed in Chapter 2, "Knowledge as a Capital Asset"). This long list of operational knowledge types would have been dismaying had it not been for "the Chip," our team member who calmly reminded us, "It's simple." But then, her logical mind found many things simple, for which she had earned the other sobriquet, "Mr. Spock's niece."

The many sessions that led to the final format of the knowledge profile were immensely rewarding for all of us. We brainstormed, analyzed, debated, argued, got huffy, laughed, and kept working. We used artistic metaphors like *sculpting, modeling,* and *crafting* to describe the work that led to the design and redesign of the prototype profile. As we continued to refine the profile, we took it to others and endured their criticisms even as we listened intently and altered our work in response to their insightful comments.

When we finally examined the finished product, laid out before us on a single page, we liked what we saw.

"A rhapsody of words," our Shakespeare-quoting team member proclaimed.

"Nice detail," Roger declared.

"It does organize the operational knowledge required for any job in the company as we intended," the Chip confirmed.

As we designed it, the profile gives both incumbents and successors extraordinary access to the critical operational knowledge they need, an overview of the resources at their disposal, and a snapshot of priorities that range from urgent items to long-term goals. The profile identifies critical knowledge, knowledge leverage points, and knowledge holes. It is comprehensive in scope, yet it can drill down to many levels of detail.

Knowledge Sections of the Knowledge Profile

The knowledge profile groups critical operational knowledge into four knowledge sections: *Operating Data, Key Operational Knowledge, Basic Operational*

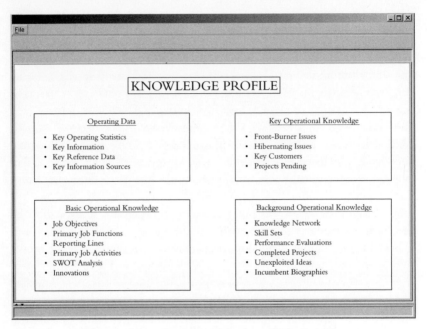

Figure 8.1   Content of the knowledge profile.

Knowledge, and *Background Operational Knowledge.* These four sections contain a total of 20 knowledge categories, shown in Figure 8.1 as a portal on a computer screen. The knowledge category is the basic structural unit of the profile. Each knowledge category contains multiple knowledge topics related to that category. The design of the profile is thus:

$$\rightarrow \text{Knowledge section}$$
$$\rightarrow \text{Knowledge category}$$
$$\rightarrow \text{Knowledge topic}$$

Each knowledge category can be clicked to display the knowledge topics it contains and expanded again to show content details.

Welcome to the Knowledge Profile

To personalize the knowledge profile and make its transfer from incumbent to successor as effective as possible, we added a special feature to the profile introduction. The introduction explains the purpose of the profile, defines its knowledge categories, and provides a set of recommended guidelines for its use. The special feature is a personal note from the last incumbent who owned the profile—that is, the new hire's predecessor. This note takes the form of a supportive message acknowledging that there is a lot to learn about the job, but expressing confidence in the successor's ability to acquire the knowledge and to succeed. The actual wording is determined by the incumbent and can be as long or as short as desired. There are no rules about format, content, or writing style. The note is what it claims to be: a personal message from the incumbent to the successor. Some incumbents have added a contact e-mail address. Incumbents who have been transferred to another part of WedgeMark are the most likely candidates for this addition, but a surprising number of others offer to be contacted, at least for a period of time and under certain circumstances. Other incumbents simply end the note with a general expression of good wishes and good luck.

When a new incumbent takes over the profile, the note from the last incumbent passes into the Incumbent Biographies knowledge category along with the biography of the person who wrote it, providing an archived history of personal notes as well as biographies. Our objective with this introduction was to keep the profile as personal, friendly, and welcoming as possible. We wanted the new hire to start out with a sense of being valued and with a sense that the knowledge profile was something important— a true legacy to which the new hire was heir as a WedgeMark employee.

Knowledge Categories of the Knowledge Profile

The knowledge profile is structured around 20 knowledge categories grouped into four knowledge sections. One of the major contributions of the profile is this categorization of critical operational knowledge, which gave us a handle on how to capture, organize, and transfer that knowledge. When the profile is created with sophisticated technology, all its knowledge is accessible through questions and key word searches. Its knowledge can also be accessed directly through the knowledge categories. While employees do not generally like to search databases for knowledge, our experience has been that new hires willingly access their knowledge profiles because their job-specific operational knowledge is virtually zero. When they can search in the form of frequently asked questions, which the WedgeMark continuity management system offers, the task is that much easier.

We created a knowledge profile template for all of WedgeMark, which was meant to be universal. Most of the knowledge categories would remain valid across WedgeMark, but not all of them would. Accounting, engineering, sales, budgeting, planning, research and development, production, and marketing might have significant differences within the knowledge categories for their positions. Our aim was to create a model profile that would allow individual customization by job classification. That necessarily meant that the model profile might include more knowledge categories than necessary for every job classification and, in some cases, fewer than might be necessary.

The following paragraphs describe the contents of each of the knowledge sections and the knowledge categories of the profile. Even the topics within the knowledge categories, however, are subject to change based on the job classification. Some classifications will require more knowledge topics and some will require fewer topics to match the profile to the job. The profile we prepared for WedgeMark was a model designed to stimulate thinking within each unit about that unit's operational knowledge and how the profile's contents should be altered to fit it precisely.

Section 1: Operating Data

Operating Data contains current, routinely used operating data, basic reference data, and the results of financial and other analyses that provide specialized information for controlling, monitoring, or decision making. The knowledge categories in Operating Data are:

- *Key Operating Statistics.* Key operating statistics that are critical to the job classification (for example, monthly sales figures, sales trends, market share, budgets, cash flow projections, and so forth).
- *Key Information.* Official corporate announcements, late-breaking news, personnel changes, and other current information about which the employee needs to be aware.
- *Key Reference Data.* This knowledge category is divided into two subcategories. The first includes personal reference data such as telephone numbers, forthcoming events, number of vacation days used, looming deadlines, and so forth. The second subcategory includes job-relevant corporate reference data such as policies and procedures manuals, market and competitor analyses, product plans, pricing sheets, service guides, user manuals, and so forth.

- *Key Information Sources.* The sources through which the data and information in this section of the knowledge profile can be obtained, whether documents or individuals.

Section 2: Key Operational Knowledge

Key Operational Knowledge contains knowledge related to current issues, customers, and projects that is crucial for successors to know. Such knowledge is often tacit rather than explicit. The knowledge categories in Key Operational Knowledge are:

- *Front-Burner Issues.* Front-burner issues include major decisions, assignments, questions, tasks, controversies, opportunities, threats, or anything else that may require quick action with potentially serious consequences.
- *Hibernating Issues.* Hibernating issues are ongoing threats, opportunities, controversies, events or other issues that carry particular risk or reward, but that are currently dormant. The incumbent must either continually monitor them or else be knowledgeable enough about them to respond quickly should they suddenly erupt.
- *Key Customers.* This knowledge category includes all of an incumbent's most important customers (those to whom goods and services are provided), whether inside the organization (internal customers) or outside the organization (external customers), including their contacts, history, special needs, requirements, expectations, and other relevant information.
- *Projects Pending.* This category includes any project in which the incumbent is involved that could have a significant impact on the organization. As pending projects are closed, they are archived and stored for future reference under Completed Projects, a knowledge category in the Background Operational Knowledge section of the profile.

Section 3: Basic Operational Knowledge

Basic Operational Knowledge contains foundational knowledge that describes the parameters of the job. It is found in mission statements, annual goals, budgets, databases, organizational charts, Web pages, policies, procedures, memos, strategic analyses, and other official documents. But it is the kind of knowledge that also grows out of on-the-job experience, arises from stories passed among colleagues, and develops from thoughtful analysis. The knowledge categories in Basic Operational Knowledge are:

- *Job Objectives.*   This category includes organizational and unit mission statements, general goals and objectives of the unit, performance goals and objectives for the coming year, and other personalized short- and long-term goals and objectives expressed in performance measurements.
- *Primary Job Functions.*   This category includes the major functions of the job classification in their approximate order of importance, the amount of time usually devoted to each function, and a list of functions that waste time, drain resources, or otherwise fail to support performance objectives.
- *Reporting Lines.*   This category includes formal reporting lines depicted in the organizational chart, informal reporting lines, and an analysis of the reporting preferences of each person.
- *Primary Job Activities.*   This category includes the primary job activities (whether tasks or responsibilities) that are conducted regularly or periodically in support of the job's functions and objectives, the amount of time devoted to each, the knowledge required for each, and the related processes.
- *SWOT Analysis.*   SWOT analysis is an analysis of the organization's internal strengths and weaknesses (including competitive advantages), and an analysis of threats and opportunities facing the organization or the incumbent.
- *Innovations.*   This is the knowledge category that captures shortcuts, better ideas, innovations, or changes in established procedures or services that the incumbent has developed, heard about, or otherwise put to use in a productive way. These are often informal, unofficial procedures or processes that are part of the incumbent's tacit knowledge base and that represent significant opportunities for increased productivity or effectiveness. Or they may be whole new processes or services that can be immediately adapted by the successor (and spread through knowledge management best practices).

The potential contribution of the Innovations knowledge category is very high. That this category will fulfill its purpose is supported, at least conceptually, by a program initiated at Deloitte Touche Tohmatsu, the professional services company. James Copeland, CEO, describes that program:

> One of the ways we've tried to capture and leverage knowledge is to find and create new ideas for services through what we call a venture board. This is an internal organization. We wanted to offer new, valuable services to the marketplace, and we figured that's best found in the minds of our people. So we told people to send in their ideas. And, of course, the response was less than overwhelming. So what we found we had to do was go out into the offices, convene meetings, and ask, "What are you doing that's smart for your clients?" We found a veritable gold mind of ideas—value that had already been created for clients. We knew those ideas worked, and there's no reason we couldn't use them for a thousand of our clients instead of just two of our clients. (Haapaniemi, 2001, p. 67)

Section 4: Background Operational Knowledge

Background Operational Knowledge contains knowledge that incumbents may not consciously use every day but is essential to their operational knowledge. The knowledge categories in Background Operational Knowledge are:

- *Knowledge Network.*   This category contains the names of the people inside and outside the organization who comprise the incumbent's knowledge network. It consists of colleagues, mentors, previous bosses, old friends, suppliers, superiors, and others on whom the incumbent relies for information, knowledge, and advice.
- *Skill Sets.*   This category describes the skills required to function well in the job.
- *Performance Evaluations.*   This category describes the process by which employee performance is evaluated, compensation is set, and promotions are earned, whether formally disclosed or not.
- *Completed Projects.*   This category contains the historical record of all major projects completed by incumbents during their tenure with the organization. It is automatically populated from the Projects Pending category in the Key Operational Knowledge section of the profile when incumbents classify their pending projects as complete and closed.
- *Unexploited Ideas.*   This category includes innovative solutions, creative ideas, and imaginative approaches developed by incumbents as

they manage the requirements of their jobs, but not yet implemented. It is the tickler file for future action and a memo pad for ideas, notions, and brainstorms.

■ *Incumbent Biographies.*   This category includes a photograph and biography of every incumbent who has contributed to the knowledge profile, beginning with the founding incumbent, who is the profile's originator. As successors become incumbents, they add their own photographs and biographies to create a personal, visual record of all those who have contributed to the knowledge profile they now possess. Biographical sketches include whatever professional achievements the incumbents select and, to the extent the incumbents are willing, personal data to personalize the profiles. These biographies personalize the process of knowledge profile construction, create a sense of ownership of the knowledge profile, act as an incentive for making the profile as complete as possible, and build identification and trust between incumbents and their successors.

■ ■ ■

With completion of the knowledge profile, the next challenge was to figure out the major topics to be covered in each of the knowledge categories and the questions that would fill those categories with critical operational knowledge from the minds of incumbents. That task was assigned to the Dream Team.

9 | Developing K-PAQ: The Knowledge Profile Analysis Questions

The Dream Team met to design the methodology for harvesting operational knowledge from incumbent employees. Rob, our tech-knight, joined us to offer technological assistance while emitting serious amounts of radiation from mysterious black objects he carried. Roger was back, of course, and the Chip was parallel processing even before we started. We were joined by assorted other experts and team members.

The Dream Team established five objectives for the proposed methodology that would harvest the critical operational knowledge from incumbents and create the knowledge profile. They were:

1. To capture the critical job-specific data, information, and knowledge that incumbents use in their jobs
2. To capture the primary sources of this critical data, information, and knowledge (whether individuals, documents, or processes)
3. To identify knowledge priorities and leverage points (i.e., knowledge with the greatest potential to increase productivity and effectiveness)

4. To identify critical knowledge that was not available because of knowledge hoarding, inefficient or obsolete reporting systems, poor knowledge needs analysis, or a variety of other reasons
5. To analyze knowledge-based strengths, weaknesses, opportunities, and threats associated with the job classification

With those objectives set and the knowledge categories of the Knowledge Profile template as our guide, we turned to the various methodologies that might be employed to harvest the targeted knowledge.

Techniques for Harvesting Knowledge

We began by examining the many different techniques through which human beings can acquire knowledge, about 100 in fact. They ranged from card sorting and simulations to process analysis and focused discussions to diagramming and concept mapping to interviews and questionnaires. Of these, we settled on two types as the most appropriate for the knowledge profile, although each type could take a myriad of forms. The first was the interview (structured or unstructured), and the second was the questionnaire, in whatever form it took. Both of these techniques depend upon questions to accomplish their task, and questions are the most often used means to gather knowledge. The obvious difference between the techniques is that the interview delivers the questions in person and the questionnaire through a form. Questionnaires can differ dramatically in form (electronic or manual, for example) as well as in format, yet they always retain the essential feature of being a list of questions presented in a logical order to achieve a specific set of objectives. Each technique has its advantages and disadvantages in relation to the knowledge profile.

Interview

An interview requires a one-on-one meeting with the incumbent employee in which a trained interviewer poses a series of questions from a prepared list. The interview is *structured* if the interviewer asks only the questions on the list and only in the exact order in which they appear. It is *unstructured* if the interviewer is permitted to change the order of the questions, delete questions, or add questions, as might happen in probing for more information. The advantage of the interview technique is the ability it confers to probe for more specific knowledge, to seek related knowledge, or to link knowledge. It offers great flexibility, and the human interaction of interviewer and interviewee often stimulates further thought and additional information.

The disadvantage of the interview is that it requires an individual who has some training in interviewing and who is reasonably familiar with the subject matter being covered. Interviewing is expensive because of the one-on-one requirement, the special training required, the time necessary to conduct a complete interview, and the additional cost that is often incurred for video recording or transcribing. These factors limit the number of employees whose knowledge can be gathered using the interview technique.

Questionnaire

Questionnaires can assume many different forms and can be administered in very different formats. The primary advantage of the questionnaire, in whatever form, is that it can be administered with standardized or customized content to a large number of people. As a result, questionnaires are highly efficient. Sophisticated electronic versions can be designed to probe with additional questions through intelligent prompts, mimicking some of the advantages of the semistructured interview. The primary disadvantage of the questionnaire technique is the other side of the efficiency coin: Its standardization eliminates deep individual probing and knowledge linking. Questionnaires may also be less successful than interviewers in getting the interviewee to provide complete data.

■ ■ ■

Our review of these two techniques led us to the conclusion that some jobs at WedgeMark would merit interviews, whereas most jobs would merit questionnaires. Interviews would be appropriate for unique positions where thoroughness, flexibility, and significant probing were important to secure the breadth and depth of knowledge warranted by the person's expertise and experience. In such cases, the knowledge being captured is so critical that it is usually knowledge that the organization itself must have, not just a successor. For example, the only person who knows how to operate the computer system or the only person who knows government contracting procedures would be candidates. Sophisticated software programs are available to assist the interviewer in these special cases.

For most job classifications, however, a well-designed questionnaire in electronic form is the most efficient way to capture critical operational knowledge for successors. Such questionnaires may not look like questionnaires, and they can be made highly interactive, but questionnaires they are in that they contain a set of ordered questions that the incumbent answers.

Knowledge Profile Creation Process

The key element that makes both interviews and questionnaires effective as knowledge-harvesting techniques is the set of questions they employ. The next task before the Dream Team was to create a set of master questions developed specifically to capture the critical operational knowledge of incumbents in any knowledge position at WedgeMark. Andre had already dubbed this set of questions *knowledge profile analysis questions,* or *K-PAQ* for short. We liked the term and continued to use it. When finished, K-PAQ would contain a complete set of questions for each knowledge category in the knowledge profile. It was not, however, the actual instrument that would be used to harvest the critical operational knowledge of incumbents. In order to understand the relationship of K-PAQ to that instrument, a summary of the process to date and a preview of the next steps might be in order. Knowledge profile creation consists of five steps:

1. *Design the knowledge profile.*   Designing the knowledge profile entails two objectives: (1) identifying the knowledge categories that make up the profile and (2) determining the knowledge topics within each category.
2. *Develop K-PAQ: the knowledge profile analysis questions.*   On the basis of the knowledge categories in the knowledge profile, it is possible to develop a master list of questions to capture an incumbent's critical operational knowledge. This database of questions for each knowledge category and its subcategory of topics provides the pool of questions from which to create the questionnaire that will be administered to harvest an incumbent's operational knowledge. The same question pool can be used to construct interviews. We called this database *K-PAQ,* which was short for *knowledge profile analysis questions.*
3. *Develop K-Quest: the knowledge questionnaire.*   K-PAQ is a master list of questions; it is not an instrument to capture operational knowledge for a specific job classification. Were K-PAQ to be administered in its

entirety as an instrument to harvest knowledge, it would take too long to complete, and many of its questions would be redundant or irrelevant. K-PAQ is merely the pool of questions from which certain relevant questions will be selected to create the instrument that will harvest the knowledge of incumbent employees. The term we chose for the harvesting instrument, whether administered by interview or electronic means, was *knowledge questionnaire.* We shortened knowledge questionnaire to *knowledge-quest,* and finally to *K-Quest,* which was the term we came to use. Development of the knowledge questionnaire is a multistage process described in the next chapter.

4. *Administer K-Quest.*   Once the knowledge questionnaire has been developed, it is administered to all incumbents participating in continuity management in accordance with a set of procedures that are also described in the next chapter.

5. *Generate the knowledge profile.*   As K-Quest is administered and completed by an incumbent, its contents are reorganized electronically into the knowledge profile for that position. The full process of knowledge profile creation, however, involves several additional stages beyond administration of the knowledge questionnaire. The stages are described in Chapter 11 ("Creating the Knowledge Profile").

This five-step process from knowledge profile design to knowledge profile generation can be diagrammed as shown in Figure 9.1.

The K-PAQ Cafeteria

The Dream Team designed K-PAQ as a buffet of questions from which individual selections could be made to create the knowledge questionnaire for any job classification at WedgeMark. The questions in K-PAQ were developed to facilitate thinking about job-critical operational knowledge as well as to harvest that knowledge. Operational knowledge encompasses

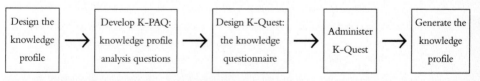

Figure 9.1   Knowledge profile design and generation.

more than data and information, although it may include data and information. It also includes formal and informal processes, procedures, and relationships; essential skills; procedures that incumbents have developed or heard about that are not official or written down, but that guide them in their work; and past experiences, successes, and failures that contain lessons for the future.

As our colleagues continually reminded us, the real need in their jobs was knowledge rather than information. But it was more than just knowledge. It was the *right* knowledge—and getting that knowledge when they needed it in a form that was meaningful to them. The same problems exist for successors as well as for incumbents: too much information, too little knowledge, knowledge that is ill-timed, incomplete knowledge, and knowledge presented in a form that is confusing or unhelpful. Like incumbents, successors require quick access to the critical operational knowledge they need to excel, and in a format that will allow them to process it quickly and to understand it in the context in which it will be applied. The knowledge profile is the means through which this knowledge is organized and accessed. K-Quest is the means by which it is gathered. K-PAQ is the bridge between the two.

Because K-PAQ is one of the key processes of continuity management, and because, in some ways, it is the heart of continuity management, I am incorporating its design and its basic questions into this journal. K-PAQ appears here in the same format in which it was provided to senior management for a briefing on our progress in implementing continuity management. Because knowledge questionnaires for any position at WedgeMark can be created out of K-PAQ, the senior executives found it useful to skim the list of questions as a means of more fully appreciating the breadth and depth of operational knowledge that K-Quest can capture. When reviewing the list of K-PAQ questions, the executives were asked to keep three caveats in mind.

The first caveat is that no knowledge questionnaire to be completed by any incumbent will ever contain all the questions in K-PAQ. Depending on the job classification, some questions will be irrelevant, others will be redundant, and still others will be too detailed. The strength of K-PAQ is the range of questions that it provides for creating highly customized knowledge questionnaires for specific job classifications.

The second caveat is that not all of the K-PAQ questions will require as much time to answer as it may appear. Some questions in K-PAQ are designated to appear in the knowledge questionnaire accompanied by prefilled answers, which are tentative answers developed by a team of peer incumbents. Such questions are referred to as *knowledge core* questions, defined as questions that tap critical operational knowledge shared by virtually all employees in the same job classification. Much of the operational knowledge in the knowledge profile is specific to the job rather than to the job classification, but not all of it. Some of it is shared by virtually everyone who holds the same position. For example, the job description, corporate mission statement, corporate objectives, operating statistics, performance appraisal standards, and so forth are likely to be very similar for everyone with the same job classification. Prefilled answers shorten the time required to complete K-Quest because such answers have only to be reviewed by incumbents for accuracy and, if necessary, modified by deletion or addition rather than created from scratch.

The third caveat is that K-PAQ is a database of questions that will continually expand as continuity management infuses an organization and more and more incumbents analyze their knowledge needs. The questions that we developed for WedgeMark are just the beginning of our K-PAQ. We anticipated (and it turned out to be true) that additional questions would be added as continuity management spread throughout the company and we developed more and more experience with it. Different industries, organizations, and job classifications will undoubtedly develop their own K-PAQs by adding highly specialized questions designed to capture the critical operational knowledge of their knowledge-based incumbents. Like knowledge itself, the bank of questions in K-PAQ will continue to change.

K-PAQ: The Knowledge Profile Analysis Questions

We keyed K-PAQ to the knowledge profile. Therefore, the four sections of K-PAQ match the four sections of the profile and are further subdivided according to the knowledge categories of the Profile. These four sections are entitled Operating Data, Key Operational Knowledge, Basic Operational Knowledge, and Background Operational Knowledge. The questions shown with a marked checkbox are likely to be fully or partially pre-answered in the knowledge questionnaire. The extent of the prefill, if any, will depend on the job classification for which the knowledge questionnaire is being developed.

Section 1: Operating Data

Operating data is the knowledge category containing current information that is routinely used, such as key operating statistics (e.g., monthly sales figures, sales trends, and market share), budgets, projections, and so forth. Reference information such as corporate telephone numbers, policies and procedures, number of vacation days used, and so forth are also included.

Potential questions for the Operating Data section include:

☑ What operating data or information do you use or require, such as key operating statistics, that is critical to your job (i.e. your productivity will suffer if you do not have it)?

☑ From what sources do you obtain this data or information?
- Documents (such as reports, databases, memos, brochures, user manuals, service guides, product plans, pricing sheets, etc.)
- Individuals to whom you can turn for assistance in providing this information

☑ What historical data or information, if any, is critical to your job?

☑ From what sources can you obtain this historical data or information, including, for example, documents and individuals?

☑ What data or information are you currently receiving that you do not need or that you do not need as often as you are receiving it? (Some data and information continue to be generated long after its usefulness has passed. Reports are often a good example of this kind of data and information.)

☑ What data or information do you suspect that you are passing on to others that has lost its usefulness or that is very time-consuming to prepare with little apparent return on that time investment?

☑ What additional data or information, if any, do you need to do your job well that you cannot get or have difficulty getting?

☑ What sources could provide this additional data or information (documents or individuals)?

Section 2: Key Operational Knowledge

Key operational knowledge, as used in K-PAQ, is current knowledge required to perform well in a position. That knowledge is often tacit rather than explicit. Tacit knowledge is the unofficial or informal knowledge stored in an incumbent's head rather than in a database and known only to the incumbent and, perhaps, to a few others with whom it has been shared. This type of knowledge is generally not written down, unless it appears in the margins of procedures manuals or as notes to the file. It develops from on-the-job experience, trial-and-error discoveries, inventive solutions, and improvisations or as lessons learned from projects that succeeded—or failed. It consists of informal rules of thumb that incumbents have devised, principles they have developed, cause-and-effect relationships they have discerned, and guidelines they have created or that others have shared with them. Tacit knowledge is sometimes handed down from employee generation to generation in the form of stories, morality tales, warnings, scribbled notes, or private files. This kind of operational knowledge is invaluable, yet it has no value outside of its context, which is everything.

The Key Operational Knowledge section of K-PAQ consists of four knowledge categories:

Front-Burner Issues

Front-burner issues include decisions, assignments, questions, tasks, controversies, opportunities, threats, or anything else that may require quick action with potentially serious consequences. Major projects, which are always front-burner issues, are excluded from this knowledge category because they are covered in a separate category, Projects Pending. Front-burner issues include current issues (issues currently "on the front burner") and acute issues (likely to arise soon because of emerging factors). Chronic issues, which are ongoing issues that can flare up at any time, demanding quick responses, are included under the Hibernating Issues knowledge category. Front-burner issues may or may not require significant time or resources, but may require quick and effective action to avoid serious consequences or to capitalize on unusual opportunities. An understanding of the context, background, pros and cons, alternatives, and possible outcomes related to these issues is imperative. The determination of whether an issue is a front-burner issue and important enough to be included in the knowledge profile is left to the incumbent.

The questions relating to Front-Burner Issues are applicable to *each* front-burner issue. Of course, not every question will be relevant to every issue, so questions that are not relevant should be deleted from K-Quest. Others could be added if necessary to provide a concise, but clear understanding of the issue.

☐ Briefly describe the issue, including its category (decision, assignment, task, controversy, opportunity, threat, etc.) and whether it is acute or chronic.

☐ Who are the main parties to the issue?

☐ What are the basic factors in this issue? In other words, what are the central facts one needs to know to make the decision, carry out the task, or meet the threat?

☐ What are your objectives related to this issue?

☐ What are the principle options related to this decision, including the pros and cons?

☐ What historical information, if any, is pertinent to this issue?

☐ What threats or opportunities to you or the organization are embedded in this issue?

☐ Who are the principle internal contacts (those from the company, whether still with the company, no longer with the company, consultants to the company, or former consultants to the company) who can help with this issue?

☐ Who are the principal external contacts (those outside the company), if any, who can help with this issue?

☐ What documents constitute the primary resources to which you turn for data, information or knowledge about the issue?

☐ Who are your primary allies, or what are the supporting forces on this issue (people, institutions, organizations, events, trends, etc.)?

☐ Who are your primary antagonists, or what are the primary opposing forces on this issue?

☐ What special insight can you offer based on your own experience with this issue?

☐ Is there any other critical knowledge related to this issue that should be included in the knowledge profile?

Hibernating Issues

Hibernating issues are dormant or semidormant ongoing threats, opportunities, controversies, events, or other issues that carry particular risk or reward and so must be continually monitored in case they erupt and require a quick response. The difference between hibernating issues and front-burner issues is this: Hibernating issues are not necessarily imminent. They may be long-standing issues simmering below the surface that *could* erupt suddenly, but might not. Or they may be regularly recurring issues that are not currently on the front burner but that will return, proving treacherous to the novice and even to the incumbent if not properly handled.

The questions relating to Hibernating Issues are applicable to *each* hibernating issue. Delete questions from K–Quest as necessary or add others as needed to provide a concise, but clear understanding of the issue.

- ☐ Briefly describe the issue, including its category (decision, assignment, task, controversy, opportunity, threat, etc.).
- ☐ Who are the main parties to the issue?
- ☐ What are the basic factors in this issue? In other words, what are the central facts one needs to know to make the decision, carry out the task, or meet the threat?
- ☐ What are your objectives related to this issue?
- ☐ What are the principle options related to this decision, including the pros and cons?
- ☐ What historical information, if any, is pertinent to this issue?
- ☐ What threats or opportunities to you or the organization are embedded in this issue?
- ☐ Who are the principle internal contacts (those from the company, whether still with the company, no longer with the company, consultants to the company, or former consultants to the company) who can help with this issue?
- ☐ Who are the principal external contacts (those outside the company), if any, who can help with this issue?
- ☐ What documents constitute the primary resources to which you turn for data, information or knowledge about the issue?
- ☐ Who are your primary allies, or what are the supporting forces on this issue (people, institutions, organizations, events, trends, etc.)?
- ☐ Who are your primary antagonists, or what are the primary opposing forces on this issue?
- ☐ What special insight can you offer based on your own experience with this issue?
- ☑ Is there any other critical knowledge related to this issue that should be included in the knowledge profile?

Key Customers

This knowledge category includes all of an incumbent's most important customers inside the organization (internal) and outside the organization (external). As used here, *customer* is broadly defined, and the definition of *important customer* is left to the incumbent. *Internal customers* include supervisors, peers, direct reports, and others in the company to whom formal or informal products or services are provided (including knowledge). *External customers* are those outside the company to whom products or services are provided on behalf of the company.

The process of identifying internal and external customers focuses attention on customer priorities, on customers *as priorities,* and on the quality of service provided to them. This analysis is helpful to incumbents, but critical for new hires. If new hires are not satisfactorily briefed on their customers and on their customers' special needs and expectations, they will encounter criticism, experience frustration, and may even lose the customer.

Potential questions for the Key Customers category include:

- ☐ Who are your key internal customers, ranked in order of importance, to whom you provide formal or informal products or services? Customers may be ranked individually or by tiers (for example, 1, 2, 3 or Tier 1, Tier 2, Tier 3). Informal customers are people to whom you provide advice and counsel, with whom you share other forms of knowledge, or for whom you provide services on an informal basis.
- ☐ Who are your key external customers, ranked in order of importance (individually or by tier)?
- ☐ Are there additional internal or external customers you intend to approach or could approach (e.g., customer prospect lists)?

For *each* of these key customers, answer the following questions:

- ☐ Customer name
- ☐ Customer priority ranking
- ☐ Internal or external
- ☐ Product or service provided to customer
- ☐ Contact and contact's position
- ☐ Customer history (if applicable)
- ☐ Special needs, requirements, procedures, or expectations
- ☐ Selling hints or peculiarities
- ☐ Customer testimonials
- ☐ If problems with customer, contact
- ☐ Other comments

Projects Pending

According to a study by Standish Group Research, 84 percent of all projects fail in some way. Of these, 53 percent are late or over budget, and 31 percent are cancelled prior to completion. The *average* project takes 222 percent longer than planned to complete and exceeds its budget by 189 percent (Projects are risky business, 2001, p. 1). While there are many reasons for project compromise or failure, one of the reasons is the transfer of key personnel off the project or the lack of personnel with institutional memory of the project who can provide assistance when potential problems arise. Some jobs are primarily project based—whether software development projects, consulting assignments, or new product development. Others are not, but all jobs involve some projects that require planning, coordination, and execution.

Projects Pending includes any project in which an incumbent is involved that could have a significant impact on the organization (in other words, a major project). The criteria for including a project in this knowledge category are left up to the incumbent to determine. If it is a project that is exclusively an incumbent's to organize, direct, or launch, then it is by definition a major project, because no one else could handle it effectively in the incumbent's absence. As pending projects are closed, they are archived and stored for future reference under Completed Projects, a knowledge profile category appearing in the Background Operational Knowledge section of the profile.

The Projects Pending questions that follow are applicable to *each* major project pending. Delete questions from K-Quest as necessary or add others as needed to provide a concise, but clear understanding of the issue.

- [ ] What is the name of this project?
- [ ] Briefly describe the project.
- [ ] What are the goals of this project?
- [ ] Who are the official parties involved in this project?
- [ ] Are there any unofficial or interested parties related to the project who play an important, if indirect, role?
- [ ] Is this project anyone's pet project, and, if so, what are the ramifications?
- [ ] What is the history of this project, if relevant?
- [ ] What are the issues, if any, associated with this project?
- [ ] What opportunities or threats to you or the organization are related to this project?
- [ ] What major decisions, if any, are likely to arise out of this project?

☐ Which individuals or forces, if any, oppose this project, and what is the best way to deal with them? Put another way, what are the biggest obstacles to completion of this project?

☐ Who are the principal internal contacts (those within the company) and the principal external contacts (those outside the company) on this project or those who know the most about this project who could be relied on to provide assistance?

☐ What are the primary documentary resources to which you can turn for data, information or knowledge about this project?

☐ What special insight can you offer based on your own experience with this project?

☐ Is there any other critical operational knowledge related to this project that should be included in the knowledge profile?

Section 3: Basic Operational Knowledge

Every job can be described in terms of six components: objectives, functions, activities, decisions, skills, and performance evaluation criteria. These six knowledge categories are examined in the *Basic Operational Knowledge* section. They are important to new hires because they describe the parameters of the jobs they are assuming. They are also important to incumbents, however, because they provide an overview of their jobs and a perspective on how they spend—or should be spending—their time on those jobs. The analysis that creates this section of K-Quest will pinpoint knowledge leverage points: areas where knowledge-based productivity gains can be achieved through changes in priorities, activities, and time allocations or through improved skills and decision making.

Basic operational knowledge is contained in mission statements, annual goals, budgets, databases, organizational charts, Web pages, policies, procedures, and other official documents. But it is also the kind of knowledge that grows out of on-the-job experience, arises from stories passed between colleagues, and develops from thoughtful analysis.

The Basic Operational Knowledge section of K-PAQ consists of six knowledge categories: *Job Objectives, Primary Job Functions, Reporting Lines, Primary Job Activities, SWOT Analysis,* and *Innovations.*

Job Objectives

Every job can be described in terms of its objectives, functions, and activities. This knowledge category focuses on employee *objectives* and on their relationship to the *operational knowledge* that incumbents possess or need to acquire.

Potential questions for the Job Objectives category include:

- ☑ What is the mission statement of the organization?
- ☑ What is the mission statement of your unit?
- ☑ What are the goals and objectives of your unit?
- ☑ What documents contain these goals and objectives?
- ☐ What are your performance goals or objectives for the coming year (i.e., those on which your performance appraisal will be based)?
- ☐ Are there other short-term goals you have set for yourself (such as sales, projects completed, customers served, or other performance measures)?
- ☐ What are your *long-term* goals and objectives, as expressed in performance measurements?

Primary Job Functions

Ideally, job objectives, functions, and activities should be aligned. Functions should support achievement of organizational objectives. Functions describe the kind of work that we do (whereas activities describe the tasks that we perform to carry out those functions). The functions of a sales job, for example, might include developing new customers, supporting present customers, or assisting other organizational units in understanding customers. For successor employees, job functions provide an overview of the job.

Potential questions for the Primary Job Functions category include:

- ☑ What are the major job functions that you perform, in the approximate order of their importance?
- ☐ How much time do you devote to these functions, on average? In other words, what does your average day look like in terms of time devoted to these functions?
- ☑ Which functions, if any, are you asked to perform that waste time, drain resources, or otherwise fail to support your objectives, and therefore should be eliminated or dispensed with quickly?
- ☑ What additional functions, if any, should you take on?
- ☑ What existing functions, if any, should be transferred to someone else?

Reporting Lines

Formal reporting lines are depicted in organizational charts, but organizational charts do not tell the whole story. As important as they are, they do not reveal informal lines of authority, the courtesy heads-up, the blind carbon copies, or the indirect reporting arrangements that are equally important to success in a given position. While invaluable for successors, these questions benefit incumbents by focusing their attention on the characteristics of those to whom they report and the most effective means of dealing with them.

Potential questions for the Reporting Lines category include:

- [ ] Who are the people to whom you report directly?
- [ ] For each direct report, provide the following information:
  - What are this person's three most important objectives?
  - What is his or her management style?
  - How does he or she prefer to communicate (through oral briefings, memos, formal reports, telephone calls, e-mail, social gatherings, staff meetings)?
  - What are his or her pet preferences?
  - What are his or her pet peeves?
- [ ] Should you have fewer or more direct reports, and why?
- [ ] Who are the people to whom you report indirectly?
- [ ] For each indirect report, provide the following information:
  - What are this person's three most important objectives?
  - What is his or her management style?
  - How does he or she prefer to communicate (through oral briefings, memos, formal reports, telephone calls, e-mail, social gatherings, staff meetings)?
  - What are his or her pet preferences?
  - What are his or her pet peeves?
- [ ] Who are the people who are neither direct nor indirect reports with whom you should share knowledge for political, personal, or other reasons, and why?

Primary Job Activities (Tasks and Responsibilities)

All job activities, whether tasks or responsibilities, should support one or more job functions, which, in turn, should support achievement of the job's objectives. The Primary Job Activities knowledge category can be invaluable to incumbents because it will:

- Allow them to increase the alignment of their activities with their job functions and objectives.
- Allow them to analyze the amount of time they devote to their primary activities in light of their objectives.
- Allow them to analyze what they do in relation to the operational knowledge they have or need to acquire.
- Identify key leverage points of productivity: activities with the greatest value added. It is these activities to which more time and resources should be dedicated.

The following chart shows the three question sets to be answered for each activity. In other words, for each primary activity, an incumbent is queried about the time spent on that activity (time relationship), the knowledge required to accomplish it (related knowledge), and the processes (related processes).

Activity Identification	Set A: Time Relationship	Set B: Related Knowledge	Set C: Related Processes

Potential questions for the Primary Job Activities category include:

Activity Identification

☑ What are the primary activities that you carry out each day (or as necessary) to support your job functions and accomplish your job objectives?

☑ Of these activities, which ones are critical to the achievement of your goals and to high performance in your position, and which ones are secondary? Rate them in order of importance or by category of importance.

☑ What activities, if any, are currently assigned to you that should be shifted to someone else?

☑ What additional activities, if any, would it be reasonable for you to take on?

Question Set A: Time Relationship.   The following questions on time relationship relate to each activity:

- ☑ How much time do you devote to each of these activities, on average? In other words, what does your average day look like in terms of time devoted to major activities?
- ☑ How much time *should* you be devoting to each of these activities, given their relative importance? In other words, which of these activities are nonproductive, waste time, drain resources, or do not warrant the expenditure of time, effort, and knowledge devoted to them?

The often-quoted Pareto principle (or the 80/20 rule) states that 20 percent of a group of people will be responsible for 80 percent of production, that 20 percent of customers will produce 80 percent of the business, and that 20 percent of our effort generates 80 percent of what we are trying to achieve. On the basis of the 80/20 rule, we can guess that something like 20 percent of our activities and 20 percent of our operational knowledge produce 80 percent of what we are trying to accomplish. The goal, therefore, is to identify that 20 percent.

Question Set B: Knowledge Identification.   Each primary activity is supported by operational knowledge. In accordance with Pareto principle, these questions focus attention on acquiring or enhancing the 20 percent of operational knowledge that generates 80 percent of achievements.

Potential questions on knowledge identification include:

- ☐ What operational knowledge, if any, could you enhance that would increase your productivity in these primary activities?
- ☐ What operational knowledge, if any, do you need, but do not have, that would make you more productive in primary activities?

Question Set C: Process Identification.   An important area of operational knowledge is understanding how things get done—the formal procedures and informal processes by which employees carry out their activities, accomplish their tasks, and achieve their objectives. If formal corporate documentation painted an accurate picture of organizational processes, it would only be necessary to read the corporate policies and procedures manual (while staying awake), various handbooks, and a few key memos in order to know everything. But corporate documentation seldom describes how things really happen in an organization.

People often set up informal processes that are more efficient and effective than those mandated by the organization. Or they devise ways to circumvent the formal processes in order to save time or to move their projects to the head of the line. Or they come up with better, faster, or more innovative solutions than official procedures describe. Social capital plays an important role in the development and communication of such knowledge, as do communities of practice, knowledge networks, and friendships. All these sources generate knowledge that is used to modify obsolete corporate procedures that fail to keep step with the demands of the rapidly changing work environment. The process identification questions in K-PAQ attempt to capture the processes that incumbents have modified or created to make their primary activities more productive.

Potential questions on process identification include:

- ☐ For each activity and its related knowledge, briefly describe the processes and procedures that you follow, especially if they are short-cuts.
- ☐ What processes or procedures have you modified or created that have enhanced productivity?
- ☐ What standard procedures or processes are particularly cumbersome or counterproductive?

SWOT Analysis (Strengths, Weaknesses, Opportunities, and Threats)

SWOT is an acronym used to describe the analysis of an organization's internal strengths and weaknesses (including competitive advantages), and an analysis of threats and opportunities facing the organization or the incumbent. Successful leaders and great organizations are aware of their strengths and weaknesses and monitor them continuously. In an ideal world, these strengths and weaknesses would be candidly assessed with the goal of eliminating the weaknesses and capitalizing on the strengths.

Potential questions on strengths and weaknesses include:

- ☐ What are the strengths of your unit or of the strengths of the organization as they affect your unit?
- ☐ What are the strengths of other units that should be taken into account in dealing with them?
- ☐ Are there ways to capitalize on these strengths that are not being pursued?
- ☐ What are the weaknesses of your unit or of the organization as they affect your unit?
- ☐ What are the weaknesses of other units that have to be considered in dealing with them?
- ☐ How might these weaknesses be reduced or eliminated?
- ☐ What are the weaknesses of outsourced suppliers that have to be considered in dealing with them?
- ☐ What are the three biggest mistakes made in your unit in the last year, and what are their lessons?
- ☐ What are the three greatest successes achieved in your unit in the last year, and what are their lessons?
- ☐ What are the three most significant improvements made in your unit over the past year?

Threats and opportunities include short-term and long-term threats and opportunities that incumbents or their organization face. Short-term threats may also have appeared under Front-Burner Issues. The following questions relate to both the incumbent *and* the organization.

- ☐ What major threats, if any, do you see developing over the next year?
- ☐ What major threats, in any, do you see developing within the next five years?
- ☐ What might be done to counter these threats?
- ☐ What major opportunities, if any, do you see developing over the next year?
- ☐ What major opportunities, if any, do you see developing over the next five years?
- ☐ What might be done to capitalize on these opportunities?

Competitive advantage is a form of opportunity. In business, competitive advantages are attributes, capabilities, ideas, resources, products, services, or anything else that makes one entity, product, or service more attractive in the marketplace than competing entities, products, or services. For purposes of K-Quest, the term *competitive advantage* is broadly applied. By answering the following questions, incumbents will have an opportunity to analyze existing competitive advantages, determine those that can be strengthened further, and identify those that need to be created.

Potential questions on competitive advantage include:

- [ ] What are the primary competitive advantages of the service or products that you develop, provide, or sell, listed by *service* or *product?*
- [ ] How do you capitalize on these competitive advantages?
- [ ] How can you or the organization strengthen these competitive advantages?
- [ ] What new competitive advantages might be created?
- [ ] What are the primary competitive advantages of the organization as they apply to you and your job?
- [ ] How might you or the organization strengthen these competitive advantages?
- [ ] What new competitive advantages might the organization create?

Innovations

Innovations is the knowledge category that captures the shortcuts, creative solutions, modified techniques, procedural revisions, new ideas, or any other changes that incumbents have developed, heard about, or otherwise applied. They are often informal, unofficial, and unreported, arising from the incumbent's tacit knowledge base and shared with one or two people, with the team, or perhaps with no one. They represent significant organizational opportunities for increased productivity and effectiveness and are a key part of the knowledge legacy that incumbents can pass to their successors.

Potential questions for the Innovations category include:

- [ ] What changes or modifications have you made to existing organizational procedures, policies, processes, rules, or requirements that have increased your productivity or effectiveness? These changes may have stemmed from your own experience or they may have resulted from conversations with your colleagues or others.

☐ If not covered by the previous question, what new ideas, creative solutions, or innovative approaches to carrying out your job functions or conducting the primary activities of your position have you developed or employed?

Some answers to the preceding questions may also appear under the Activity Identification knowledge category.

Section 4: Background Operational Knowledge

Background operational knowledge is knowledge that incumbents may not consciously use every day but that is an essential part of their operating knowledge. Background operational knowledge is often analytical knowledge compiled by incumbents from official and unofficial sources and synthesized into strategic concepts and principles that support their strategic thinking and lead them to networking resources. This knowledge category is vital to successors if they are to grasp the nature of the job they are assuming and move quickly to high productivity. But this knowledge category is also important to incumbents, because it forces them to analyze key components of their knowledge base and to keep them current.

The Background Operational Knowledge section consists of six knowledge categories: *Knowledge Network, Skill Sets, Performance Evaluations, Completed Projects, Unexploited Ideas,* and *Incumbent Biographies.*

Knowledge Network

Key knowledge suppliers are individuals connected to incumbents by mutual knowledge needs. Together, these individuals form a *knowledge network,* which can be defined as a web of formal and informal relationships composed of people inside and outside the organization connected by mutual knowledge interests. An incumbent's knowledge network includes internal and external suppliers, colleagues, competitors, consultants, mentors, and others to whom incumbents turn for knowledge and the social and political relationships through which to grease the wheels of decision making, cut red tape, get a higher priority for requests and projects, or otherwise speed up the processes on which high performance depends. People who know the ropes or know where the bodies are buried are especially important network members.

These continuity sages can often provide knowledge and ensure knowledge continuity when no other reliable source can.

Some of the individuals named on this list of key knowledge suppliers will be useful to successors and some will not be, but the list itself will be invaluable. Although successors still have to re-create the knowledge relationships, they can do so with greater efficiency and understanding if they know whom to contact and why they are contacting them. For a new hire to start from scratch to create a knowledge network is very time-consuming. It will take weeks or months for a new hire to recreate the knowledge network of the predecessor. Without access to the knowledge network, however, new hires will find it difficult if not impossible to retrieve needed information or obtain the necessary cooperation and collaboration to be productive quickly.

Knowledge networks can be traced through a mapping process, which is built into K-PAQ. The process identifies people within the organization and external to the organization who are joined by shared knowledge requirements, mutual knowledge opportunities, and social ties that lead to knowledge exchange. In a larger sense, knowledge mapping describes how people influence each other and relate to each other on the basis of knowledge. It traces organizational knowledge flow among incumbents and others inside and outside the organization, tracking three types of flows:

- Critical knowledge inflow (knowledge from sources external to the organization)
- Critical knowledge outflow (knowledge from the organization to external sources)
- Critical knowledge cross-flow (knowledge shared only within the organization) that is essential to the work incumbents do

Knowledge mapping provides an overview of an incumbent's knowledge network that facilitates prioritization of knowledge relationships that support their work, identifying those that need to be strengthened and those that can be deemphasized.

The names of some people in the knowledge network may also appear in response to other K-PAQ questions (for example, if they are important to specific functions, projects, decisions, or activities), but this section on key knowledge suppliers provides an integrated overview of the contacts on which incumbents regularly (or occasionally) depend to function well in their jobs. When the knowledge profile is created electronically in high-technology continuity management systems, any key knowledge supplier reported elsewhere will be summarized under this heading. Key knowledge suppliers can be referenced by expertise, by work or project experience, by knowledge application (cutting red tape, general advice, political insights, confidential knowledge, and so forth), by corporate function (marketing, budgeting, planning, and so forth), by job classification (sales manager, accountant, and so forth), and by other useful categories.

Potential questions for the Knowledge Network category include:

- ☐ Who are your key informal and formal *internal* knowledge suppliers (e.g., knowledgeable supervisors, peers, subordinates, or mentors)?
- ☐ Who are your key *external* knowledge suppliers (e.g., customers, suppliers, consultants, or mentors)?
- ☐ Which peers (those holding the same job classification) do you turn to for assistance when you need it?

The following questions relate to *each* key knowledge supplier. Questions can be added as necessary.

- ☐ Name
- ☐ Expertise or knowledge function provided
- ☐ Position (if internal) or position and organization (if external) with contact information
- ☐ History of the relationship with the key knowledge supplier (if relevant)
- ☐ Anything else about key knowledge suppliers that should be included in the knowledge profile

Skill Sets

In an era of turbulent change, continuous learning is a necessity. An important aspect of continuous learning and of operational knowledge is developing the set of job-related skills required for high performance. This knowledge category will help incumbents and successors compare their existing skills to the ideal skill set. From that analysis, they can determine the additional training they need to improve those skills or acquire new ones.

Potential questions for the Skill Sets category include:

☑ List the key skills that are necessary to perform well in your job. Rank each skill as 1, 2, or 3, with 1 being the most important. Conflict resolution, time management, emotional intelligence, managing change, team building, negotiating, delegating, closing a sale, and prospecting customers are examples of such skills. Proficiency in software programs such as Excel or Word is an example of a technical skill that might be critical to a job classification.

☐ What additional training or education would be helpful in your job? For example, would you benefit from an introductory course in accounting, budgeting, marketing, finance, or logistics offered through an in-house training session, an online course, or a course offered by a local college? What additional technical skills should you acquire?

☑ What technical skills are necessary in your job? For example, training in special software programs.

☐ Are there any additional technical skills that would be useful to you?

Performance Evaluations

This knowledge category describes the criteria and processes through which employee performance is evaluated, compensation is set, and promotions are earned. Although it is primarily for the benefit of successors, it benefits incumbents by crystallizing their thinking about how success is achieved in their positions. In some cases, the questions should not be answered, but nonetheless considered by incumbents as they develop their career strategies. The goal of the knowledge category, however, is to have incumbents include as many answers as they feel comfortable in revealing.

Potential questions for the Performance Evaluations category include:

☐ Who is officially responsible for your performance evaluation?

☐ Who else has input in that evaluation?

☑ What are the official criteria for measuring performance (i.e., performance goals), earning promotions, and receiving increased compensation for this position? How should they be prioritized?

☑ What are the *unofficial* criteria for measuring performance, earning promotions, and receiving increased compensation for this position? Unofficial criteria may be as important as official criteria. How should these criteria be prioritized?

☑ What is the official process through which performance is evaluated?

☐ Is there an informal evaluation process that bears on the official process?

☑ What characteristics does it take to succeed in this position?

☑ What characteristics would likely cause you to fail in this position?

☐ To what extent is your performance judged on the basis of what you do versus what your group does?

Completed Projects

This knowledge category archives all major projects completed by incumbents during their tenure with the organization. The category does not appear in K–PAQ or K–Quest because it is automatically populated by completed projects from Projects Pending. When incumbents update their knowledge profiles and designate a pending project as having been completed, it is automatically moved to the Completed Projects knowledge category of the profile.

Unexploited Ideas

One of the challenges for incumbent employees in any organization is setting aside the time and finding the discipline to exploit the new ideas they have generated. Innovative solutions, creative revisions, and imaginative approaches often occur to employees during the course of their work. Sometimes they pursue these ideas; often they do not. This knowledge category requires incumbents to examine ideas that have not been developed or exploited to their full potential. Not every incumbent, of course, has such ideas, but these questions apply to those who do.

Potential questions for the Unexploited Ideas category include:

☐ What ideas, suggestions, or recommendations for improving operations have you developed that you would like to pursue?

☐ Who might be of assistance in helping you exploit these ideas, either through further development or through wider implementation?

☐ What ideas or recommendations were made by your predecessor that have not yet been developed or implemented?

☐ Who might be of assistance in helping you develop or implement those ideas?

Incumbent Biographies

Each knowledge profile contains a biographical sketch of every incumbent who has contributed to it, along with that incumbent's favorite photograph of himself or herself. The originator of the profile is called the *founding incumbent* and is especially honored.

The purpose of the biography is to personalize the profile and to connect the incumbent emotionally to it. The biography may be of any length. We encourage a biography that includes both professional aspects (such as jobs held or special areas of expertise) and personal aspects (such as hobbies, interests, home town, family members, and so forth), or anything else that incumbents would like to say about themselves in this biography. Incumbents should provide their favorite photograph of themselves, which will be scanned into the profile for inclusion with their biographies.

Feedback on the Methodology

Because continuity management at WedgeMark is a work in progress, the Dream Team was very interested in feedback on the K-PAQ questions. For that reason, we developed a final section that did not relate directly to the knowledge profile, but rather to the design and administration of the knowledge questionnaire itself. For example, we recommend that these three questions be included in each K-Quest to ensure that no critical operational knowledge was omitted:

- What operational knowledge critical to your position has not been captured by the previous questions but should be included in the knowledge profile?
- What additional questions, if any, should be added to capture this knowledge?
- What questions do you remember asking during the first few weeks or months of your employment in this position that were not raised in K-Quest?

The Dream Team was also interested in the incumbents' experience of taking the knowledge questionnaire. Therefore, we recommended these questions as well:

- What was the most helpful thing about taking K-Quest?
- What was least helpful thing about K-Quest?
- How could the design, format, or administration of K-Quest be improved?

K-PAQ was the source for the questions that would populate the knowledge questionnaire, but the process of choosing those questions and creating the questionnaire itself was still to be devised. Because each knowledge questionnaire would differ according to the job classification for which it was designed, we would have to develop principles and procedures for creating the questionnaire and for administering it. To this task, the Dream Team next turned its attention.

10 | Developing K-Quest: The Knowledge Questionnaire

As the members of the Dream Team reconvened, our spirits were high. All of us, however, felt the need to pause and review what we had accomplished in relation to where we were going. The more we worked with continuity management, the more its principles, steps, and techniques became clear, and the easier it was to fit them into the larger framework that was developing. Now it was time to reassess that framework, to see the big picture into which these emerging elements fit. So we turned to Sarah, whose digital mind could create a conceptual photograph of any management model, theory, or process—from any desired perspective, angle, or distance. Wide-angle shot of the concept from beginning to end? No problem. Close-up of a single component? You bet. Telephoto shot of the end result? Any time you want. So we asked Sarah for the big picture of what we had done and where we were going.

"Here's the deal," she said. "There are four major knowledge processes in continuity management, and each process is implemented through an instrument designed specifically for it. If you understand these processes and how they are implemented, you understand continuity management."

The four instruments and their corresponding processes are:

- *Knowledge continuity assessment* for assessing knowledge continuity in the organization
- *K-PAQ* (*knowledge profile analysis questions*) for analyzing operational knowledge
- *K-Quest* (*knowledge questionnaire*) for harvesting operational knowledge
- *Knowledge profile* for transferring operational knowledge to successor employees

"Because we had to develop the continuity management process from scratch," Sarah said, "our major contribution has been to create model instruments for each process. Still, every organization that implements continuity management will have to develop its own version of these instruments. Their task will be much easier thanks to our planning, but what we have given them is a set of guidelines and a model for the instruments—nothing more. K-PAQ, for example, isn't definitive."

"I was hoping it might be . . . *kind of* . . . definitive," Roger said.

"Impossible. Each instrument is unique to its organization—created by the organization for the organization. We can create a universal model for K-PAQ, but not a universal K-PAQ."

"In other words," Andre said, "at this point, we are three-quarters through the development process. We have conducted the knowledge continuity assessment, designed our knowledge profile, and developed K-PAQ. Our next step is to design the knowledge questionnaire."

"Right," Sarah confirmed.

Designing the Knowledge Questionnaire

As the Dream Team conceived it, K-Quest was to be a highly individualized instrument for harvesting critical operational knowledge from incumbent employees. It was the means by which the questions contained in K-PAQ could be converted into the answers contained in the Knowledge Profile. Every K-Quest is customized to fit the special knowledge characteristics of the job classification and the unique knowledge needs of the unit, department, or organization in which it is administered. Each K-Quest is different, painted from the palette of questions contained in K-PAQ. K-Quests designed for relatively uncomplicated jobs, for example, might contain fewer questions than those designed for more complex knowledge-based positions. K-Quests for different industries will likely contain very different questions. A service company will not create the same knowledge profile as a manufacturer. A salesperson will not be given the same knowledge questionnaire as a project engineer. K-Quests can vary significantly in content and length from one job classification to another and from one organization to another. There is no *standard* K-Quest, just as there is no standard K-PAQ and no standard knowledge job in the Information Age. It would have been impossible for the Dream Team to create a knowledge questionnaire for all of WedgeMark, much less for any other organization. The content and format of each K-Quest is determined by the organization creating it.

Content Criteria for the Knowledge Questionnaire

Because the knowledge questionnaire for each job classification is unique, the Dream Team established six principles to guide K-Quest developers in their choice of K-PAQ questions and the design of K-Quest.

Principle 1. *K-Quest should be tailored to each job classification and position.*

K-PAQ contains a bank of questions that cover every job classification. Because K-Quest must be customized to fit the job classification in which it will be administered, some of these questions will have to be eliminated. Question selection involves two issues: *how many* questions to choose and *which* questions to choose. That choice is made on the basis of these criteria:

- The job classification for which the K-Quest is being prepared.
- Individual variations in the job among incumbents who share the same job classification.
- The uniqueness or importance of the job to the organization as a factor in determining the type and number of questions selected for the K-Quest.
- The depth of operational knowledge to be captured in the knowledge profile for the specific job classification.
- The form of K-Quest administration (for example, interview or electronic questionnaire). In those cases where an incumbent's knowledge is unique and so critical to the company that its loss would be devastating, a semistructured interview may be more appropriate than a written questionnaire.

- The degree of technological sophistication in K-Quest administration. More sophisticated technology generally speeds up administration of K-Quest and might allow additional questions.
- The number of pre-answered questions. Pre-answered questions speed up administration of K-Quest.
- The length of employment with the organization. Longer-term employees generally have more operational knowledge to impart and more knowledge that is important to preserve in the institutional memory.

In developing K-Quest, incumbents have two central tasks: Choose the most appropriate questions for the job classification, and determine additional questions that should be added to K-Quest and to K-PAQ.

Principle 2.   *Each organization should add its own questions to K-PAQ as necessary, to tailor K-PAQ to its special requirements.*

It was our expectation that K-PAQ would be regularly reviewed to ensure its continued relevance and completeness and expanded as necessary to satisfy emerging knowledge requirements. We do not presume to have included every potentially valuable question. Even if we had, new questions would have to be added and old ones modified as the position's operational knowledge evolved.

Principle 3.   *K-PAQ questions that analyze knowledge requirements and usage should be included in K-Quest whenever possible.*

Our objective was to make K-Quest valuable to incumbents as well as to their successors. Given the importance of knowledge in the Information Age, we realized that a well-designed analysis of knowledge requirements could contribute significantly to the incumbent's productivity as well as to the successor's. Therefore, we built a knowledge analysis into K-PAQ that would identify knowledge leverage points, establish knowledge priorities, and guide the day's activities toward the greatest possible level of knowledge-based productivity and effectiveness. This analysis is one of the reasons that organizational time devoted to completing K-Quest is time well spent for incumbents. This analytical process can reorder incumbent thinking about knowledge, about its relationship to job objectives and functions, and about its most effective utilization. For some incumbents, it may be the first time they have ever examined their operational knowledge base and considered how they could sharpen, focus, or expand that knowledge to achieve greater productivity.

Principle 4.   *Convert as many questions to pre-answered questions as possible.*

Pre-answered (knowledge-core) questions shorten the administration time of K-Quest and stimulate additional thinking about knowledge. Knowledge-core questions harvest knowledge that is common to many or all incumbents with the same job classification. Knowledge-core questions that appear in the knowledge questionnaire have been pre-answered by a peer incumbent team and inserted into K-Quest prior to its administration. They require only verification by the incumbent or modification by deletion or addition; they do not have to be created from scratch. As a result, knowledge-core questions can be answered more quickly. For that reason, and because of the discussions among peer incumbents required to produce them, it is desirable to convert as many questions to the knowledge core as possible.

Principle 5.   *Specific instructions are necessary to guide peer incumbents in completing their knowledge questionnaires.*

In those instances where sophisticated technology is employed in K-Quest and incumbents have the choice of recording their answers in different media, they should be provided with criteria for choosing among the alternatives: typed, audio, or video. Because the answers themselves will be shaped by governing principles determined by the medium, incumbents should be provided with the requisite guidelines. Typed answers, for example, should use bullets to encourage conciseness and clarity and to reduce the time spent on revisions by those seeking to produce a flawlessly crafted document. It is not as important to use complete sentences as it is to make statements that are short and clear, but comprehensive and complete.

Principle 6.   *Employ the most sophisticated technology possible for K-Quest.*

All else being equal, the more sophisticated the technology employed in K-Quest administration, the faster, easier and more useful the resulting knowledge profile will be. It is not necessary to create highly sophisticated technology to administer K-Quest, but the more sophisticated the technology, the more effective K-Quest is in harvesting knowledge. Sophisticated software facilitates an orderly progression through K-Quest with helpful prompts and links, and it allows incumbents to respond in whatever medium they find most comfortable, including audio and video.

The Peer Design Team

The knowledge questionnaire for each job classification should be developed by a peer design team drawn from peer incumbents in that classification. The responsibilities of the peer design team are:

- Select the K-PAQ questions that will appear in K-Quest.
- Work with HR to develop pre-answers for K-PAQ questions that relate to job specifications, policies and procedures, performance appraisal criteria, organizational history, and so forth.
- Develop answers to all knowledge-core questions that will be pre-answered in K-Quest.
- Determine the format for K-Quest.

The knowledge analyses that the design team conducted and the pre-answers it developed expanded its members' knowledge networks and deepened their support for continuity management.

With the K-Quest design principles established, it was time for Roger's take-aways. Herewith, half a dozen of what one of the irreverent members of the team refers to as *Roger's out-takes:*

ROGER'S TAKE-AWAYS

Content Criteria for the Knowledge Questionnaire
- K-Quest should be tailored to each job classification and position.
- Each organization should add its own questions to K-PAQ as necessary, to tailor K-PAQ to its special requirements.
- K-PAQ questions that analyze knowledge requirements and usage should be included in K-Quest whenever possible.
- Convert as many questions to pre-answered questions as possible.
- Specific instructions are necessary to guide peer incumbents in completing their knowledge questionnaires.
- Employ the most sophisticated technology possible for K-Quest.

Conducting the K-Quest Pilot

We chose three different job classifications for our K-Quest pilot to see how the knowledge questionnaires would vary among them and to gain additional experience with the design and administration processes. We developed a nine-step process for conducting the pilot.

Step 1.   Our technowizard created a simple program to house K-Quest temporarily so that a prototype could be administered in the three job classifications chosen for the pilot.

Step 2.   We submitted the K-Quest prototype to HR for its evaluation and input.

Step 3.   Following the HR review and the modifications it brought, we took the prototype to the three employees we considered to be the most effective in each job classification, and we asked them to complete it. What would they add, what would they eliminate, and what did they think about K-Quest? On the basis of their feedback, we made further modifications to the questionnaire.

Step 4.   We decided to ask five managers who were buddies of ours to take a Saturday and work with us on K-Quest, promising some form of reward, if nothing more than praise and a night on the town. They agreed. We explained K-Quest, administered it to them, and then conducted what was essentially a focus group on its format, content, and administration procedures.

Step 5.   For each job classification, we assembled a small group of incumbents who shared the classification and who were highly regarded. We asked these peer incumbents to complete only those questions in the K-Quest prototype that had been designated knowledge-core questions (the questions that would be preanswered in the final version). These peers then met in a facilitated focus group to discuss their answers to each question and to reach consensus on official pre-answers for the questionnaire.

Step 6.   On the basis of input from all these activities, we prepared an official knowledge questionnaire for each of the three job classifications participating in the pilot. K-Quest was now ready for administration to all employees in these job classifications in our unit at WedgeMark.

Step 7.   Once K-Quest had been designed, administration procedures had to be developed. The procedures we developed for administering K-Quest are described in detail later in this chapter.

Step 8.   We administered K-Quest to all employees in the three job classifications that comprised the pilot.

Step 9.   We synthesized everything we had learned from the pilot and finalized K-PAQ and its administration procedures. Out of this pilot came many small modifications and some large ones, including the addition of new questions to K-Quest and to K-PAQ. All that remained was to expand the pilot program to the whole of our unit at WedgeMark.

But first:

ROGER'S TAKE-AWAYS

Nine Steps to Piloting the Knowledge Questionnaire

1. Create a simple software program to house the K-Quest prototype.
2. Submit the K-Quest prototype to HR for feedback.
3. Administer the K-Quest prototype to the three most capable employees in each job classification.
4. Beta-test K-Quest with a small group of managers.
5. Assemble a group of peer incumbents from each job classification to pre-answer the knowledge-core questions.
6. Prepare the official knowledge questionnaire for each job classification in the pilot.
7. Devise the administration procedures for K-Quest.
8. Administer K-Quest to all incumbent employees participating in the pilot.
9. Revise K-PAQ and K-Quest on the basis of feedback from the pilot and finalize the content of the knowledge questionnaire for administration to all participating job classifications.

Because WedgeMark is a large company, and because senior management wanted to evaluate continuity management for a possible roll-out to the entire company, our pilot was detailed and comprehensive. It was made more so because continuity management had never been implemented before, requiring us to feel our way along. For business units or smaller organizations, the pilot will resemble the full process through which K-Quest is developed and administered.

Rolling Out the Knowledge Questionnaire

With completion of the pilot, we were ready to expand the process of developing K-Quest to all job classifications in our unit at WedgeMark that had been designated to participate in continuity management. The lessons we had learned from the pilot were enlightening and resulted in tangible outcomes:

- An expanded K-PAQ (more questions and some better ones from which to draw in creating K-Quests for each job classification).
- Solid procedures for administering K-Quest.
- A thorough understanding of the process that took us from the universality of K-PAQ to the specificity of K-Quest. We could now design a knowledge questionnaire for any job classification.
- Confidence in the validity of including preanswers for knowledge-core questions.

In order to administer K-Quest more broadly, we had to develop a process for creating knowledge questionnaires for every participating job classification. We accomplished this objective through these steps:

Step 1.   Appointment of an overall coordinator with responsibility for K-Quest development and administration throughout the unit.

Step 2.   Selection of a peer design team for every job classification for which a knowledge questionnaire would be prepared. This small group of peer incumbents within each job classification would develop the pre-answers to the knowledge-core questions for their job classifications, which would be inserted into K-Quest prior to its administration.

Step 3.   Selection of appropriate K-Quest and knowledge profile technology to harvest the critical operational knowledge from incumbents and reformat it into the knowledge profile. This process is discussed in detail later in the chapter.

Step 4.   Development and finalization of the content and format of K-Quest for each job classification participating in continuity management.

With completion of the fourth step, we had a knowledge questionnaire for each job classification. Now, we had only to administer it to the participating incumbents.

Administering the Knowledge Questionnaire

For reasons that are described later, we decided that a full day should be devoted to K-Quest administration. We flirted briefly with the idea of a Western theme (as in Knowledge Roundup), a sports theme (as in Knowledge Plays), and a space theme (as in Knowledge Launch), but all three ideas lost out to the simpler and more direct Continuity Management Orientation Day. While one of our members objected to "a whole day away from work," it was hardly that.

The orientation day served several purposes, the most important of which was to signal a change in the way in which WedgeMark would approach knowledge continuity in the future. A second, but no less important, function was to make K-Quest administration a collaborative endeavor. We were well aware that it was much easier to harvest knowledge that was volunteered than knowledge that was demanded, so we wanted to make the process of harvesting that knowledge a group effort, with constructive and supportive competition and collaboration among incumbents.

We were also intent on ensuring that incumbents were aware of the K-Quest benefits that would accrue to them as well as to their successors. Incumbents had to perceive that the K-Quest process that created value for WedgeMark and future successors would also create value for them if we were to get the full cooperation we wanted. With that in mind, we emphasized the insights generated by the knowledge analyses in K-Quest and the ongoing reference capabilities of the profile.

Finally, we wanted a full day to ensure that all incumbents had time to reflect on what they *knew* or needed to *learn*. Ironically, reflection time is increasingly scarce in the rush of the Information Age, despite the fact that it has never been more necessary. Reflection organizes existing knowledge and creates new knowledge; it grows the knowledge asset. A full day of orientation makes reflection time available and allows managers to explore their knowledge bases and knowledge needs in a structured way.

The underlying themes of Continuity Management Orientation Day were the value of knowledge and the value of WedgeMark employees who create that knowledge. Knowledge workers completing K-Quest were continually reminded of their knowledge contributions and encouraged to build those contributions by taking full advantage of the questionnaire. During the administration process, peer incumbents were grouped together in twos and threes and were supported in working together to complete their knowledge questionnaires.

Continuity Management Orientation Day included the following elements:

- An explanation of the acute and chronic threats to WedgeMark profits and productivity posed by knowledge loss through job turnover and impending baby-boomer retirements.
- An introduction to continuity management and why it effectively counters these threats, including an explanation of its principles, concepts, and methodologies.
- An explanation of the competitive advantages that accrue to the organization and its members as a result of implementing continuity management.
- A discussion of the benefits to incumbents of participating in continuity management.
- A description of the revised promotion, performance appraisal, and reward systems being introduced to support continuity management.
- An introduction to the knowledge profile, including its purpose, content, and use, so that incumbents would better understand K-Quest and its role in the development of the knowledge profile and the continuity management process.
- Instruction and training in how to complete K-Quest and how to update the knowledge profile, including an explanation of associated technologies.
- Questions from participants.
- Administration of K-Quest to each participating employee.

Continuity Management Orientation Day was surprisingly successful. Discussions about knowledge loss and knowledge discontinuities struck home with participants. Incumbents were excited by the prospect of stemming the knowledge loss at WedgeMark, increasing their productivity, and building a competitive advantage.

Selecting Technology for K-Quest and the Knowledge Profile

K-Quest turned out to be much more than a questionnaire. It was an analytical tool composed of a set of questions that we could deploy in whatever format we chose in order to identify, analyze, and harvest an incumbent's critical operational knowledge. The selection of K-Quest technology proved to be crucial because it was this technology that would:

- Take the incumbent's critical operational knowledge harvested through the knowledge questionnaire and convert it into the operational knowledge for the successor contained in the knowledge profile. In other words, this technology would bridge the differing perspectives of the supplier of knowledge and the consumer of knowledge.
- Allow incumbents to continually update their knowledge profiles and to integrate this process with other job activities.
- Make the knowledge profile an integral part of the knowledge management system.

So while we were approaching the selection of technology from the perspective of K-Quest, we were also approaching it from the perspective of the knowledge profile. It was this dual perspective on technology that we had to accommodate as we developed the guidelines for selecting K-Quest technology.

"But technology isn't everything," Sarah reminded us, as we began our exploration of available options.

"No," Rob agreed, "it isn't. But since it *is* an integral part of both K-Quest *and* the knowledge profile, and since the knowledge profile *is* everything, technology is one very high priority."

It was certainly that. Through meetings with the IT department and interviews of key people, we examined a broad spectrum of technological options for K-Quest and the resulting knowledge profile. These options ranged from simple technology to highly interactive technology at the cutting edge. Data entry, for example, could proceed along a spectrum from handwritten notes to word processing to e-mails to voice-activated dictation to audio and video to portals that encompassed all these methods. We examined the full spectrum of technological sophistication, beginning with a paper-based system, progressing to stand-alone PCs (with or without video and audio capabilities), then to data-based systems, and finally to Web-based systems (without or without video capabilities). Every point on this spectrum had advantages and disadvantages: cost capabilities, user preferences, and so forth. Those of us who were not technologically oriented encountered a mind-numbing array of technological terms: groupware, data mining, mind mapping, crawling search engines, push technology, portals, and acronyms and cleverly phrased terms of all kinds. It seemed to make sense to the technology people, however, and we left it up to them to develop specific proposals with pros and cons. There were, however, some general guidelines that we gave them to guide their work and their decision making as they took on the task of developing alternatives.

The goals we had in mind for the K-Quest and knowledge profile technology were based on ideals that we might not be able to fully realize because of cost constraints and other limitations, but that were, nonetheless, worthy targets. Our fundamental objective was to choose technology that would enable us to realize as completely as possible the full potential of the profile and its operational knowledge. The more sophisticated the technology we could employ, the more likely we were to achieve that objective, but the more expensive that technology would be. As we explored the options, we realized that continuity management could work through less sophisticated technology that utilized the single PC as well as through more sophisticated Web-based technology that utilized a corporate portal.

The basic trade-off, therefore, was cost versus functionality. The right technology would have to satisfy the competing and, to some degree, mutually exclusive factors of cost and system capabilities. The costs that we were most concerned about were those associated with developing, implementing, updating, and maintaining the technology; training people in the technology; and the opportunity costs of using the technology (technology that is easier to use has lower usage opportunity costs, but often higher setup costs). We wanted a knowledge profile that was as easy to use, update, and access (and a K-Quest that was as easy to administer) as funding would allow. Ideally, we wanted technology that would allow employees to access the operational knowledge they needed *at the time they needed it,* providing the immediate access to knowledge that emerging problems and opportunities often demand.

At the high end of technological sophistication, rather amazing things can happen with continuity management. For example, as employees are completing their K-Quests, technology can automatically cross-fill and cross-link knowledge data that appears under more than one knowledge category and link the profile to all relevant data and information resources. The profile itself can be a permanent link on the corporate portal, providing instant access to all 20 knowledge subcategories and instantaneous updating when necessary. Created in this way, the profile becomes a virtual partner in the planning and execution of decisions and activities that contribute mightily to knowledge continuity and to increased productivity. What we discovered in guiding the selection of the technology, however, was that we did not require high-end technology to achieve knowledge continuity at Wedge-Mark. It could be accomplished through a savvy modification of existing knowledge management software.

As the Dream Team closed out its work on K-Quest, we looked back with a sense of accomplishment and a hint of nostalgia. Not that we were at the end of our project yet, but we were beginning to see it. We were in the last quarter of the continuity management implementation process, and we had arrived at the knowledge profile. What remained was to take the knowledge captured in K-Quest, convert it to the knowledge in the profile, and then develop the procedures that would transfer that knowledge to the successors of our departing incumbents. So, in the words of Mr. Spock's niece, we were about to "boldly go where no one has gone before." We moved on to creating the knowledge profile.

11

Creating the Knowledge Profile

Knowledge Profiles carry the knowledge DNA of an organization. As transporters of the genetic code of corporate knowledge, knowledge profiles transfer to successive employee generations the critical operational knowledge through which an organization builds its productivity, its quality, and its capacity for innovation. The cycle of knowledge preservation and creation that the profile enables makes it possible for each employee generation to profit from the lessons of preceding generations and so produce a powerful knowledge legacy and a true learning organization. This virtuous cycle enhances employee competencies and delivers the prized competitive advantages that characterize a continuity-managed organization.

K-Quest is the instrument through which critical operational knowledge is harvested from incumbent employees, but the knowledge profile is the means through which successors acquire it. The focus of K-Quest is on knowledge capture and the incumbent employee. The focus of the knowledge profile is on knowledge acquisition and the successor employee. The two instruments reflect two different goals, and two different perspectives even though they deal with precisely the *same* knowledge.

Once technology has converted the completed K-Quests into knowledge profiles, a three-part process is employed to validate the operational knowledge and ensure its currency:

1. Meetings of peer incumbents to discuss and validate the operational knowledge harvested through K–Quest
2. Regularly scheduled updates of the knowledge profile and as needed
3. Updates of the knowledge profile resulting from annual peer incumbent meetings and quarterly online meetings

The following section explains the process in more detail.

Meetings of Peer Incumbents

The Dream Team had determined early on that a review of the knowledge gleaned from K–Quest and contained in the knowledge profile was warranted. Everyone liked the idea of peer incumbents meeting formally to discuss what they had learned from completing their knowledge questionnaires. Therefore, we proposed a one-day meeting of peer incumbents to discuss, validate, and expand the operational knowledge they had identified in K–Quest. If the knowledge profile provides a structure for WedgeMark employees to understand the critical operational knowledge they use, peer incumbent meetings give them the opportunity to analyze that knowledge structure, test its validity, and monitor its contents. Peer incumbent meetings generate knowledge because they force incumbents to analyze their knowledge bases and their evolving knowledge needs in light of existing and emergent knowledge requirements, but always in the context of achieving individual and corporate objectives. No other forum at WedgeMark affords incumbents such a rich opportunity.

While the meetings were made up of incumbents in the same job classification, none of us particularly liked the term *peer incumbent meeting,* because we thought it sounded formal, forced, and nonproductive. Some of us lobbied for *peer incumbent gathering* because it better described the collaborative nature of these learning opportunities for employees with common interests. But we decided that the phrase was disingenuous (we weren't gathering, we were attending) and then the acronym—PIG—posed a problem.

The term we finally settled on was *PEAK meeting,* with PEAK an acronym for *peer evaluation of accumulated knowledge.* PEAK meetings were held for all incumbents within a single job classification. The format of the meeting was straightforward. Each PEAK group selected one of its members to serve as informal leader. The purposes of the meeting were to assess the effectiveness of the knowledge questionnaire, validate the operational knowledge gathered through K-Quest, develop additional pre-answers for K-Quest, generate new questions of K-PAQ, and expand the knowledge networks of the participants.

K-Quest Assessment

PEAK participants were asked to evaluate the instructions, format, content, and administration of K-Quest and to make recommendations for improving them. Some of the questions that we suggested PEAK leaders propose included:

Instructions
- Were the K-Quest instructions clearly stated, and did they provide adequate guidance for answering the questions? Two concerns that surfaced in the meetings were how much knowledge should be included in an answer and how the answers should be formatted (bullets, phrases, complete sentences, etc).
- Was it clear how and when to modify pre-answered questions?
- Were the instructions for the technology used in completing K-Quest comprehensive and easy to understand?
- Was it apparent that peer collaboration was encouraged during K-Quest administration?

Format
- What suggestions do you have for improving the format of K-Quest?
- Did the knowledge categories and related questions appear in the proper order?
- Was the technology effective?
- How could the technology be improved?
- What format changes would have facilitated the development of your answers or improved their quality?

Questions in K-Quest
- In relation to your job classification and, again, in relation to your specific job: What questions, if any, were redundant, irrelevant, unclear, or in need of being combined with other questions?
- What questions should be added to K-Quest to better harvest the operational knowledge for your position or your job classification? These questions will be added to future versions.

Administration
- How could Continuity Management Orientation Day be improved?
- How could the administration of K-Quest be improved?

Operational Knowledge Validation and Transfer

One of the primary purposes of the PEAK meetings was to validate the answers to K-Quest and, hence, to validate the operational knowledge content of the knowledge profiles. We asked the peers to help each other in validating knowledge that was held in common across the job classification. In this way, the peer incumbents vetted the operational knowledge of the profiles. The methodology employed was for the leader to take the group through K-Quest, knowledge category by knowledge category (sometimes question by question), calling on those who were willing to share their answers with others and managing the sometimes lively discussions that followed.

In the process of validating their answers, incumbents shared operational knowledge among themselves, often for the first time. This aspect of the PEAK meeting integrates continuity management and knowledge management by combining knowledge harvesting with knowledge sharing. As a result, incumbents were challenged to create new knowledge, which they did, as well as to incorporate new knowledge from their peers into their own operational knowledge bases. In some cases, they corrected perceptual or knowledge errors that had constrained their productivity and performance. The PEAK meetings thus facilitated the sharing of best practices.

Some of the most fruitful discussions centered around the knowledge analysis in K-Quest: knowledge leverage points, missing knowledge, and obsolete knowledge. The analysis of job characteristics also produced important insights, especially in the area of job functions and the relationship of productivity to knowledge. Many of the incumbents confirmed that they left the PEAK meeting with a clearer understanding of how they used knowledge and also of the kind of knowledge they needed to jump-start their performance. Incumbents also came away with a better understanding of their goals, skills, and resources and how they could be marshaled for high-yield activities. The results were subtle and, in some cases, not-so-subtle job redesigns that capitalized on new opportunities.

Identification of Additional Knowledge for Pre-answered Questions

Knowledge that is relatively uniform across the job classification is captured by pre-answered questions developed by the peer design team. Some pre-answers are complete and some are not, requiring additions or modifications. A complete pre-answer might be the corporate history or mission statement of WedgeMark. Performance appraisal, by contrast, may contain official doctrine provided by HR as well as amendments developed by incumbents that more accurately reflect the process.

The pre-answered questions in K-Quest speed its completion, because incumbents have only to modify these answers rather than create them from scratch. The PEAK meeting provides an opportunity for all peer incumbents in the job classification to expand the pre-answers or to propose new ones.

Generation of New Questions for K-PAQ

K-PAQ is a databank of knowledge-focused questions for all job classifications and positions at WedgeMark. It describes the comprehensive structure of operational knowledge at WedgeMark, offering a concise look at the core knowledge used by the company to develop, produce, and sell its products and services and to generate its revenue and profits. The operational knowledge structure at WedgeMark (i.e., the 20 knowledge categories that define operational knowledge at WedgeMark), is expected to vary little over time. But the subcategories and knowledge content of those categories is constantly changing as the operational knowledge itself changes.

Expansion of Knowledge Networks

PEAK meetings were designed to create a setting for personal interaction that would expand an incumbent's knowledge network, encourage the formation of future communities of practice, and build excitement for continuity management. At WedgeMark, they facilitated knowledge sharing throughout the job classifications by creating a sense of community, a common purpose, and a mutual commitment among incumbents. The meetings also encouraged employee buy-in of continuity management processes and increased the motivation to participate.

We found that the benefits gained from group conversation and knowledge exchange could be recreated in follow-up PEAK meetings held annually. These annual meetings contributed to the evolving operational knowledge of incumbents. But they did something else. They added knowledge input from new incumbents—successors who had never participated in a PEAK meeting before—to the collective knowledge of their peers. These meetings were also used to revalidate preanswers to the knowledge core questions in K-Quest.

Follow-up PEAK meetings were so successful that we instituted quarterly PEAK forums on operational knowledge. These relatively short conferences were conducted entirely on the corporate intranet and were focused on high-impact knowledge updates and refinements developed over the past quarter. For a few job classifications, semiannual PEAK forum meetings were more appropriate than quarterly meetings. Some of these meetings evolved into communities of practice, which are discussed later in this chapter.

PEAK Meeting Attendance and Format

The number of PEAK meetings that were held for a single job classification was a function of the number of incumbents in that job classification as well as certain other factors, such as the number of people at a given location. PEAK meetings were not limited in size. When the meeting consisted of seven or more members, however, we divided the peers into PEAK groups of three to four participants. At the conclusion of the small group meetings, someone from each group reported the high points of the discussion to the meeting as a whole, so that the knowledge exchange was complete. In large organizations with many incumbents in the same job classification but at different sites, we found that holding a special meeting with representatives from all the sites was a helpful follow-up. These meetings made it possible for incumbents from different sites to exchange knowledge and viewpoints, an example of the integration of knowledge management and continuity management.

Although peers were not forced to reveal their answers, almost all of them did. They were enthusiastic in these discussions and conscientious in their responses. They had been looking for the opportunity to engage in this kind of knowledge exchange—the kind that had previously occurred only around the watercooler, in ad hoc gatherings at lunch, and informal meetings at the end of day. By providing a forum for incumbents to compare notes on their K-Quest answers, PEAK meetings allowed them to share their knowledge bases and to explore differences in their knowledge. As a result, the PEAKs stimulated exciting knowledge trades and spread new operational knowledge among incumbents.

Not all WedgeMark employees have a peer incumbent. In some job classifications, there are no peers at all. In other classifications, employees holding the same job classification perform such different tasks that they are barely peers. For employees in these positions, the task of completing K-Quest can be an isolating experience. To reduce that sense of isolation, we had them complete their K-Quests as full participants in Continuity Management Orientation Day and attend the PEAK meeting for the most closely related job classification. While not ideal, this proved to be an effective solution.

Communities of Practice

The emphasis in continuity management on identifying and sharing critical operational knowledge creates a natural environment for the creation of *communities of practice*, which are important elements of both continuity management and knowledge management. Communities of practice are relatively small groups of people with a common knowledge need and a common sense of purpose who choose to work together. Generally, they operate outside of the formal organizational hierarchy. Communities of practice can be encouraged and even catalyzed, but not mandated. They are usually self-selecting and often self-creating, but not always. They are permeable in the sense that members are free to come and go.

Communities of practice may be made up of peers who share a common job classification or employees from different job classifications who share a common project, task set, or goal. Communities of practice are, in the strictest sense, networks for knowledge exchange, validation, and creation. They promote the transfer of knowledge between experts and novices as well as among experts, who find their own knowledge augmented or corrected by newer or better ideas. A need for knowledge is the irritant around which the community-of-practice pearl is created.

The most important knowledge exchanges in an organization are likely to take place around the watercooler, whether literally or figuratively, as people meet to gather knowledge, sort through alternatives, or seek new solutions. Knowledge thus creates and uses its own networks—or takes advantage of existing networks perceived to be authentic. Communities of practice are a common form of these knowledge networks and are especially good at providing knowledge that can be brought to bear on specific problems.

At WedgeMark, true communities of practice developed from the PEAK meetings. Some of the peers who had profited from the knowledge sharing and had enjoyed the interaction of the PEAK meetings instituted informal meetings among themselves. Others inaugurated online exchanges that evolved into ongoing conversations with other WedgeMark employees, both within their own peer groups and, when warranted, across peer groups. Still others created bulletin boards that served the whole community of peers and became virtual communities of practice. The virtual communities proved to be especially exciting because they later spread throughout WedgeMark and often evolved into cross-disciplinary communities of practice.

Deloitte Research, a thought leadership organization established by Deloitte & Touche and Deloitte Consulting, reports on a similar phenomenon at Chevron. More than 100 such communities at Chevron (dubbed *collaborative knowledge networks*) link different professions around such diverse topics as process engineering, Web application development, and nonconventional drilling. The advantage of these virtual communities is their extraordinary capability for rapid knowledge sharing. This exchange results in improved processes, quicker responses to changing customer needs, streamlined product development, greater innovation, and higher productivity.

Ultimately, some of the communities of practice at WedgeMark became quite cohesive. The most famous declared itself a *peer incumbent tribe,* coined a name for itself, developed its own logo, referred to its meetings as *PEAK experiences,* and put up an electronic bulletin board that it shared with other peer groups. Perhaps inevitably, this peer incumbent tribe (PIT) referred to its bulletin board as the *PIT Stop,* which became the slang for all bulletin boards for PEAK groups and other communities of practice at WedgeMark. What started out as a need for sharing existing knowledge had turned into a knowledge genertor for incumbents as well as their successors.

The knowledge profile creates a virtual community of practice between new hires and their predecessors. Knowledge profiles make possible a kind of dialogue between incumbents and their successors, one that is grounded in mutual objectives, similar contexts, shared competencies, and common information needs. Modern technologies provide various means through which this dialogue can take place—from interactive databases to video-streamed storytelling to historical narratives to frequently asked questions. Multimedia-based material is a powerful means of incumbent knowledge transfer and successor acquisition. Through the knowledge profile, a successor has access to the thoughts, perceptions, and insights of generations of previous incumbents. Properly constructed and populated, the knowledge profile provides virtual mentors for every new hire.

Updating the Knowledge Profile

The one aspect of technology that is critical to the knowledge profile but not relevant to K-Quest is the updating function. Because knowledge profiles are created through K-Quest but updated as profiles, this function is supremely important. The value of the knowledge profile, whether to incumbent or successor, is dependent on the timeliness and relevance of the operational knowledge it contains. Because the value of such knowledge is time- and situation-specific, that value rises or declines as a function of relevancy. Obsolete or missing information is worthless in the Information Age, and a knowledge profile that is not complete and up to date quickly losses its potency. New material must be added to the profile as it becomes relevant, and obsolete material must be eliminated or archived as it becomes irrelevant. Regularly scheduled updating of the profile is therefore mandatory. In an ideal continuity management system, technology facilitates this process by integrating the update with other knowledge operations. Because some job classifications are characterized by faster-changing knowledge than others, profile updates should be based on how rapidly the content of the profile changes. Knowledge categories that feature common knowledge shared by all incumbents in the same job classification, such as Key Operating Statistics or Key Information, might be updated daily by a knowledge profile Webmaster.

Beyond keeping the knowledge profile current, however, updating serves another function. It expands and enriches the operational knowledge in the profile. Incumbents know more about what they know and can access what they know in greater detail when they are *using* their knowledge than when they are trying to *recall* it. While K–Quest harvests basic operational knowledge and provides a framework for that knowledge, updating adds details and nuances that are remembered only as they are used.

The Lite Profile

As a result of the knowledge continuity assessment, we knew that certain WedgeMark employees would require less comprehensive knowledge profiles than others. Therefore, we divided the knowledge profiles into two types. We dubbed the less comprehensive version the *knowledge profile lite,* or, as we finally came to call it informally, the *lite profile.* Formally, we referred to it as *profile-2.* Each profile type follows a different developmental process. The lite profiles are easier and less costly to develop than the full profile because they harvest less operational knowledge, but they serve their purposes just as well. The following paragraphs describe the development processes for the lite profile and the circumstances under which such profiles are warranted.

Lite Profile Criteria

The nature of the job-specific operational knowledge determines whether a full knowledge profile or a lite profile is appropriate. A lite profile is selected when the following criteria apply:

- The operational knowledge is mostly explicit (contained in documents or databases).
- Whatever tacit knowledge is contained in the profile is not unique, but is generally shared by all employees in the position.
- The tacit knowledge changes little from one employee generation to another or can easily be converted to explicit knowledge for transfer to a successor.
- Job activities are largely routine, involving few unique events or interactions with others that require complex decisions.
- The job is not related to the core competencies of the organization, and its potential impact on the organization is low.
- An analysis of knowledge leverage points, knowledge needs, or knowledge strengths and weaknesses can be conducted for the entire job

classification and need not be conducted for individual positions within the classification.

Although the types of profiles (full and lite) appear dichotomous, they are actually points on a spectrum. Within the lite category, for example, there can be significant variations in the complexity of the operational knowledge. A sophisticated lite profile will approximate a less complex full profile. However, the two profile categories are developed through different processes. The developmental process for the full profile has already been described. The process for developing the lite profile is described in the paragraphs that follow.

Developing the Knowledge Questionnaire Lite (K-Quest Lite)

The knowledge questionnaire for the lite profile is developed from the same K-PAQ database as the full profile. The major difference is that most of the questions in K-Quest Lite will be pre-answered, and little incumbent modification of those answers will take place. A peer design team composed of peer incumbents from each job classification is appointed to develop K-Quest Lite. Team members are selected on the basis of job performance and productivity. The team's objectives are:

- To determine which K-PAQ questions are suitable for the job classification.
- To determine which K-Quest Lite questions should be preanswered.
- To develop preanswers for all appropriate questions by either generating new preanswers or by adapting preanswers from K-Quest.

Continuity Management Orientation Day for K-Quest Lite

The continuity management orientation day for K-Quest Lite is similar in format to the orientation day held for administration of K-Quest. The content is adapted from the full day to meet the needs of the particular job classification. Generally, less than a full day is required, because K-Quest Lite is less complex than K-Quest and so requires less time to complete. We believe strongly in holding the orientation day even for K-Quest Lite, however, because it focuses employees' attention on the need for knowledge continuity, familiarizes them with the nature of their operational knowledge, and commits them to regular profile updates.

Technology for K-Quest Lite

Technology for K-Quest Lite may be less sophisticated than the technology employed for K-Quest. For example, the audio and video options in highly sophisticated K-Quest systems are not necessary for K-Quest Lite.

PEAK Meetings for K-Quest Lite

We debated whether PEAK meetings should be held so that incumbents could discuss and validate their answers to K-Quest Lite. We finally decided that it would depend on how comprehensive the resulting lite profiles were. At the less comprehensive end of the spectrum, we concluded that PEAK meetings were simply not necessary. Instead, meetings were held to brief incumbents on best practices that arose out of the meetings of the peer design team. At the more comprehensive end of the spectrum, however, PEAK meetings proved to be useful. One determining factor was whether we thought that the development of communities of practice for that job classification was desirable. If it was, we tended to recommend PEAK meetings; if it was not, we did not.

Lite Profile Updates

Lite profile updates were made by the peer design team and communicated to peer incumbents at semiannual meetings held for that purpose. These updates were related to changes in explicit knowledge or new best practices that needed to be shared.

Profile Improvements

The knowledge profile is the central transfer vehicle for critical operational knowledge, but it is only a snapshot of knowledge taken at a moment in time. If the profile is to accurately reflect the dynamic process of knowledge creation, transfer, and acquisition, it must be continually updated, which may mean content, format, and process changes. *Knowledge interviews* conducted three months into a new hire's employment address form and process issues. In the knowledge interview, new hires are asked to evaluate format, content, and transfer procedures, including the effectiveness of their profile partner or phased mentor (profile partners and phased mentors are discussed in Chapter 12, "Operational Knowledge Transfer and Acquisition.") The evaluation of the knowledge profile included:

- The ease with which the operational knowledge could be accessed, applied, and understood
- The value of the operational knowledge, including most valuable and least valuable aspects
- How well the profile technology facilitated or enhanced profile use, especially the acquisition or utilization of operational knowledge and the ease with which knowledge links and other profile-associated documents could be accessed
- How well the profile-partner or phased-mentor system worked, including suggestions for improving it
- Additional knowledge categories or subcategories or frequently asked questions
- Additional questions for K-PAQ
- Process suggestions regarding any aspect of profile creation or transfer
- Process suggestions regarding K-Quest administration or PEAK meetings

We also asked the PEAK meetings to address these same process-improvement issues on a regular basis in order to ensure that the profiles remained as current in design and administration as they were in content.

Profile Caveats

Three caveats emerged from our conversations and debates about the continuity management process and the design of the knowledge profile. The caveats are not negatives as much as they are realities that have to be considered in implementing continuity management.

Start-Up Costs

The start-up cost of developing a knowledge profile is significantly higher than the cost of maintaining it, because everything has to be created from scratch, including K-PAQ and K-Quest. The initial investment in time and technology to create the continuity management structure as well as the original contents of K-PAQ and the profiles should be allocated across the participating positions and amortized over the life of the job classifications.

The Value of the Profile

The value of any knowledge profile is inevitably greater for the organization and for a successor than it is for the incumbent who created it. While many rewards come from the analysis that K-Quest completion requires and from incumbent participation in PEAK meetings and communities of practice, the value of the profile to the incumbent cannot compare to its value to the successor or to the organization itself. Knowledge continuity is more meaningful (and, hence, important) to successors than to incumbents, and it is for this reason that intrinsic and extrinsic reward systems must be aligned to support continuity management. However, significant benefits accrue to incumbents, and it is imperative that management continue to emphasize those benefits and to construct an organizational culture that supports continuity management.

Using the Profile

The knowledge profile was created for successor employees. That context determines the design and implementation of the profile and is the basic criterion by which it should be judged. The knowledge profile is the means by which successor employees with little or no job-specific operational knowledge can learn their jobs in a quick, efficient, and effective manner. While few experienced employees will spend time searching extensive databases for answers to specific questions, new hires will spend time in extensive exploration of their knowledge profiles in order to acquire the basic operational knowledge they need to succeed in their new positions. The mechanisms of *knowledge management* transfer—and how well they are accepted by diverse employees—should not be confused with the mechanisms of *continuity management* transfer—and how well they are accepted by successors.

The two mechanisms are not the same, because they were not designed to achieve the same purpose. The knowledge profile is highly effective in transferring critical operational knowledge to successors, particularly when it is used in a comprehensive knowledge transfer program involving a profile partner or phase mentor and supported by the organizational culture and reward system.

Transferring the Knowledge Profile

With the creation of the knowledge profile, our last remaining task was to determine how to transfer to successor employees the critical operational knowledge gathered through K-Quest and contained in the knowledge profile. The focus of our work thus shifted from capturing operational knowledge to passing that knowledge legacy to the next generation of employees.

"There are two processes we need to consider," the Chip said as we took up the task. "The first is how to get people to keep their profiles current so they still have value when they leave. The second is how to handle the knowledge transfer itself."

"You're talking motivation," Roger responded.

"In the first instance," the Chip agreed. "In the second, we're talking about knowledge transfer procedures and opportunities."

"I'm motivated," Roger said enthusiastically.

"But you're . . . *unusual,* Roger," the Chip suggested. "And you've been so involved in the process of developing continuity management that you've bought in to it."

"Our next project," Andre said, "is a comprehensive realignment of the organizational reward systems if we intend to make this work. While there are a lot of internal rewards to continuity management, it will fail if K-Quest administration, knowledge profile creation, profile updating, and knowledge transfer are not rewarded."

"We also have to develop the transfer procedures for the knowledge profile," Roger reminded us.

When we had finished that task, our design for continuity management at WedgeMark would be complete. Because we were learning as we went along, we knew that many changes were yet to come. These changes would collectively refine continuity management as it became an integral part of what we did at WedgeMark.

I was among the first to produce a knowledge profile. Although I had played a major role in creating continuity management at WedgeMark, I was not alone in developing a sense of ownership about my profile and a feeling that it was something valuable I had created. While operational knowledge may be personal, it is also an organizational asset. It belongs not just to us but to the organization that helped us create it and to our successors for whom it is destined. Many of us came to take great pride in our profiles and to regard them as true knowledge assets that we wanted to pass on to our successors. The profile was our handoff in the knowledge relay we were running. It was a worthy legacy.

Part III

Knowledge Asset Management

Brett's journal in Part II, "Confessions of a Continuity Manager," is a literary device through which to study the principles and concepts of continuity management as they might have been developed in an American company. Its chapters describe the continuity management processes through which critical operational knowledge could be harvested from incumbent employees in an efficient, effective, and comprehensive way, yielding benefits for incumbents, their successors, and their organizations.

Part III departs from the format of Brett's journal and returns to the voice of the authors. While it continues with the practical implementation of continuity management, its subject matter is *knowledge transfer and acquisition* rather than knowledge harvesting. In other words, it explores the processes through which operational knowledge harvested from incumbent employees can be effectively transmitted, internalized, and acted on by their successors. Knowledge transfer and acquisition is the final set of processes in continuity management. The process of identifying critical operational knowledge and harvesting it from incumbents is incomplete and, ultimately, unproductive unless that knowledge can be successfully transferred to, and applied by, successor employees. We use the term *knowledge acquisition* in conjunction with *transfer* in Part III to emphasize that the transfer of knowledge from one employee to another does not constitute continuity management unless the receiving employee also internalizes and applies that knowledge.

Continuity management is designed to ensure both the *acquisition of existing operational knowledge* transferred by the predecessor and the *creation of new knowledge* by the successor. In continuity management, knowledge transfer and acquisition form an integrated whole. Increased productivity rests on this duality of knowledge acquisition and creation. For literary purposes, *knowledge transfer and acquisition* is sometimes abbreviated to *knowledge transfer*, but acquisition is always implied.

Part III consists of three chapters. Chapter 12 describes the principles and procedures of knowledge transfer and acquisition as they are applied in continuity management. Chapter 13 examines the context in which that transfer and acquisition take place: the organizational culture and reward system. Chapter 14 describes the integration of continuity management and knowledge management.

In Part I, we use the phrase *knowledge asset management* to refer to an overarching process that integrates the two processes of continuity management (the vertical transfer of knowledge between employee generations) and knowledge management (the horizontal transfer of knowledge within an employee generation). In Chapter 14, we return to this concept of knowledge asset management by describing how knowledge continuity and knowledge management processes can be merged into a holistic process of knowledge asset management that expands an organization's knowledge base and maximizes the exploitation of its knowledge asset.

12

Operational Knowledge Transfer and Acquisition

The primary goals of continuity management are to preserve and then enhance the critical operational knowledge of departing employees by transferring that knowledge to their successors in such a way that the successors can internalize that knowledge, apply it, and create new knowledge from it as quickly as possible. This phase of continuity management—knowledge acquisition—is focused on the goal of moving new hires quickly up the learning curve, making them as productive as possible as rapidly as possible, and turning them into high-performing employees for whom innovation and knowledge creation are both facilitated and characteristic.

The harvesting of knowledge, the transfer of knowledge, and the acquisition of knowledge are three different, but related, processes. In continuity management:

- *Knowledge harvesting* is accomplished primarily through the knowledge questionnaire (K-Quest) administered to all participating employees and supplemented by knowledge gathered, compared, and exchanged in the PEAK meetings of peer incumbents and other forums for sharing knowledge among peers.

- *Knowledge transfer* is accomplished primarily through the knowledge profile, which contains the critical operational knowledge for each job classification and for each job within that classification.
- *Knowledge acquisition* is accomplished primarily through the design and content of the knowledge profile, the process through which the profile is presented to successor employees, and the organizational culture and reward systems, which support both the creation of the profile and the acquisition of the knowledge it contains.

Knowledge transfer does not ensure knowledge acquisition. It is tempting to focus on knowledge transfer at the expense of knowledge acquisition and to settle for an elaborate transfer system that nonetheless fails to result in the acquisition and subsequent application of operational knowledge by new hires. The knowledge transfer and acquisition process is governed by various principles that determine the most effective processes, procedures, and activities. These principles are derived from:

- Research on the nature of knowledge and on how it is acquired
- Lessons from successful and unsuccessful knowledge management initiatives over the last decade in many different organizations
- The particular knowledge transfer and acquisition problems and opportunities of continuity management

Knowledge Transfer and Acquisition Principles

Knowledge is contextually based and highly personal; so personal, in fact, that it is an essential part of our identity as human beings. The knowledge we have gained—and, in a very real sense, *earned*—is part of our concept of self and is precious to us. We take pride in what we know, whether acquired through formal instruction or personal experience, because it is often hard won and because it is the basis of how we see the world. The extent to which we are willing to share our knowledge depends on the circumstances in which it will be shared and on the individuals with whom we will be sharing it, including *how* the knowledge will be transferred to, and received by, the object of the transfer. Knowledge management has provided some important lessons regarding the personal nature of knowledge and the conditions under which it is most likely to be shared and acquired. From these lessons, two major principles have emerged regarding knowledge transfer and acquisition, one dealing with trust and the other with compensation:

- *We are more likely to share knowledge in an atmosphere of trust that relieves our fears about sharing our knowledge than in an atmosphere where trust is absent.*   In other words, we are more likely to share knowledge with people in whom we have confidence or with people we believe will value our knowledge by being attentive and appreciative *even if they don't agree with it.* Conversely, we are reluctant to share our knowledge with anyone we think might disparage it or dismiss it. For the same reason, we are less likely to expose our knowledge in a public or semipublic forum or to send it to an anonymous repository (such as a database) than we are to share it privately.
- *We are more likely to share knowledge when we believe that we will receive something in return for sharing it.*   That return can take many forms, from direct compensation for overcoming our fears of sharing knowledge to expressions of appreciation as a reward for giving knowledge.

Both of these general principles have to be applied if knowledge transfer and acquisition are to be successful.

Create Opportunities for Knowledge Exchange

A simple but powerful idea in knowledge transfer and acquisition may seem self-evident: Opportunities to exchange knowledge will increase the likelihood that existing knowledge will be shared and that new knowledge will be created. Continuity management capitalizes on this principle in the design of its processes, which create collaborative environments. These processes take advantage of the relational aspects of knowledge sharing, the influence of social processes, and the importance of peer participation and encouragement. They include:

- K-PAQ (knowledge profile analysis questions) development
- K-Quest (knowledge questionnaire) development
- Pre-answer construction for the knowledge-core questions in K-Quest, which is accomplished by the peer design teams
- K-Quest administration, including the discussion of answers by peer incumbents during continuity management orientation day
- Knowledge sharing and creation during PEAK meetings
- Annual and quarterly follow-up PEAK meetings of peer incumbents through which incumbents keep their knowledge bases current and relevant

- New-hire orientation, which introduces new employees to continuity management and its procedures (described in detail later in this chapter)
- Implementation of mentoring and peer-support programs and changes in organizational rewards, which encourages continuity management activities (as described in the next chapter)

Facilitate Mutual Knowledge Sharing between New Hires and the Organization

Knowledge transfer and acquisition is not a one-way street. The knowledge profile is designed to be a means of transferring knowledge *to* new employees *and* a means of transferring knowledge *from* new employees to established employees and to the organization itself. The profile solicits three categories of new knowledge from new hires, making knowledge acquisition a reciprocal process between the organization and its employees. These categories of knowledge are described in the following paragraphs.

Existing operational knowledge that new hires bring with them from their previous positions that has direct application to their new positions.   Because most new hires take positions that are related, similar, or even virtually identical to their old positions, they bring valuable operational knowledge with them from the organizations they have left. This knowledge can take many forms: knowledge of superior policies, better procedures, enhanced processes, improved approaches, and so forth. It is not that new hires don't have any operational knowledge; it's that they don't have job-critical operational knowledge related to their new positions.

In fact, it is well recognized that new hires have valuable knowledge. Some employees are hired specifically to obtain their knowledge. A statement that this knowledge should be systematically harvested by the new organization would seem unnecessary, were it not that so few organizations are doing so. The problem is not a lack of understanding of the value of such knowledge, but the failure to institute an organized structure to harvest, evaluate, and share the knowledge. Without such a structure, new knowledge will be lost to the hiring organization. The knowledge profile provides that structure for transferring the new employee's knowledge to the organization.

New knowledge created by the employee through direct application of the operational knowledge contained in the profile.   Because new knowledge is based on old knowledge and because knowledge is constantly changing in response to changing circumstances, new employees often synthesize the knowledge they bring and the knowledge they derive through the knowledge profile to create new knowledge of great benefit to the organization. Such knowledge is new knowledge for both the employee and for the organization. New employees also create new knowledge by applying profile knowledge in different ways from their predecessors to create new organizational knowledge for the organization.

Knowledge created as a result of the fresh perspective new employees bring to their position and to the organization. New hires invariably bring a fresh perspective to their jobs that exposes organizational problems that have been undetected or ignored by established employees. Generally, however, new hires have no power to correct the inconsistencies, absurdities, or counterproductive policies and procedures they observe. An organization can take advantage of the new perspectives of incoming employees by creating a vehicle to harvest their insights as part of the knowledge transfer and acquisition process. The knowledge profile is designed to serve this purpose.

A new employee can often very quickly spot counterproductive situations to which established employees have become inured. The recently appointed dean of an eastern university observed an odd situation. While 40 percent of the students in his school attended late afternoon and early evening classes, most student services—such as registration, records, student loans, and so forth—closed at 5 P.M. The new dean's reaction was bewilderment, because the out-of-synch office hours were highly detrimental to the students and contrary to the goals of the university. Yet the situation had continued for years without attracting the attention of anyone in authority. How was that possible? The apparent reason was timing. The shift from virtually all daytime class attendance to over 40 percent late-afternoon and evening attendance had occurred so gradually that the administrators had never seen it as a problem. The dean's new perspective made it easy for him to see the absurdity of closing student services during the hours when 40 percent of the students needed them. Because he was dean of the school, he was in a position to correct the situation, which he did. But what if he had not been the dean?

The Innovations knowledge category in the knowledge profile contains three topic areas specifically designed to harvest knowledge from new employees. These knowledge topics, which are regularly updated by new hires during the first months of their employment for routine review by their superiors, are:

- *Transferred knowledge.* This knowledge was brought by new employees from their previous positions but is new knowledge to the hiring organization.
- *New knowledge.* This knowledge is created by new employees when they apply their existing knowledge to the circumstances of their new positions.
- *New perspectives.* This knowledge takes the form of recommendations for revising policies, processes, or procedures based on the employees' previous experience or as a result of their fresh perspective.

Continuity management thus provides a structure for capturing the recommendations and new knowledge of employees in the first months of their tenure.

Transfer Both Tacit and Explicit Knowledge

Like knowledge management, continuity management relies on two basic sources for knowledge transfer: documents and people. The processes through which these sources are utilized in knowledge transfer are:

- *People to documents to people.* Tacit knowledge is transferred from the heads of incumbents to the knowledge profile for future transfer to the heads of successors or other incumbents.
- *People to people.* Tacit knowledge is transferred from the heads of incumbents to the heads of successors or other incumbents through personal interaction.

Continuity management uses people-to-people knowledge-transfer processes whenever possible, because not all relevant tacit knowledge can be made explicit and codified in documents. Knowledge networks, peer incumbent meetings, profile partners, and phased mentoring are utilized whenever possible. However, people-to-documents-to-people transfer is also necessary, because much tacit knowledge can be converted to documentary form for future transfer. In addition, various documents are an essential part of operational knowledge.

The primary vehicle for knowledge transfer and acquisition in continuity management is the knowledge profile, but knowledge transfer through the profile can be supplemented by tacit transfers through incumbents (when they are available through phased mentoring or overlapping employee arrangements), profile partners (who introduce new hires to their knowledge profiles and coworkers), members of the new employees' knowledge networks, and other peers when predecessors are not available. Because operational knowledge is clarified, expanded, and generated through social interaction, continuity management provides for such interaction as frequently as possible.

Without some form of continuity management, knowledge transfers are likely to be unstructured, limited in perspective, relatively inefficient, and incomplete. With no peer collaboration, no content guide, and no other check on what is passed to the successor, an incumbent can easily transfer knowledge that is tangential or even incorrect. There is little, if any, quality control in such transfers and virtually no assistance in helping the successor acquire the knowledge. This assessment is valid for both people-to-document and people-to-people transfers when there is no continuity management.

Without some equivalent form of the knowledge profile, tacit knowledge transfers between incumbents and successors must rely solely on short-term overlap between employee generations due to retirements or transfers or postretirement initiatives that temporarily reunite successor employees with their predecessors. Yet these knowledge transfers are possible only in limited situations: retirements, job transfers, instances in which employees quit with adequate notice, and other instances in which budgetary and scheduling requirements permit employee overlap. Even in such situations, however, the operational knowledge may not have been analyzed for accuracy or relevance or been structured so that the content is comprehensive and the transfer is effective. If there is no incumbent–successor interaction, tacit knowledge transfer between predecessors and successors does not occur at all.

Without some form of knowledge profile, incumbents cannot pass their explicit operational knowledge to successors either, unless there is incumbent–successor interaction. The only knowledge available to successors is likely to be contained in pages and pages of official documents or hidden in files that cannot be readily accessed. Like the tacit knowledge in the heads of the departing employees, it may be beyond retrieval, lost to the organization and the successor.

Make Knowledge Creation a Principal Objective

Continuity management provides a different perspective from knowledge management, but it is very much aligned with the perspective of organizational learning. The primary objectives of knowledge management are to identify, extract, and codify knowledge in order to transfer it as widely as possible throughout the organization and thereby take advantage of innovation and avoid having to reinvent the wheel. Yet knowledge management has emphasized knowledge *preservation* at the expense of knowledge *creation*. In the Information Age, maintaining the existing knowledge base is not sufficient to achieve competitive advantage, which requires the continuous creation of new knowledge. Preserving existing operational knowledge is a crucial *element* of continuity management, but it is not, ultimately, the primary *goal* of continuity management, which is to create new knowledge from existing knowledge.

Knowledge profiles enable new hires to internalize operational knowledge quickly, adapt it to their current problems and opportunities, and apply it to new situations as they arise. Their profiles allow new hires to access other knowledgeable individuals who can add to their operational knowledge and help them understand how to be more productive in their new positions. In essence, the profiles marshal existing knowledge resources in the service of creating new knowledge and new applications for old knowledge as such knowledge is needed. Just-in-time knowledge acquisition provided by the profile is highly advantageous in a rapidly changing, uncertain environment. The context in which the profile is presented to the new hires reinforces the objective of knowledge creation and emphasizes the availability of peers and coworkers to assist in the knowledge acquisition and creation process.

Nancy Dixon, an authority on knowledge management and author of *Common Knowledge: How Companies Thrive by Sharing What They Know* (Dixon, 2000), points out that one of knowledge management's major contributions has been to help us see that *every* knowledge worker possesses valuable knowledge, not just a few people and not just the "best" people. "What we have learned," says Dixon, "is that people have a greater capacity to create knowledge out of what they do than we had previously realized"

(Dixon, 2002). Best practices, in other words, exist throughout an organization and throughout its job classifications.

Through the knowledge profile, continuity management encourages employees to identify their best practices, adapt the best practices of their predecessors, and generate new best practices. These best practices are then shared with everyone in the same job classification through the knowledge profiles and PEAK meetings. This approach to knowledge generation is grounded in community, knowledge networks, social interaction, and peer collaboration. It rejects rules, procedures, and dictates that constrain knowledge creation.

The focus in continuity management is not on what might be termed *hierarchical knowledge,* but on what could be called *hands-on knowledge.* Hierarchical knowledge is declared superior and prescribed. In stable times, this approach is acceptable; but in times of turbulence and constant change, it is likely to be ineffective and resented. In contrast, hands-on knowledge is generated by the person doing the work, enriched by peers, and enhanced through knowledge networks. Hands-on knowledge is local, relevant, current, modifiable, and effective. It is not decreed by management, but sought by it.

Internalize Knowledge by Incorporation, Application, and Re-creation

Famed Swiss developmental psychologist Jean Piaget, whose primary research interest was how knowledge developed in the human organism, has made an enormous contribution to our understanding of knowledge. Piaget's work makes it clear that knowledge is not static, but dynamic. In some ways, it is more *process* than content. It is continuously reordered, recreated, and reapplied by individuals as they engage in social interaction, respond to changes in their environment, and make sense of their world. Our knowledge is constantly changing because our world is constantly changing. Knowledge as a process is easy to discern in groups when synergy is present. Synergy does not result from the simple transfer of knowledge among members of the team, but from the active synthesis and application of that knowledge. Team members create new knowledge by reinterpreting, reapplying, or reusing their shared knowledge.

Knowledge profiles are the primary mechanism of knowledge transfer in continuity management, but the ultimate purpose of the profile is knowledge creation. The profile is not a prescription, but a stimulus. No knowledge created by one person or drawn from one situation is perfect for another person or another situation; it must be modified to fit the specific individual and the circumstances. The shape of the profile, its manner of transfer, and the content of its knowledge categories all recognize that the operational knowledge that incumbents transfer to their successors must be reinvented by those successors if that knowledge is to be meaningful to them and productive for their organizations.

William Seidman, CEO of Cerebyte, Inc., the company that produces knowledge harvesting and replication software, suggests that three phases are required for successful knowledge *absorption,* which is the term he uses for the process that takes place when an employee integrates new knowledge with existing knowledge in a productive way (Seidman, 2002). These phases are:

1. Initial determination that the knowledge is useable
2. Subsequent interaction with the knowledge that engages the employee and creates a sense of ownership of the new knowledge
3. Follow-up application of the knowledge in a systematic way that leads to integration with existing knowledge and increased productivity (absorption)

Each of these phases takes place in the required interactions between new hires and their knowledge profiles, which are described in more detail later in this chapter.

Make Knowledge Transfer and Acquisition Demand-Driven Rather than Supply-Driven

As an assumption, "build it and they will come" may work for baseball fields and better mousetraps, but it does not work for databases and other static means of knowledge transfer. One of the lessons from knowledge management is that the availability of knowledge does not mean that employees will actually access the knowledge and put it to use. In the past, knowledge management has been *supply-driven* (that is, focused on creating a supply of knowledge) rather than *demand-driven* (that is, focused on creating a demand for knowledge). Supply-driven knowledge management initiatives are more concerned with the providers of knowledge than with the users of knowledge.

Continuity management is a demand-driven approach based on the new hires' urgent need for critical operational knowledge. As a result of this compelling need, new hires are in a learning-receptive frame of mind. They are more likely to utilize the knowledge profile than, for example, established employees are to utilize a best-practices database. New hires perceive that the operational knowledge contained in the profile yields a direct competitive advantage. This pro–knowledge acquisition learning mode is an enormous advantage that the knowledge profile is designed to exploit. On the other hand, continuity management also reflects a recognition of the importance of human motivation, attitudes, and feelings in determining the success of knowledge transfer and acquisition. The result is a greater emphasis in continuity management on user-relevant knowledge, people management issues, and organizational processes that encourage and facilitate the use of knowledge than is typically the case with knowledge management.

Develop a People-Centered, Not Technology-Centered, Process

Continuity management is not primarily a technological solution to the threat of knowledge loss, but a management solution that enables technology. The astute management of critical operational knowledge that leads to the acquisition and creation of new knowledge is its objective. Historically, knowledge management has been focused less on knowledge acquisition than on knowledge transfer, focused more on technology than on the human–technology interface. Technology is merely one medium for the transfer of knowledge; it is not synonymous with knowledge transfer and certainly not with knowledge acquisition. Knowledge acquisition is a complex process more dependent on human issues than on technological factors. A requisite concern for the quality of the human–technology interface leads away from an emphasis on the tools, systems, and databases of technology toward the feelings, needs, and desires of people.

Knowledge acquisition is a loose process, which means that its success is dependent on messy human-related factors like motivation, commitment, fears, hopes, and rewards. It is more driven by community and trust than by logic and edicts. Any attempt at knowledge transfer and acquisition that fails to account for human characteristics cannot succeed. In this regard, continuity management and the learning organization have much in common. At the core of all learning organizations—all knowledge-acquiring organizations—is an emphasis on human learning and, hence, on human beings. Processes that facilitate learning and knowledge creation recognize the unique role of knowledge in the human experience and are woven into the fabric of the learning organization. Continuity management is a management *function,* not a management *program,* because it requires a people-focused commitment to employee development and empowerment and to cultural transformation that supports knowledge sharing, acquisition, and creation.

Involve Human Resources

Because continuity management is demand-driven rather than supply-driven, people-centered rather than technology-centered, and user-focused rather than provider-focused, human resources (HR) must be involved in its implementation. Continuity management is not a short-term program, a piecemeal approach, or a procedural response to ensuring knowledge continuity between employee generations. It is a new management function that benefits both incumbents and successors and that requires the integration of other management functions if it is to succeed in preserving existing knowledge, creating new knowledge, and improving organizational productivity. From initial implementation to ongoing maintenance, HR has a significant role to play in continuity management.

Consider, for example, these six applications of the knowledge profile to HR decision making:

- *Employee selection criteria.* Knowledge profiles describe the skills and competencies needed to excel in all knowledge-critical positions in the organization and provide excellent summaries of the functions and activities of those positions. The profile is a highly efficient way to get a sense of a given job and its requirements. It is a powerful tool for writing job descriptions, developing employee selection criteria, and choosing among potential candidates.
- *Career counseling and planning.* Knowledge profiles contain a summary of skills, accomplishments, and basic competencies that can assist incumbents in charting their professional development and

future career paths and in working with HR and career counselors toward that end.

- *Succession planning.*   For the same reason that knowledge profiles are useful in developing employee selection criteria, they are constructive additions to the succession planning process. Because they detail the skills, processes, projects, decisions, and activities of the job, they improve the likelihood of making the best choice among candidates. When we discussed continuity management with Mike Ruettgers, EMC Corporation executive chairman, he pointed out the advantage of the knowledge profile in succession planning and recognized its contribution to building competency, two critical processes in a knowledge-centered organization. According to Ruettgers, "The knowledge profile would be invaluable in charting the careers of EMC employees so that both the employee and the company are maximally benefited" (Ruettgers, 2001).

- *Downsizing choices.*   When downsizing or reorganization is mandated, knowledge profiles identify the knowledge and expertise that will be lost with each position that is eliminated. The profiles can be used to make downsizing decisions, sculpt a more strategic workforce, and prevent later regret at having eliminated critical positions. In fact, this function of the profile is a powerful means of avoiding the kind of knowledge-loss disasters that plague organizations when they down-size on the basis of criteria that do not take into account the critical operational knowledge of each incumbent position.

- *Promotion criteria.*   Because knowledge profiles contain the objec-tives, skills, functions, and activities of the job, they provide a snapshot of the position, which facilitates development of promotion criteria.

- *Recruiting tool.*   Continuity management can be a significant recruit-ing tool, because new hires gain immediate and extensive access to the operational knowledge they need. Availability of the knowledge profile can be a persuasive incentive in attracting highly desirable applicants, particularly in a tight job market, and in convincing them to accept an offer.

■ ■ ■

With a nod to Roger, nine take-away principles relating to knowledge trans-fer and acquisition:

TAKE-AWAYS

Nine Principles of Knowledge Transfer and Acquisition

1. Recognize that knowledge is personal.
2. Create opportunities for knowledge exchange.
3. Facilitate mutual knowledge sharing between new hires and the organization.
4. Transfer both tacit and explicit knowledge.
5. Make knowledge creation a principal objective.
6. Internalize knowledge by incorporation, application, and re-creation.
7. Make knowledge transfer and acquisition demand-driven rather than supply-driven.
8. Develop a people-centered, not technology-centered, process.
9. Involve Human Resources.

Knowledge Transfer and Acquisition Processes

Various knowledge profile–based activities motivate, facilitate, and enrich the knowledge transfer and acquisition process and speed the new employee up the learning curve. These activities are based on the principles of knowledge transfer and acquisition that are discussed in the following paragraphs.

New Employee Orientation

Knowledge transfer and acquisition generally begins on the first day of work and typically involves some form of orientation. That orientation may be formal or informal, complete or incomplete, elaborate or simple, well coordinated or uncoordinated. A great deal of research has been conducted on the effectiveness of orientation programs, and well-developed designs are available to ensure a solid launch for new employees. Standard orientation components often include a briefing on official policies, employee benefits, office procedures, start times, and so forth. It is imperative that orientation programs be well designed, comprehensive, and relevant.

At Cisco, a collection of employee-orientation initiatives dubbed *Fast Start* was initiated to increase the rate at which new employees reached full productivity (Birchard, 1997). The program ensures that each new employee arrives with a fully functional workspace and a day of training in the use of computers, voice mail, and so forth. It includes the assignment of a company peer, called a *buddy,* who answers the new hire's questions. New Cisco employees also attend a two-day course called *Cisco Business Essentials,* which describes the company's business units and history and the networking market in which it sells its products and services.

The process of bringing new hires to full productivity requires more than an information-based orientation, however. It requires job-specific operational knowledge. Such knowledge is transferred to new employees through a knowledge-acquisition program, which may be well designed and productive, poorly conceived and unproductive, or largely nonexistent and counterproductive. Too often, it is left to well-meaning colleagues or to no one at all—and fails. When knowledge acquisition is chaotic or haphazard, it wastes the time of new hires and established employees alike and squanders the productivity potential of both. Formal programs therefore play a vital role in speeding the transfer of operational knowledge to new employees. In continuity management, the knowledge profile is the basic text around which a new employee's orientation program, training sessions, and teaching curriculum are built.

As a knowledge-transfer device, the strength of the knowledge profile is its ability to transfer critical operational knowledge from an incumbent to a successor *even in the absence of the incumbent.* In the case of job openings that result from retirements and transfers, incumbents may be available to assist in the knowledge transfer, but such opportunities exist in a relatively small percentage of total job turnovers. Even in such cases, the structured format of the profile provides a more orderly, concise, and effective means of transferring critical operational knowledge than would be the case with unstructured attempts by incumbents to pass on their knowledge to successors. The power of the profile in these cases is the careful analysis of operational knowledge that went into its construction, the links to human and documentary resources, and the macro- and microviews of the job it provides to orient new employees and equip them with the operational knowledge they need.

By linking orientation and training programs to the knowledge profile and to the phases of productivity described in Chapter 4 ("The Knowledge Learning Curve"), the skills training and knowledge transfer offered in formal programs is made relevant to new hires. Because this just-in-time training and on-demand operational knowledge are received when they are *needed,* they are more quickly internalized and applied than operational knowledge and training offered prior to need.

On the first day of a typical continuity management–based orientation, new hires receive a standard orientation program that delivers basic information on the organization (its history, market, benefits, etc.) and basic instruction in the use of essential equipment and data sources. New hires are given the knowledge profiles developed by their predecessors (or the knowledge profiles of colleagues in the same job classification when they are assuming a new position) and instructed in how to access the profile, update its content, and use it to maximum potential. Each new hire also meets his or her *profile partner.* Profile partners are individuals who have been assigned to introduce them to their coworkers, familiarize them with their profiles, and serve as their temporary advisors until they have selected more permanent mentors.

Based on their knowledge profiles, new employees are asked to compare their existing skill sets to the skill sets required for their positions, and, therefore, to participate in determining their own training needs. On the basis of their self-assessment and additional training assessments, HR devises the teaching and training curriculum appropriate for each employee and each productivity phase so that all training and knowledge are relevant at the time that employees receive them.

Before their first week is over, new hires have begun the process of familiarizing themselves with the contents of their knowledge profiles and making contact with the members of their knowledge networks. They are also briefed on performance expectations for the first 90 days of employment. They receive regular performance appraisals during their first year, because feedback during the early phases of productivity will help new employees reach their performance potential sooner.

Profile Partners

Profile partners are peer incumbents assigned to new hires to take them through their knowledge profiles and move them quickly up the learning curve. They are similar to the buddies or temporary mentors that some organizations utilize to provide an informal orientation to new employees, introduce them to coworkers, and answer their questions about the new job.

Whereas mentoring is geared more toward advice and counsel and the development of the individual both from the standpoint of managerial experience and increased personal competency, profile partners are more concerned with the transfer of operational knowledge during a set time period, using the knowledge profile as the basis of that transfer.

Like traditional buddies, profile partners help new hires understand the culture and systems of the organization, provide a temporary mentoring relationship, and introduce them to their coworkers. As peer incumbents, profile partners are uniquely equipped to explain the contents and operation of the knowledge profile to new employees, guide them in its most effective utilization, and help them understand its full capabilities. Profile partners introduce the newcomers at their first PEAK meetings of peer incumbents—whether in person or online—and to their communities of practice in order to facilitate their assimilation into these groups. Finally, they assist in one-to-one knowledge transfer by answering their questions and directing them to additional resources. By taking full advantage of their knowledge profiles and their profile partners, newcomers accelerate their rate of knowledge acquisition and experience the knowledge acquisition process as highly participative and rewarding.

Profile partners operate in three different types of profile-transfer situations. In each of these situations, their roles are slightly different:

- *When there is a direct successor.*   In most cases, the new hire replaces a previous employee and so receives the predecessor's knowledge profile. As a peer incumbent, the profile partner is well equipped to lead the newcomer through the profile and assist in the acquisition of knowledge, often through questions and answers that provide additional knowledge.
- *When there is an indirect successor.*   When downsizing and reorganizations result in fewer employees, but no less work, there is no direct successor. There are, however, indirect successors: surviving employees who are charged with carrying out the departed employees' activities. In these cases, a copy of the knowledge profile from each downsized position is transferred to each surviving employee who serves as an indirect successor. Ordinarily, a profile partner would not be necessary in these situations. If there is a high degree of specialization associated with a position, however, it may be necessary to assign

a profile partner who is knowledgeable in that specialization to assist the indirect successor.

- *When there is no predecessor.*   When an organization is expanding and there is no predecessor for a specific position, the newcomer receives the knowledge profile that most resembles the one that would have been transferred had there been a predecessor. A profile partner is appointed from peer incumbents within the job classification. When the job is entirely new or is an amalgamation of existing jobs, the new hire receives the knowledge profiles of the most closely related positions and is paired with a profile partner from the most similar job classification.

A fourth situation exists when there is no direct successor and no indirect successor, as happens in the case of massive downsizings or reorganizations that temporarily or permanently eliminate whole units, markets, products, services, and the like. In these cases, no profile partner is needed, but the knowledge profiles themselves are archived in case circumstances warrant adding employees at a later date.

Newcomer Interaction with the Knowledge Profile

Because the knowledge profile is the basic vehicle for knowledge transfer and acquisition (including the harvesting of new employee knowledge), it is imperative that new hires use it immediately. Furthermore, meaningful and structured interaction with the profile creates ownership of the operational knowledge it contains and a commitment to knowledge creation. From the beginning, newcomers are allowed to change their profiles—in fact, they are encouraged to do so in order to become involved with the operational knowledge they need and to apply that knowledge immediately. The modifications they make in the profile contents personalizes the profile for them and creates a sense of accomplishment. In addition to knowledge ownership and integration, the goal in encouraging immediate profile interactions is to instill in newcomers the habit of integrating their profiles into their regular management activities. To achieve these objectives, new hires are given a series of assignments related to their profiles:

- *Familiarization tour of the profile.*   During orientation, new employees are expected to familiarize themselves with the format, contents, purpose, and use of their knowledge profiles. Following orientation, a built-in tutorial (available in sophisticated systems) will lead them through the profile, describing each knowledge category, the contents of the category, how to update the profile, and how to make most effective use of the profile. Pop-up screens in sophisticated systems remind profile users of the contents of the various knowledge categories, which ones require updating, and how they are updated.

- *Review of incumbent biographies.*   Newcomers should review the Incumbent Biographies section of their profiles, including the welcoming letters from their predecessors, the biography of the founding incumbent, and the biographies of subsequent incumbents who have added to the profiles. They should also begin their own biography.

- *Review of frequently asked questions.*   Within the first week of employment, new hires should review the Frequently Asked Questions (FAQ) section. These questions were originally developed by peer incumbents, but were later expanded through the addition of questions contributed by new successor employees.

- *Knowledge profile exercise.*   New hires are expected to answer a series of questions based on their knowledge profiles; these must be completed and submitted to their supervisors by the end of their first week and their first month. These exercises encourage new hires to use their profiles from the beginning, to become familiar with the contents of the profile and comfortable with its use, and to acquire job-critical operational knowledge quickly.

- *Knowledge network contacts.*   Also during their first week, new hires will begin the process of contacting key individuals listed in the Knowledge Network category of their profiles.

- *FAQ preparation.*   At the end of their first and second weeks, new hires are expected to make a list of questions they have developed but that have not been answered in the profile or that have not been easily answered through the profile. As appropriate, these questions will be used to expand the FAQ section of future profiles or to add to the contents of the knowledge categories.

- *Profile usage.*   To the extent possible, supervisors are expected to encourage their new employees to use the profile regularly as a means of developing the operational knowledge they need to perform well in their new positions and to accustom them to regular profile use.

- *Orientation critique.* At the end of their second week and their second month of employment, new hires are expected to critique the orientation process and to make recommendations for improving it. These recommendations will be entered in the Innovations category of the knowledge profile.
- *Process and procedures critique.* At the end of their first, second, third, and sixth months of employment, new hires are expected to critique the various systems, processes, and procedures they have encountered in their new jobs and to record recommendations for improving them. These recommendations will be entered in the Innovations knowledge category of their profiles. This assignment takes advantage of the different perspectives that new employees bring to their jobs.
- *Security designations.* When new employees take control of the knowledge profiles for their positions, they inherit the security designations assigned by the previous incumbents. These designations restrict access to certain parts of the profile. By the end of the third month or so, new employees should have reviewed these security designations for each of the knowledge categories in their profiles, approving or changing them.

Following implementation of continuity management, additional means of integrating the profile quickly and effectively into daily management activities will undoubtedly emerge as the organization becomes more and more knowledge-conscious and continuity management–based.

PEAK Meetings of Peer Incumbents

Peer incumbent meetings (which Brett called *PEAK meetings* at Wedge-Mark) play an important role in the transfer of critical operational knowledge to new employees. The annual PEAK meetings, the quarterly online meetings, and the communities of practice that develop out of them are personal means through which newcomers can enrich their knowledge profiles by seeking additional information or specific advice relating to decisions or issues confronting them. Because all PEAK members are peer incumbents, they operate in relatively similar environments and share a great deal of common knowledge. They are, therefore, an incredibly rich source of operational knowledge for newcomers and for each other.

Because learning is best accomplished when it is most needed and through a structured, experiential method, peer incumbents supplement the knowledge profiles with human interaction and deeper knowledge resources. The profiles cannot contain all the operational knowledge needed for a given position, but they do point the newcomer to additional knowledge sources and make it easy to access those sources. PEAK meetings, communities of practice, and knowledge networks provide a pool of experts to whom the newcomer can turn for advice, counsel, and additional knowledge.

Phased Mentoring

Mentoring of new hires is recognized as an important contributor to employee productivity and satisfaction, and continuity management takes full advantage of it. In addition to a regular mentoring program, however, continuity management calls for a unique program called *phased mentoring,* which is used when retiring or transferring employees remain available to mentor their replacements. Under the phased-mentoring program, retiring employees retain a contractual relationship with the organization to mentor their successors for an agreed-on period of time. The process is called *phased mentoring* because it ties the activities of the mentoring program to the knowledge profile and the phases of productivity.

Phased mentoring allows successors to integrate experientially the knowledge they acquire through their profiles *under the guidance of their predecessors,* acquiring that operational knowledge as it is needed, in a direct knowledge exchange with their mentors that is nonetheless structured by their profiles. As new employees work their way through the phases of productivity, they interact with their mentors less frequently. To some degree, the knowledge profile serves as a new employee's personalized and highly interactive "mentor," but it cannot replace its human counterpart.

William M. Mercer, Inc., the New York–based human resources consulting firm, surveyed 232 large employers for a 2000 report and found that 23 percent of those responding offered a formal phased-retirement program, whereas 53 percent relied on individual arrangements (Few employers, 2001). This data suggests that almost three-quarters of the surveyed companies have some form of phased retirement that could be adapted to the phased-mentoring component of continuity management. EMC Corporation, the data storage company with $9 billion in sales in 2000, has instituted a retirement-based mentoring program that is similar to phased mentoring, but without the knowledge profile. Employee retirements at EMC are activity-driven rather than age-driven (retirement at 65 is not mandatory). EMC encourages its retiring employees to provide a year's notice by offering them incentives for doing so. According to Executive Chairman Mike Ruettgers:

> We encourage employees who are contemplating retirement to give us as much notice as possible so we can have their successors shadow them before they leave. Our objective is to ensure that when they do leave, their accumulated operational knowledge doesn't leave with them but stays in the heads of those who will carry on in their functions. To be sure, retirees often have a financial incentive to maintain a relationship with us because of their incentive packages. But most of the time their sustained connection to EMC goes beyond that practical reason. I think it really grows out of our culture of accountability, execution, and cross-functional cooperation. EMC's culture tends to attract people who are intensely dedicated to their work and our customers, and therefore to the future prosperity of the company. Many retirees want to be able to continue to make a contribution after they have left. We've found that when you give them something on the other side and make it rewarding for them, you're able to maintain access to them, and their knowledge isn't completely gone. This continuing relationship works well for EMC and it works well for its "retired" employees. (Ruettgers, 2001)

Incumbent–Successor Overlap

In those cases in which an employee is not retiring, but is leaving on good terms with some time remaining on the job, it may be possible to arrange a short mentorship with the successor if an overlap exists or can be arranged. Incumbent–successor overlap is possible only if the incumbent is being replaced by a successor who is readily available or if the incumbent can be persuaded to delay starting the new job. Although short-term, such mentoring can be effective and productive when used in conjunction with the knowledge profile and modeled after the early stages of phased mentoring.

Without knowledge acquisition, knowledge transfer is meaningless. While knowledge transfer may be technology-enabled, knowledge acquisition is human-driven. This chapter explores principles and procedures that create a favorable environment for the acquisition of critical operational knowledge. The following chapter examines a larger set of circumstances that are no less important: the environment in which knowledge acquisition occurs, including the characteristics of the organizational culture and reward systems that support or impede it.

13 | Realignment of the Organizational Culture and Reward System

Richard A. Kleinert, global practice leader of the human resources strategy group that specializes in human capital advisory services at Deloitte & Touche LLP, nicely sums up the new role that organizational knowledge has assumed in the management of an organization:

> To me, knowledge has three Ms: message, medium, and motivation. Message—you have to define the business critical information in your organization. Medium—you need some sort of system to provide the right type of information to the right people at the right time. But most important, I think, is the motivation side. You have to motivate people both to populate a system and to use it. And that gets into the amorphous cultural area comprised of rewards, both monetary and non-monetary; communications, both pull and non-pull; measurement; and finally, but not least, leadership. (Haapaniemi, 2001, p. 73)

The unique characteristics of knowledge described in Chapter 2 ("Knowledge as a Capital Asset") mandate a holistic approach to its harvesting, transfer, and acquisition. Preceding chapters have examined many of the complex, interrelated factors that affect continuity management implementation and practice. This chapter examines another crucial factor: the organizational environment within which operational knowledge is transmitted.

Two environmental influences have a direct—and even decisive—effect on the implementation and effectiveness of continuity management and knowledge management: organizational culture and organizational reward systems. "You cannot do knowledge management," says John Kunar, President of Delphi Group Canada, the management consulting firm, "unless you change the existing culture of the organization. The overwhelming majority of companies that have actually done knowledge management have claimed that the cultural barrier is the greatest barrier" (Buckler, 2001). Similarly, organizational rewards support or impede continuity management implementation by motivating employees to participate in the continuity management initiative or to reject it. An appreciation of knowledge, a willingness to share it, and a commitment to preserving and enhancing it cannot be dictated by fiat. Such attitudes can, however, be grown, and the soil in which they grow is organizational culture, fertilized by focused rewards shrewdly designed and carefully administered.

Realigning Organizational Culture

Organizational culture is a concept that organizational theorists have borrowed from anthropology as a means of understanding why organizations behave collectively as they do and how they influence the individual behavior of their members. It refers to values, beliefs, assumptions, practices, and norms shared by members of the organization that shape their behavior and provide a sense of identity for them. Simply put, organizational culture is who we are and how we do things. It is largely tacit and, hence, is mostly invisible. Yet it is extremely powerful in determining organizational characteristics and individual behavior. Organizational culture can generate intense commitment or deep antagonism to an organization's mission and goals, and it directly affects organizational performance levels. Culture is particularly important in continuity management. The success of the continuity management process is highly dependent on individual behavioral responses, particularly positive attitudes around sharing and acquiring knowledge, which are either supported or discouraged by the organization's culture.

Organizational culture can be intentionally reshaped by altering the factors that create and sustain it so that it directly supports continuity management. In fact, such reshaping is mandatory if the existing culture is not open to knowledge sharing. Yet changing an organization's culture is a complex process, because the factors that influence it are many, highly interrelated, and subtle. They emerge as much as they are created, and so they are hard to manage. Yet, ignorance or denial of the importance of culture in an organizational change effort dooms that effort to failure. An American businessperson would never attempt to manage a company in Japan or the Middle East without understanding the culture of that country. Similarly, no leader can expect to manage an organization without understanding that organization's culture or to manage knowledge effectively without understanding the extent to which the culture values it.

Whatever degree of cultural change may be required to implement continuity management, it can be achieved through a two-pronged initiative. The first effort is to identify, overcome, or remove existing obstacles and impediments that block continuity management implementation. The second, launched simultaneously, is to develop new forces or strengthen established forces that support continuity management implementation. An analysis of those factors that affect continuity management should be conducted to determine where these obstacles and opportunities lie.

The Sources of Culture

Many good books have been written on organizational culture and how to change it, most notably John Kotter's book, *Leading Change* (Kotter, 1996), and the excellent multiple works of Edgar Schein. It is not necessary to repeat the contents of these books in this chapter. The objective here is to create an awareness of organizational culture rather than to provide specific instructions on how to change it. Nonetheless, an understanding of the components that create an organization's culture makes it possible to identify what has to be changed. The following paragraphs describe the primary determinants of organizational culture.

Official Organizational Beliefs. This determinant consists of formal statements of position and principle that define an organization's purpose, mission, and goals and that are presumed to embody the ideals of the organization and its employees. Such beliefs are often contained in mission statements, declarations of corporate purpose, and lists of goals repeated by executives and managers and often appearing in official communications. These stated beliefs may or may not reflect the true purpose, goals, and beliefs of the organization and may or may not be supported by the culture or by organizational structure and personnel policies. Nevertheless, official beliefs promulgated and repeated by the organization and its executives and managers are a starting point of cultural change. The vision of the organization must be embraced by employees if they are going to adopt behaviors that reflect it. Therefore, knowledge-based objectives embodied in continuity management should be written into the vision of the organization through its statements of principle, mission, and objectives. Knowledge continuity should be a stated goal of management that is communicated through every available medium.

Unofficial Organizational Assumptions. This determinant of organizational culture consists of assumptions held by employees about the way things really work and beliefs about the way things are that may or may not reflect the official beliefs and stated positions of the organization. For example, a university may claim that it values the quality of a professor's teaching whereas, in fact, what it values is the quality of a professor's research. The quality of teaching may have little effect on a professor's status, class assignments, compensation, or promotion. The official university position sounds good to parents, but the professors know that, despite administrative protestations to the country, advancement depends on the quality (and quantity) of their research, not on the quality of their teaching.

When official beliefs and unofficial assumptions are not aligned, a dysfunctional organization results. Ordinarily, unofficial assumptions that guide employee behavior are based on what employees see as being rewarded or on what is reinforced by their peers rather than on what they hear. Because unofficial assumptions are more important than official statements of belief, cultural change can be brought about only when actions are in line with official statements. Realignment of the reward system is discussed later in this chapter.

Organizational Norms and Values. Norms and values prescribe what is acceptable and unacceptable behavior within an organization, define success and failure, and assist in ethical and strategic decision making. They influence, for example, how employees treat each other, how they deal with customers, how they dress, and how punctual they are at meetings. Because norms and values shape what is honored and what is ignored, they are particularly important in the acceptance or adoption of new behavior. In the case of continuity management, norms and values must be changed to support the importance of knowledge to the organization, the need to leverage and increase it, and a willingness to share and acquire it. The preservation of knowledge continuity between employee generations must become a central value of the organizational culture.

Human Resources Department.   HR oversees human resource planning, development of job descriptions, recruitment and selection, training and development, performance appraisal, and compensation. HR can play a powerful role in cultural change and the incorporation of continuity management into the fabric of an organization through the policies it issues, the personnel it hires, the training it conducts, the evaluations it performs, and the compensation it sets. Cultural change requires the marshalling of all organizational resources and communication capabilities if it is to succeed, especially those available to HR. A respect for knowledge and a commitment to continuity management can be instilled in new hires through orientation and training efforts and can be strengthened in established employees through performance evaluation criteria and personnel policies.

Organizational Rewards.   Rewards are an important means through which an organization supports desirable behavior, punishes undesirable behavior, and shapes its culture. This topic is discussed in more detail later in the chapter.

Rituals and Ceremonies.   These symbolic aspects of organizational culture provide meaning and structure at work and indicate what an organization values. Ceremonies tend to be more formal than rituals, somewhat grander, less frequently occurring, and more celebratory, such as ceremonies associated with employee awards, promotions, or other honors. Examples of rituals include staff meetings, annual performance reviews, quarterly results, annual shareholder meetings, and so forth. Ceremonies should be developed to honor successful examples of continuity management, and rituals can be designed to support continuity management practices. An example of the former might be honoring an established manager for innovative use of the knowledge profile or a new employee for a comprehensive update of the profile. Examples of a ritual might be opening the knowledge profile portal as soon as the workday begins and always updating it, if necessary, at the end of the day.

Initiations and Rites of Passage.   Initiations confer organizational acceptance on newcomers. They confirm membership in the organization, make that membership valuable, and introduce new members to the norms and values of the group. Initiations may be formal or informal, planned or spontaneous, but they will always occur. They are essential to bringing a new employee from outsider status to insider status. Rather than leaving such initiations to chance, savvy leaders design and implement meaningful initiation ceremonies, including those that emphasize continuity management as an important practice of group members.

Rites of passage formally convey a new status. Baptism and bar mitzvah are examples of formal religious rites of passage in American society. Promotion ceremonies are rights of passage, as they formally convey a new title, new authority, and new responsibilities. As employees work their way though the phases of productivity and up the learning curve, their enhanced states of operational knowledge should be acknowledged and honored through rites of passage designed for that purpose.

Organizational Structure.   This determinant of organizational culture includes the lines of authority in the organization, the division of labor, and the policies, procedures, job descriptions, and objectives that guide organizational activities. A rigid hierarchical structure with many management layers and strict policies and procedures will create a more inflexible, less responsive culture than one with few management layers, widely dispersed decision making, and an emphasis on vision and mission. Policies and procedures, job descriptions, and corporate objectives that emphasize continuity management will positively affect its adoption and incorporation into the organizational culture.

Myths and Stories.   These transmitters of culture reinforce or redefine fundamental organizational beliefs, describe appropriate role behavior, and unify members. Myths and stories transmit what is valued and rewarded by the organization, reinforce organizational goals and objectives, provide role models, prescribe guidelines for success, and motivate employees. Because they have a powerful effect on organizational culture, the stories that leaders and managers tell should foster continuity management and recount examples of how to do it well. Myths serve the same purpose. Whereas stories are true, myths are technically not, although they communicate truth by describing core values. Stories of George Washington's courage are true. The myth that he never told a lie is not likely to be, but it nonetheless conveys a core value of American culture.

Jargon.   Jargon, or slang, is the specialized language that develops within an organization. Jargon helps to define the organization, unify it, and create a sense of belonging among its members. The deliberate introduction of new slang words into an organization can help reshape its culture by creating a common language through which to discuss and internalize the new characteristics that are sought. Usually, slang emerges naturally out of the culture, but it is possible to introduce it through explanation and repetition. *Knowledge continuity,* for example, is not a common phrase in contemporary organizations, and yet it would be quite common in an organization that has implemented continuity management. In fact, introduction of the phrase would be necessary because it is a central continuity management concept, and employees must have that phrase (or one like it) to understand and talk about continuity management and its advantages.

Brett's journal provides numerous examples of the jargon that became part of the culture at WedgeMark. Some of the jargon, such as *barrier reefs* and *ghost work,* emerged from the continuity management process itself. Other terms, such as *PEAK meetings, K-Quest, knowledge vacuum,* and *knowledge collapse,* were chosen to explain new concepts that had to be discussed. The knowledge questionnaire, for example, was often called *K-Quest* at WedgeMark, which was short for *knowledge quest.* Knowledge quest has the favorable connotation of an adventure involving a search for knowledge. The term *knowledge Profile* was chosen, in part, because it connoted something personal through its association with the human profile and even with the head, which contains the mind, where knowledge is stored. Likewise, the term *K-PAQ* (knowledge profile analysis questions) was chosen because of its positive connotation of a "knowledge pack" that could be employed in the knowledge quest. Choosing the right words to introduce the continuity management initiative is a first step in building acceptance of continuity management into the culture.

Metaphors.   Metaphors use analogies to express complex ideas simply, and so they clarify the ambiguity and uncertainty that characterize work. Organizational metaphors may come from the military ("Let's nuke 'em"), football ("It's fourth and ten"), medicine ("We need a tourniquet, not a band-aid"), horticulture ("It's time for heavy pruning"), engineering ("That group can't carry its weight"), and so forth. Metaphors have an important impact on organizational culture because they influence the way in which employees perceive the organization and their own roles within it.

Shifting the Culture

Continuity management represents a dramatic shift from the archaic perspective of knowledge as a byproduct of work—and thus largely expendable—to a contemporary recognition that knowledge is the driving force of work and thus is essential to high performance. This paradigm shift in perspective requires a change in organizational culture. Fortunately, a culture that supports continuity management is likely to support knowledge management, organizational learning, innovation, and vice versa. The critical role of culture in the success of knowledge management initiatives is now clear. But culture is only one ingredient in a successful implementation of continuity management. A related factor of equal importance is the system of organizational rewards.

Realigning the Organizational Reward System

Years of research have confirmed that managers get what they emphasize, what they measure, and what they reward. "Ultimately, to make knowledge management work and work well," observes James Copeland, CEO of Deloitte Touche Tohmatsu, "it's going to require a fundamental change in the way we do business and the way we reward our people" (Haapaniemi, 2001, p. 71). Organizational rewards can be used to create a new organizational perspective on knowledge, a willingess to share existing operational knowledge and, beyond that, a strong desire to *acquire* knowledge in order to create *new* knowledge. Organizational rewards can help create a culture in which exiting knowledge is enthusiastically offered, shared knowledge is passionately acquired, and knowledge creation is vigorously pursued. Organizational rewards can be divided into two types: extrinsic and intrinsic. Each is approached differently, and each is described in the following paragraphs.

Extrinsic Rewards

Extrinsic rewards are tangible organizational rewards offered or granted to employees in order to motivate them to engage in specific behavior. This reward category includes bonuses, promotions, stock options, employee honors, salary increases, and the like. To ensure alignment of these rewards with the goals of continuity management, an analysis should be conducted of every organizational reward as well as the strategic planning, goal-setting, and performance evaluation systems. In every case, two criteria should be applied:

- Do the existing rewards support (or work against) continuity management?
- How can the existing reward system and its elements be modified to support continuity management more effectively?

The results of this analysis are likely to reveal virtually no organizational reward support for continuity management. This discovery, while not surprising, is ironic. Executives frequently talk of the need for knowledge continuity or at least bemoan its absence. And the majority of managers have suffered knowledge-starved job transitions of their own or the loss of valued subordinates that deprived them of much-needed operational knowledge. Yet, many companies are not, as it turns out, knowledge continuity–valuing companies at all, at least not from the standpoint of the rewards they offer, the measurements they employ, or the goals they set.

Extrinsic rewards are based on measures of performance, which may be relatively objective (as in the case of sales volume awards) or relatively subjective (as in the case of "employee of the month" awards, when the selection is not made on the basis of purely quantitative measures). These performance measures, in turn, are derived from a set of performance standards. Therefore, the examination of an organizational reward system begins with *standards of performance,* which, at least in theory, originate from the organizational vision and mission statements. These statements are official pronouncements of what an organization intends to reward and so are part of the organizational reward system. Vision and mission statements orient employees and set the presumed ideals that they should be trying to achieve. Although these statements do not always reflect what is actually rewarded, when they do, they can be significant motivators. Therefore, the goals of continuity management should be written into the vision and mission of the organization. The long-term process that leads to such an incorporation is more complicated than the simple statement sounds. Such a revision may, in fact, reflect a radical realignment of individual and organizational goals and values, but it must be made.

The standards of performance defined by the organizational vision and mission statements are generally broken down into specific performance criteria or objectives that the organization sets in order to achieve the vision. Attainable objectives with deadlines for achievement are powerful motivators of human behavior. The establishment of organizational continuity management–based goals and objectives provides an opportunity to explain concretely how continuity management is to be implemented and practiced and what its advantages are in terms that are meaningful to each employee. Knowledge itself is an abstract concept. Honoring knowledge is an unfamiliar paradigm that requires explanation so that people can relate to it and buy into it. Without concrete reasons for participating in knowledge sharing, acquisition, and creation, people may be hesitant to do so simply because they don't understand why it benefits them and why their lives will be better for it.

Specific objectives related to continuity management help incumbent employees realize that their competitive advantage is not based on static knowledge, but on knowledge that is growing—not on a knowledge base, but on a dynamic knowledge process in which they are the leading participants. This new value proposition emphasizes knowledge enhancement and creation, not knowledge hoarding or even knowledge transfer. Understanding knowledge as a *process* rather than as a commodity is critical. Such a statement is not a contradiction of continuity management's basic tenet that critical operational knowledge is a commodity. Critical operational knowledge *is* a commodity that can be transferred to new employees and then acquired by them. But the assumption in continuity management is that, *at the moment of transfer,* the operational knowledge that was a *commodity* for the predecessor becomes a *process* for the successor—a means to knowledge acquisition and to new knowledge creation.

Once specific continuity management objectives have been set, some form of measurement system must be established to determine whether the objectives have been met. Measurement is an essential part of any reward system, because it serves as the basis for choosing the recipients of the rewards as well as the kind of rewards that will be given for achieving different objectives. At least two types of measurements can be used in continuity management. The first type is a measurement of the *number of times* a targeted behavior is performed (for example, how many times employees update their knowledge profiles). The second measures *how well* the behavior was performed (for example, the quality or comprehensiveness of the profile updates). The task of choosing what behavior to measure is not as difficult as determining how to measure the quality or effectiveness of that behavior. For example, completion of K-Quest, regular updating of the knowledge profile, and attendance at PEAK meetings are obvious candidates for the first type of measurement. But what criteria will be used to judge how well the knowledge profile is updated or how comprehensively the knowledge questionnaire was completed? These issues will have to be addressed by each organization. To a large extent, the resolution of these issues will depend on how committed the organization is to continuity management and to making it an inherent part of management activities.

With performance objectives, criteria, and measurements in place, it is possible to determine the appropriate extrinsic rewards for each objective. These rewards take many forms, but they can be divided into three basic categories: promotion, compensation, and recognition.

Promotion.   Promotion criteria should be revised to include continuity management. Criteria for K-Quest completion, PEAK meeting participation, and knowledge profile updating should appear as specific objectives in employee goal-setting and as performance review criteria in conducting employee evaluations. For example, employees who fail to complete K-Quest, regularly update their knowledge profiles, or participate in PEAK meetings should not be considered appropriate candidates for promotion.

Compensation.   Salaries, raises, and bonuses should all be tied, in part, to the achievement of continuity management goals set by the employee and the organization. Joseph E. Griesedieck, CEO of San Francisco–based Spencer Stuart, a $365-million executive recruiting firm, described what it took to implement knowledge management at his firm. While his experience relates to knowledge management, it applies to continuity management, as well:

> When we started pushing knowledge management, we made speeches about it, we tried to make it part of the culture. But at the end of the

day, we finally had to just get serious and say it's also going to impact your compensation. Today, 20% of a person's total compensation sits within this area. I don't care how big a rainmaker you are, if you aren't putting information in the database, you're going to get 20% of your compensation taken away. So you can do everything you want to change the culture of the organization, but at the end of the day, you also have to tie it to some kind of measurement system, which we have on a monthly basis, and to the compensation system. (Haapaniemi, 2001, p. 74)

Recognition.   Various forms of recognition, such as awards, accolades, more exposure to superiors, better assignments, and so forth, can be used to reward employees for continuity management behaviors. Such recognition serves multiple purposes. Not only does it publicly reward the employee, but it also provides a role model for others and examples of continuity management in action that are both instructive and inspirational.

Intrinsic Rewards

While extrinsic rewards are tangible and granted by the organization, intrinsic rewards are intangible and are experienced as a result of the work itself. Anyone who has felt a sense of accomplishment from completing a difficult project or satisfaction from helping another person overcome an obstacle has experienced an intrinsic reward. Indeed, such rewards can be the most deeply satisfying and motivating of all. But they are also more difficult to manage than extrinsic rewards. Management can grant extrinsic rewards directly to an employee. Intrinsic rewards, on the other hand, can only be facilitated through setting up environments that are appropriate to their development. Yet these "soft" motivators of human behavior are essential complements to the "hard" motivators of extrinsic rewards and must be considered in any analysis and design of an organizational reward system.

In fact, one of the reasons continuity management is effective in getting people to share their knowledge and to internalize and apply the knowledge of others is the many intrinsic rewards that are built into its design through the structured opportunities it creates to experience them. These rewards include knowledge-based opportunities to share, to feel connected to other human beings, and to be valued. Continuity Management Orientation Day, PEAK meetings, the annual follow-up PEAK meetings, online meetings, peer design teams, communities of practice, and knowledge profile creation allow people to be of service to others in ways that are personally rewarding and professionally enriching. These opportunities for knowledge sharing confer peer acceptance, confirm the value of individual knowledge contributions, and recognize the worth of participating employees.

Intrinsic rewards not only develop out of our relationships with others, they also develop out of our relationship with ourself. Learning, for example, is an inherently pleasurable undertaking when it adds value to our activities or satisfies our curiosity. It is an intrinsic reward. Learning is the centerpiece of continuity management because its primary activities are built around knowledge analysis, sharing, acquisition, and creation. Continuity management makes possible an exchange of credible knowledge structured for ease of access, transfer, understanding, and application. It encourages discovery, self-discovery, and continuous learning, facilitating the development of new insights, perspectives, frameworks, and ways of doing things.

Another rich intrinsic reward of continuity management is the opportunity to create, one of the fundamental pleasures of human existence. Continuity management challenges employees in competitive and collaborative ways to engage in creative endeavors that can be very satisfying. Updating knowledge profiles, expanding knowledge networks, developing new means to capitalize on knowledge leverage points, and creating knowledge in PEAK meetings are stimulating processes that can be intrinsically rewarding.

Somewhat related to creating is another intrinsic reward: the opportunity to leave a legacy. Every knowledge profile is a knowledge legacy. To personalize these profiles and increase incumbent and successor buy-in, each profile contains a biography and photograph of the founding incumbent who originated the profile and the biographies of each successor incumbent who followed in the position. These biographies contribute to the value of the profile as a personal legacy left for future generations of employees. Through their profiles, incumbents leave a record of their insights, accomplishments, and actions. They leave something of themselves. Through their biographies, incumbents personalize their legacy and sign their work.

An examination of an organization's reward system is a comprehensive task that forces hard questions. There is a tendency to rely on the obvious and the easy (paying people more) rather than the subtle and the difficult (creating opportunities for knowledge sharing that are satisfying). In manual labor, extrinsic rewards are effective—but only up to a point, as seven decades of management research have proven. In knowledge work, extrinsic rewards are also important, but intrinsic rewards may be even more so.

This chapter completes our discussion of operational knowledge transfer and acquisition and the realignment of the organizational culture and reward system. The following chapter examines the relationship between continuity management and knowledge management in more detail, explores aspects of continuity management that have already been implemented and are working well, and speculates on what knowledge asset management might look like in its fullest expression in the knowledge economy.

14 | Continuity Management in Practice

Knowledge continuity initiatives have been launched in thousands of American organizations wrestling with knowledge loss in the face of high job turnover, downsizing, and impending retirements. Such initiatives are in evidence in EMC Corporation's earnest attempt to preserve the knowledge of its retiring employees through an innovative mentoring program that matches retirees with their successors and in Deloitte Consulting's Senior Leadership Program to preserve the knowledge of its retiring employees. Designed to meet different threats, knowledge continuity initiatives have in common their attempt to preserve some degree of operational knowledge and to transfer that knowledge to other employees before it is lost.

Knowledge Continuity Initiatives

The end of the Cold War brought significant downsizing and consolidation to the defense industry. At that time, Northrop Grumman Air Combat Systems (ACS) found itself in a difficult situation with its B-2 stealth bomber. The plane was nearing the end of its production cycle, but Grumman, as lead contractor, would have to retain support and maintenance capabilities for the remaining decades of the bomber's useful service. As B-2 production wound down and employees prepared to leave, Grumman faced the loss of critical expertise and experience that had been built over decades. In the late

1990s, it instituted a program to preserve the tacit knowledge of B-2 experts by identifying 200 of them in 100 different subject areas, harvesting their knowledge, and creating an expert locator system to cross-reference it. The effort was deemed successful and became the basis for a much larger initiative that encompassed the entire ACS unit when a 25 percent reduction in its workforce was announced in 1999, creating the potential for a dramatic loss of critical operational knowledge.

Pfizer, the giant pharmaceutical company, has instituted a knowledge retention program that focuses on key individuals in strategic decision-making roles who are transferring or retiring. As with continuity management, the goal is to transfer critical knowledge from the incumbent to the successor and to other people who need it. This process resembles phased mentoring in continuity management except that it applies only to key positions. Using extensive interviews, Pfizer determines the knowledge that needs to be transferred and then uses various forms of documented knowledge as well as face-to-face meetings to assist the successor in knowledge acquisition and application.

The Pfizer model concentrates on four categories of knowledge that will help the successor reach competency in the shortest possible time. These categories are *task* (activities of the work day), *process* (how things are supposed to be done in order to succeed in the position), *behavioral system* (what it takes to really get something done), and *environmental model* (how things are connected). According to Victor Newman, chief learning officer of the European Pfizer Research University, "We've so far had good experiences with our approach to retaining knowledge. It has made a difference for us, especially in the speed of succession and improved time to competence. We've been very happy with how quickly it has become effective." (Transferring high-value knowledge at Pfizer, 2002, p. 15). This initiative has also identified potential decisions that carry substantial risk, experts who provide knowledge assistance, and areas where additional study would be beneficial for the employee.

Public-sector organizations, like their counterparts in the private sector, face a common threat of knowledge loss. And like them, they have responded with knowledge continuity initiatives. The Tennessee Valley Authority (TVA), which is America's largest public power company and operator of 47 power facilities and over 17,000 miles of transmission lines, launched a three-step program to avoid knowledge loss from departing employees. The program consisted of (1) identifying the knowledge that needs to be preserved from employees planning to leave; (2) capturing that knowledge through employee training that transfers the knowledge, through apprenticeship, or through knowledge codification and storage; and (3) retaining that knowledge though processes that are similar to those of many knowledge management programs. As innovative and even bold as this initiative is, it only applies to those employees known to be leaving.

In Canada, various governmental agencies have adopted methods to preserve knowledge continuity that are consonant with continuity management. For example:

- An organizational yellow pages, organized by employee area of interest and expertise, to enable employees to locate internal sources of knowledge
- An alumni directory that provides contact information for former employees who have offered assistance in supplying needed knowledge
- A database through which employees make lessons learned available to other employees in order to eliminate repetition of the same mistakes
- A list of the top 10 questions new employees have, each of which has been answered by seasoned employees
- Incumbent–successor overlap, when possible, to permit direct knowledge transfer to the successor before the incumbent's retirement
- Emeritus programs that bring retired employees back specifically to transfer their knowledge to their successors

The U.S. Army is also deeply concerned with preserving and leveraging its intellectual capital. As part of its transformation strategy to create a network-centric, knowledge-based force, the Army launched Army Knowledge Online (AKO) in November 2000 (Grant, 2001, p. 1). One of the Army's original objectives was to provide its personnel with ready access to current information, such as a library of after-action reviews or the addresses of former classmates, and to enable online services such as leave applications. The Army's objectives were broadened, however. All AKO users were given e-mail accounts to use for the rest of their active careers and even after retirement. AKO quickly became the means for managing its knowledge assets and providing knowledge continuity in the Army.

The U.S. General Accounting Office (GAO), which ensures accountability in the federal government and helps Congress maximize the performance of federal agencies, is at the forefront of identifying key operational knowledge for preservation and transfer, both throughout the agency and for the next generation of employees. It also provides mentoring programs for new employees and assigns buddies to new hires when they come on board. The knowledge that is harvested from a broad array of incumbents (not just key employees in major agencies) includes their knowledge contacts, the processes they use in their positions, and the skills they require. As with all knowledge-harvesting efforts, a key problem has been helping incumbents to determine the knowledge and skills that are critical to their work.

A realignment of the organizational reward system, alignment of the communication system, and changes in the organizational culture to support these efforts were also required. The Honorable David M. Walker, comptroller general of the United States and head of the GAO, says of continuity management, "It shifts the mentality from knowledge ownership to knowledge stewardship . . . with the goal of better positioning employees and the organization for the future" (Walker, 2001b).

Knowledge continuity initiatives in both the public and private sectors are generally implemented to ensure knowledge continuity for senior management positions or in crisis situations that involve employee retirements or downsizing. Such initiatives are enormously valuable to an organization; in fact, they can be invaluable.

But knowledge continuity initiatives do not constitute continuity management. Knowledge continuity initiatives recognize the payoff in preserving knowledge continuity between employee generations, including the analysis necessary to generate that knowledge. But they usually omit one or more of the critical elements that define continuity management, and they lack the breadth and depth of a full continuity management implementation.

Continuity management has been implemented only when each of its elements has been employed. It is these five elements that distinguish knowledge continuity initiatives from continuity management:

1. *A knowledge audit to determine who should participate in continuity management in the organization or unit.* Without such an audit, critical knowledge workers may be excluded.
2. *A set of analytical questions (such as those embodied in K-PAQ) that define the critical operational knowledge of the organization or unit.* K-PAQ

ensures that only critical knowledge is captured and that tangential or obsolete knowledge is omitted.

3. *A knowledge questionnaire (such as K-Quest) that defines critical operational knowledge for each targeted job classification in the organization or unit and that harvests that knowledge from incumbents.* What K-PAQ does for the organization, K-Quest does for the job classification. It ensures that critical operational knowledge is preserved and provides a methodology for harvesting it.

4. *A structured means of transferring the knowledge to successor employees (such as the knowledge profile).* Without a well-designed structure, knowledge transfers are inevitably inefficient and incomplete. It isn't possible for incumbents to analyze their knowledge base and transfer their critical operational knowledge without being prompted to do so by some form of structure.

5. *Support in the organizational culture and recognition and reward system for the harvesting, transfer, and acquisition of operational knowledge.* Without such support, incumbents are less likely to analyze their knowledge, ensure that it is current, and make it available to their successors in a form that is usable to them.

With knowledge continuity initiatives, several of these elements may be employed, but not all five as in continuity management. Some knowledge continuity is better than no knowledge continuity. The temptation always exists to choose one, two, or three of these elements and abbreviate the process as a means of shortening the time required, the effort expended, or the funds spent to preserve knowledge continuity. Such efforts will yield results and will produce a form of knowledge continuity, but one that is less comprehensive, less effective, and, ultimately, less satisfactory than could have been achieved with continuity management. Nonetheless, knowledge continuity initiatives are precursors of continuity management and leading indicators of the emergence of continuity management as an organizational goal and a management function.

Continuity management does not have to be implemented in an entire organization to be continuity management. Scale, in other words, is not an a priori determinant of continuity management, although the larger the scale, the more effective continuity management is likely to be. Two of the points that we have made throughout this book are that continuity management can be implemented by any manager at any level of the organization and that some continuity management is better than none. We are confident of the validity of these statements. The only requirement for full continuity management implementation in a given organizational unit is that all five of its elements be included.

A Paradigm Shift

Revolutionary in its effect, but evolutionary in its practice, continuity management is part of a tidal wave that is reshaping organizational knowledge flow and creation in the new century and transforming the way we think about knowledge. Its distinctive contribution is a focus on the structured preservation and transfer of knowledge between employee generations in the service of *knowledge creation* by both the incumbent and successor employees. In retrospect, the emergence of continuity management was inevitable, forced by the quickening transformation of the industrial economy into the knowledge economy, the labor-based enterprise into the knowledge-based enterprise, and the effective management of the knowledge asset from a tangential aspect of management to a central function. The ultimate acceptance of continuity management as a goal, a commitment, and, finally, a function of management is virtually predetermined by the highly competitive, rapidly changing business environment; the constant innovation it demands; and the flattened hierarchies and dispersed decision making it requires of organizations operating successfully within it.

Continuity management is the harbinger of a new paradigm that recognizes the organization as a network of thoughts rather than a hierarchy of positions—and knowledge as the force that binds, directs, and vitalizes it. Like many transforming ideas, the emergence of continuity management was driven by urgent needs and great opportunities, and its development was based on antecedents that became clear only in retrospect. Such antecedents lie buried in the governing paradigms of the time and so are missed as predictors until a paradigm shift occurs, and the antecedents suddenly coalesce into a whole picture that is startling, provocative, and promising. Because the forces that drive such transformations can be subtle, they are seen individually rather than collectively in their nascent period, and so their significance is often missed until they come together suddenly—no longer scattered pieces of a puzzle, but a photograph of the future.

Continuity management will play an essential role in the development of the knowledge-centric organization. Many of its elements are already widely practiced across the organizational landscape in the form of knowledge continuity initiatives. As organizations move inexorably toward continuity management, driven by the new imperatives of the knowledge economy, these knowledge continuity initiatives will increase in number and expand in depth, breadth, and technological sophistication. Although continuity management is emergent, it resonates instantly with managers and executives, who say, "Yes, we need that. We're doing some of it, but we need to do more."

When continuity management is integrated with knowledge management, an organization leaps from twentieth-century thinking to twenty-first-century thinking, from following the swells of change to riding the crests of it. All of the great management ideas of the past quarter century—organizational learning, continuous improvement, process reengineering, and a commitment to innovation—find their fullest expression in the integration of knowledge management and continuity management. A careful analysis of what the business enterprise is and will become in the new century confirms the accuracy of that assessment.

Continuity management is a perspective, a mind-set that arises through a concerted, coordinated effort to exploit the knowledge asset to its maximum potential. Knowledge continuity initiatives pass into continuity management when a critical mass is reached, and employees begin to think of knowledge as the driving force of their work. In planning the day's activities, the central question is no longer "What do I need to do today?" but "How do I leverage my knowledge today?" In this context, *leverage* is an encompassing word that raises the questions, "How do I identify the knowledge I need? How do I build that knowledge through knowledge networks and documents? How can I apply my knowledge in the most effective way possible? And how can I create new knowledge?"

Continuity management exists when knowledge analysis becomes second nature to employees, when knowledge is harvested as part of the natural order of business, readily transferred between employee generations and across employees in the same generation, acquired by eager learners, and applied to create new knowledge, which is then returned to the other points of the knowledge network to create a virtuous cycle of knowledge creation and expansion. When knowledge is seen as the binding force in an organization, things change. Knowledge becomes more than a critical asset to be invested—it becomes a dynamic process to be embraced and nurtured. Knowledge analysis of what constitutes critical operational knowledge becomes as natural for knowledge workers as knowledge sharing, acquisition, and creation. Their thinking moves through "What can I share?" or "What's my best practice?" to "How can I grow my operational knowledge or apply it more productively?"

When continuity management and knowledge management have been integrated into a process that we have referred to as *knowledge asset management,* they make possible achievement of an enviable competitive advantage in the knowledge economy: the focused transfer of critical operational knowledge within and among employee generations so that it can be readily accessed, quickly internalized, and effectively applied by its intended recipients in the service of knowledge creation and increased productivity. What is the potential of this new organizational capability? James E. Copeland, Jr., chief executive of New York City–based Deloitte Touche Tohmatsu, says:

> Sharing intellectual capital, leveraging intellectual capital, however you want to describe this process—can produce another amazing round of productivity improvement. If you look at what happened to the U.S. over the last 15 years—the quality circles and then the real focus on re-engineering businesses in order to make them more competitive, and then we came up with enterprise-wide software products that had best practices baked into them. And all of a sudden you saw those enormous productivity gains—not at the margins, but fundamental productivity and value-creation gains that were made. The good news is that this area offers the same kind of opportunity. (Haapaniemi, 2001)

Copeland predicts on a large scale what we are already observing anecdotally on a small scale: Knowledge continuity makes employees more productive than would otherwise be the case, not only moving them more quickly up the learning curve, but providing critical knowledge resources that will be significant to their productivity long after they have attained the status of incumbent. The result is a sustained increase in organizational productivity that we believe will continue to grow as employees develop greater continuity management skills.

In the Information Age, knowledge continuity and creation are a vital part of leadership. A decade ago, Peter Drucker addressed the urgent need for management succession in a business environment of increasing complexity and competition. Drucker wrote, "The question of tomorrow's management is, above all, a concern of our society. Let me put it bluntly— we have reached a point where we simply will not be able to tolerate as a country, as a society, as a government, the danger that any one of our major companies will decline or collapse because it has not made adequate provisions for management succession" (Moulton, 1993, p. 29). Drucker's observations were true a decade ago, and they are true today, as management copes with high job turnover and impending baby-boomer retirements. But his comments have acquired an added dimension in the decade since. The twentieth-century problem of management succession has been transformed into the twenty-first-century problem of *knowledge* succession.

Key operational knowledge is no longer the sole province of top management or middle management or even lower management. Knowledge is spread throughout an organization, and the need to preserve knowledge succession or knowledge continuity is spread just as widely. Because operational knowledge is crucial to management effectiveness and organizational productivity, its preservation is an essential aspect of ensuring leadership continuity. With flattened hierarchies, dispersed decision-making authority, and self-managing work teams, more and more employees are leaders as well as managers and subordinates. The need for leadership continuity now extends well beyond the top executives for whom succession planning traditionally has taken place, into the ranks of middle and lower-level managers and their decision-making subordinates, on whom the success of the organization depends. The kind of knowledge continuity and knowledge creation required across an organization to preserve that degree of leadership continuity can be achieved only through the processes and systems inherent in continuity management. Continuity management ensures that the critical operational knowledge required to effectively manage the organization is preserved between leadership generations, but it also ensures that the knowledge is quickly acquired by new leaders and put to effective use.

A sea change is taking place in the management of the knowledge asset, and it has only begun. Its long-term consequences will transform the structural, cultural, human resource, and political characteristics of organizations, making knowledge preservation and creation a core competency of those that are successful. Most of the benefits of a paradigm shift such as this one cannot be imagined in advance. It is only when the process of change has begun—and the paradigm is shifting—that the old ways appear as they are—antiquated and counterproductive. Then participants look back in wonder at how and why they ever did what they did. In the midst of it, however, the future is not nearly so obvious, except to the prescient few who read it in the tea leaves of the present.

Knowledge continuity initiatives foreshadow the broad adoption of continuity management and development of the decisive new organizational capacity it generates—the capacity to know, to remember, to create. This capacity will be one of the defining competitive advantages of the knowledge economy, an extraordinary opportunity for leaders and managers who build it and a great peril for those who do not. Knowledge continuity is the fulcrum on which the fortunes of organizations will turn in the new century. Those that preserve it will rise; those that do not will decline. This is the new law of the knowledge economy. It is also its great opportunity. Of such opportunities, careers are built, reputations are established, and history is made.

References

Acquisition 2005 Task Force. 2000. *Shaping the civilian acquisition workforce of the future final report*. Washington, D.C.: Acquisition 2005 Task Force.

Amidon, D. M. 1995. The momentum of knowledge innovation. Entovation International. www.entovation.com/innovation/momentum.htm.

Anthes, G. H. 2001. The learning curve. *ComputerWorld,* 35(27):42.

Arquiette, Steven. 2000. Interviewed by authors. Washington, D.C. 27 October.

Basla, Michael. 2001. Interviewed by authors. Washington, D.C. 14 August.

Bassi, L. J. 2000. Profiting from learning: Do firms' investments in education and training pay off? Research White Paper. Washington, D.C.: ASTD & Saba.

Birchard, Bill. 1997. Hire great people fast. *Fast Company,* August, 132.

Brown, J. S., and E. S. Gray. 1995. The People are the company. *Fast Company,* 1:78.

Buckler, Grant. 2001. Six keys to unlocking the power of knowledge management. *Canadian Business and Current Affairs,* 9(9):28–34.

Charles, Keith. 2001. Interviewed by authors. Washington, D.C. 10 July.

Clark, J., and S. Pobulan. (2001). Oil, gas industry makes advances in managing data, knowledge. *Oil & Gas Journal,* 99(50):74–82

Collie, H. C. 2001. Knowledge management: Taking information strategy to the next level. *Mobility,* April, 5.

Congressional Management Foundation. 1999. Senate staff employment study. Washington, D.C.: Congressional Management Foundation, 95.

Cuviello, Peter. 2002. Interviewed by authors. Washington, D.C. 22 February.

Cvitanich, Anthony. 2002. Interviewed by authors. Boise, Idaho. 15 January.

DeBare, I. 2000. Keeping a packed bag at work: Employees today are more apt to job hop than ever before. *San Francisco Chronicle,* 17 October.

Dixon, N. M. 2000. *Common Knowledge: How Companies Thrive by Sharing What They Know.* Boston: Harvard Business School Press.

———. 2002. Interviewed by authors. Washington, D.C. 8 March.

Drucker, P. F. 1993. Post-Capitalist Society. New York: HarperCollins.

———. 1994. The age of social transformation. *Atlantic Monthly,* 274(5): 53–80.

———. 1999. *Management Challenges of the 21st Century.* New York: HarperCollins.

———. 2001. The new workforce. *The Economist.* www.Economist.com /displaystory.cfm?Story_10=770847&CFIO=1589482&CFTOKEN= 29459c0-7Oea.

Eisenhart, M. 2001. Gathering knowledge while it's ripe. *Knowledge Management,* 4(4):48–54.

Essex, D. 2000. Employee turnover: The costs are staggering. *ITworld.* http://itworld.com/Career/1993/ITW2491/.

Few employers have a plan to manage baby boomers nearing retirement. 2001. *HR Focus,* 78(4):8.

Figura, S. Z. 1999. Leadership void. *Government Executive,* 31(9):20–24.

Gates, B. 1999. *Business @ the speed of thought.* New York: Warner Books.

Geber, B. 2000. Who will replace those vanishing execs. *Training,* 37(7):48–53.

Grant, D. A. 2001. Army knowledge online accounts now mandatory. www.dtic .mil/armylink/news/Aug2001/a200110823armyknowledgeonline .html.

Grier, P. 2001. The civil service time bomb." *Air Force,* 84(7):10.

Haapaniemi, P. 2001. Leveraging your hidden brainpower. *Chief Executive,* 169:62–75.

Hiltebeitel, K. M., and B. A. Leauby. 2001. Migratory patterns of entry-level accountants. *The CPA Journal,* 13(4). www.nysscpa.org/cpajournal /2001/0400/dept/d045401.htm.

Kornberg, R., and M. Beattie. 2002. Embedding KM into HR at Schumberger. *KM Review,* 4(6):18–21.

Kotter, J. P. 1996. *Leading Change.* Boston: Harvard Business School Press.

Manasco, B. 2000. Leading companies focus on managing and measuring intellectual capital. www.webcom.com/quantera/IC.html.

Martin, Murray. 2002. Interviewed by authors. Stamford, Connecticut. 24 March.

McMahan, M. 2001. Interviewed by authors. Washington, D.C. 10 November.

McGinn, D. 2001. A grim job snapshot. *Time,* June 17. 37.

Ministry of the Premier and Cabinet. 1999. *Passing the torch—Managing succession in the Western Australia public sector.* Sydney: Government of Western Australia.

Moulton, H. W. 1993. *Executive development preparing for the 21st century.* New York: Oxford University Press.

Nakashima, E. 2001. Bush opens 40,000 jobs to competition. *Washington Post,* 8 June, A27.

Nobscot Corporation. 2001. Turnover rates for *Fortune* magazine's 100 best companies. www.nobscot.com/survey/surveyrresults.cfm?id=2.

O'Toole, B. 2001. Orientation vs. integration, Part I: Orienting the new employee. www.humanresources.about.com/library/weekly/uc022601a.htm.

Projects are risky business. 2001. *CPM Solutions.* www.CPM-Solutions .com/projectsfail.html.

Rasmusson, E. 2000. Look Out Below. www.workingwoman.com.

Ruettgers, Mike. 2001. Interviewed by authors. Boston, Mass. 19 November.

Sahl, R. J. 2001. Retention reigns as economy suffers drought. *Workspan,* 44(11):6–8.

Samuells, J. 2001. Putting knowledge management to work for real estate organizations. *Real Estate Issues,* 26(1):35–38.

Seidman, William. 2002. Interviewed by authors. Portland, Oregon. 7 March.

Scorca, Marc. 2001. Interviewed by authors. Washington, D.C. 12 November.

Shanley, A., and others. 1999. Striking out on their own: Independent contractors in the CPI. *Chemical Engineering,* 106(6):92.

That means I'm fired. 2001. *Time,* 158(11):22.

Transferring high-value knowledge at Pfizer. 2002. *KM Review,* 4(6):15–17.

Voinovich, G. V. 2001. Dangers of an aging federal work force. *Washington Post,* 28 March, A 23.

Walker, D. 2001a. Hearing report: High-risk: Human capital in the federal government. Senate Governmental Affairs Subcommittee on Oversight of Government Management, Restructuring and the District of Columbia. Washington, D.C.: Comptroller General of the United States.

———. 2001b. Interviewed by authors. Washington, D.C. 28 August.

———. 2001c. Maximizing human capital in the government workforce. Washington, D.C.: Comptroller General of the United States.

Ware, B. L. 2001. Win the war for talent, www.kimco.com/reten_kimfin.pdf.

Webb Partnership. 2002. Knowledge management: Tales from the darkside. http://thewebbpartnership.com.

Whimper fi: The decline of loyalty. 2001. *Washington Post,* 11 July, C1.

Web-programmers rule: Recruitment and retention are major issues. 2001. *Wired,* 9(1):154.

Wisconsin State Government Workforce Planning Team. 2001. State government workforce planning. Madison: Wisconsin State Government Workforce Planning Team.

Woodward, John. 2001. Interviewed by authors. Washington, D.C. 27 September.

Working for fun after retirement. 2000. *USA Today,* Snapshots, 26 October, A1.

Acknowledgments

During the course of writing this book, it was our pleasure to meet with a group of remarkable leaders across the public and private sectors who are reshaping the business, military, and governmental enterprises of the new century. In a time of extraordinary change, these visionaries are recreating the way in which organizations operate in response to a turbulent and exciting environment. We cannot thank all those with whom we have met or who deserve to be acknowledged, but we do want to express our gratitude to the following people who gave so generously of their time and their ideas.

The Honorable David Walker, Comptroller General of the United States and head of the Government Accounting Office (GAO); Alfred Berkley III, Vice Chairman and former President, NASDAQ; Marc Scorca, CEO and President, Opera America; Lieutenant General Harry Radegue, Director of the Defense Information Systems Agency (DISA) and Manager of the National Communications System (NCS) and White House Communications Agency; Michael Ruettgers, Executive Chairman, EMC Corporation; Otto Hoernig, CEO, Space Link International; Lieutenant General John Woodward, U.S. Air Force Deputy Chief of Staff for Communications Information and Deputy Chief Information Officer, Headquarters U.S. Air Force; Arunas Aslekys, Vice President, Corporate Marketing, Hughes Network; Lieutenant General Peter Cuviello, U.S. Army Chief Information Officer; Major General Michael McMahan, Commander of the United States Air Force Personnel Center; and John Landon, Principal Director, Office of the Secretary of Defense Command Control Communications all contributed to the ideas in this book.

We would like to thank Colonel Douglas Lengenfelder, Keith Charles, Colonel Michael Basla, Major Ken Hirlinger, Bobbi Nielson, Patrice Flynn,

Lieutenant Colonel Scott Erickson, Newt Crenshaw, Michael Kull, and Robert Ferguson, who likewise provided valuable input.

Our special thanks go to Mike Boenisch and John Barnet for their careful review of the manuscript and for their many good suggestions. We are indebted to Nancy Dixon, who brought her expertise in knowledge management to bear in her review of the manuscript and who offered many insights that substantially enriched the final work.

We also want to express our thanks to Doris Michaels, our literary agent at the Doris S. Michaels Literary Agency, who was an early and dedicated proponent of the book, and to Paula K. Sinnott, our editor at John Wiley & Sons, Inc., whose careful analysis of the manuscript added significantly to our work. Our thanks also to Larry Alexander, our publisher at John Wiley & Sons, Inc., for his support and wise counsel.

Hamilton Beazley would like to thank Andrew Callaway, his godson, for the late-night calls of encouragement and for being Andrew; Gloria Germanow Acker, a treasured friend and great Realtor, whose gifts and laughter have been a joy for decades; and Father Tom Butler, his long-time Texas friend and spiritual mentor—all of whom have provided loving support during the writing of this book. Hamilton is also grateful to his late brother, to whom the book is dedicated, for a lifetime of encouragement for his literary endeavors and for his brother's particular enthusiasm for this project, although he did not live to see its publication. Hamilton would like to thank his sister-in-law Norma Beazley for her support of his writing career and for the faith and kindness that support represents.

Jeremiah Boenisch is grateful to Mike and Kathy Boenisch, his parents, whose wisdom and love continue to guide him; Armand Boudreau, a long-time friend and mentor, who taught him how to lead; and Nancy Boenisch, his grandmother, who inspired him and showed him how to reach for the stars. Jeremiah would also like to thank his wife and daughters, to whom this book is dedicated, for their love and undying support.

David Harden would like to thank his parents, Tom and Gwen Harden, for loving a boy and raising a man; Ed and Glenda Tooley, for their continued love and support; and Do and Glenn Reynolds, who inspire by overcoming life's challenges every day. Dave would also like to thank his beautiful wife and kids, to whom this book is dedicated, for believing, loving, and dreaming with an imperfect man.

Finally, all three authors would like to thank collectively their families, friends, and colleagues who have supported them through the months of research and writing. We couldn't have done it without you.

—*Hamilton Beazley*
—*Jeremiah Boenisch*
—*David Harden*

Index

About the Authors

Hamilton Beazley is chairman of the Strategic Leadership Group and former associate professor of organizational sciences at The George Washington University, Washington, D.C. He received his BA degree in psychology from Yale University, his MBA degree in accounting from the Cox School of Business at Southern Methodist University, and his PhD degree in organizational behavior from The George Washington University.

Prior to his academic career, he served in various financial and strategic planning positions in the American oil industry, as a founding member of the board of directors of DyChem International (U.K.), Ltd., as founding chairman of the Oxy Houston Credit Union, and as former president of the National Council on Alcoholism and Drug Dependence, Inc., New York. He is a member of the board of trustees of the Educational Advancement Foundation, a member of the advisory board of the Discovery Learning Project at the University of Texas at Austin, and a former member of the board of trustees of the Episcopal Radio–TV Foundation.

He is coauthor (with the Episcopal Bishop of Texas) of *Reclaiming the Great Commission: A Practical Model for Transforming Denominations and Congregations,* a case study of organizational transformation under a visionary leader (Jossey-Bass Publishers, 2000); author of the forthcoming *Quantum Leading: Servant-Leadership in the Century of Hyper-Change,* a study of servant-leadership and how it is practiced in leading American companies (John Wiley & Sons, 2003); and author of the forthcoming *Letting Go of Regret: A Spiritual Approach to Reclaiming the Present,* a spiritual and psychological program for overcoming burdensome regrets (John Wiley & Sons, 2003). He is cocreator of *Secrets Out,* a television series that aired on the BBC, London, during the 1984 to 1987 seasons. His simulation with John Lobuts Jr., CommSpan: Content and Process in Multi-Cultural Communication, was selected as one of the top 20 multicultural management training games in the world in 1999.

His areas of expertise are servant-leadership, spirituality in organizational settings, and maintaining knowledge continuity between employee generations. He has been interviewed on NBC, CNN, CNBC, and a variety of radio programs. He has been quoted in the *New York Times,* the *Washington Post,* the *Los Angeles Times, USA Today, Newsweek, Fortune,* and numerous other newspapers and periodicals, and he has testified before committees of both the U.S. House of Representatives and the U.S. Senate as an expert witness. He is a member of the American Psychological Association, the International Society of Simulation and Gaming, the Academy of Management, and the Organizational Behavior Teaching Society.

■ ■ ■

Jeremiah S. Boenisch is an officer in the U.S. Air Force whose specialty is communications and information. He received his BS degree in environmental science and his BS degree in political science with minors in environmental health and aeronautical science from Oregon State University and his MA degree in organizational management from The George Washington University, Washington, D.C.

He is a standout officer with experience in Air Force combat communications systems and in metropolitan, wide-area, and local-area networks and has served in a variety of leadership and technical positions. His areas of expertise are team building, leadership, and continuity management.

He has led combat communicators overseas on deployment to Kuwait; has commanded 80-person teams; and has controlled sizable budgets. He is a former chief of both networks and mission systems, Holloman AFB, New Mexico; a test director within the National Missile Defense Program, Colorado Springs, Colorado; an acquisition analyst within the Office of the Secretary of Defense for Command Control Communications and Intelligence, Pentagon, Washington D.C.; and an information systems project manager at Headquarters Air Force, Pentagon, Washington D.C.

■ ■ ■

David B. Harden is an officer in the U.S. Air Force. He earned his BS degree in electrical engineering at the U.S. Air Force Academy and his MA degree in organizational management at The George Washington University, Washington, D.C. A C-17 pilot with over 1,600 flight hours, including combat time in Bosnia and Kosovo, he has served in Washington, D.C., on the Joint Chiefs of Staff as a political-military planner for Baltic affairs and NATO, at the Pentagon on the Air Force staff developing personnel policy for more than 20,000 pilots and navigators, and at North American Aerospace Command (NORAD) in Colorado Springs, Colorado, implementing systems and policy in counterdrug operations. His areas of expertise are leadership, team building, personnel policy, and continuity management.